Instructional Technology

A Systematic Approach to Education

Instructional Technology
A Systematic Approach to Education

Frederick G. Knirk
University of Southern California

Kent L. Gustafson
University of Georgia

HOLT, RINEHART AND WINSTON
*New York   Chicago   San Francisco   Philadelphia   Montreal
Toronto   London   Sydney   Tokyo   Mexico City
Rio de Janeiro   Madrid*

Notice

APPLE is a registered trademark of Apple Computer Inc.
DIALOG is a registered trademark of Dialog Information Services, Inc.
PLATO is a registered trademark of Control Data Corporation.
THE SOURCE is a registered trademark of Source Telecomputing Corp.
VISICALC is a registered trademark of VisiCorp.

Library of Congress Cataloging in Publication Data

Knirk, Frederick G.
  Instructional technology.

  Includes bibliographies and index.
  1. Educational technology. I. Gustafson, Kent L.
II. Title.
LB1028.3.K59 1986   371.3'07'8   85-10036
ISBN 0-03-071649-7

Copyright © 1986 by CBS College Publishing
Address correspondence to:
383 Madison Avenue
New York, N.Y. 10017
All rights reserved
Printed in the United States of America
Published simultaneously in Canada
6 7 8 9 038 9 8 7 6 5 4 3 2 1

CBS COLLEGE PUBLISHING
Holt, Rinehart and Winston
The Dryden Press
Saunders College Publishing

Preface

A quarter-century old, instructional technology (IT) remains an evolving concept as indicated by its many definitions. Its popularity is due in part to its applicability to a wide variety of settings including all levels of education as well as military and industrial training. However, owing to their unique environments, each group of education or training professionals has tended to develop its own definitions and terminology. Even the graduate professional preparation programs differ somewhat in their approaches. Although this diversity is healthy in an evolving field, there has been a tendency to magnify differences rather than identify commonalities.

The primary purpose of *Instructional Technology* is to present the common base of theory and practice associated with IT. From this base, it is then possible to expand in selected areas depending on one's orientation. Both theory and practical tools and techniques are described to illustrate how they may be applied in analyzing, designing, producing, evaluating, implementing, and managing instruction. In the final chapters, readers are alerted to emerging but as yet unproven technologies.

Instructional technology provides a methodological focal point for solving instruction or performance problems. Once a problem has been perceived, it is necessary to collect data to further refine and define it. This analysis may lead to designing and developing an instructional solution. However, it may also lead to alternative solutions such as redesigning the work environment or modifying the psychological climate. For example, redesigning a piece of equipment or changing the motivation or reward structure may, even without additional training, improve performance. It is essential for instructional technologists to keep in mind that application of the analytical procedures associated with IT does not always result in instructional solutions. Basic to the process is allowing data, rather than preconceptions, to dictate the solution.

To apply the IT process, technologists must be competent in many areas including administration, instructional design and development, writing objectives, materials production, research and evaluation, and diffusion of innovative ideas and products. Each of these areas is presented in detail in one or more chapters. However, simply reading about a skill does not make one competent in its application. Readers will find it necessary to practice the procedures and obtain feedback on their efforts.

The format and sequence of the chapters is arranged to reflect an instructional development model. A history of the development of instructional technology and the instructional development model itself are presented in Chapter 1. Chapter 2 illustrates procedures for assessing a problem and determining whether it is even appropriate to apply the balance of the IT process. These needs-assessment and task-analysis procedures are usually the first steps performed in attempting to define and understand the problem. Subsequent chapters examine in detail individual elements of the instructional development model.

We assume the reader has little background in the areas of instructional media, instructional design, administration, or educational psychology. The material has been written at an introductory level but includes extensive references for those desiring to explore topics in greater depth. We view this book as helping you to enter the exciting and challenging world of instructional technology. If it extends your horizon and raises more questions than it answers, it will have served its purpose. The future of IT is far more interesting than its past. We believe it has enormous potential for unleashing the almost untapped creativity and productivity of people.

The application of IT to a wide variety of settings provides a powerful tool for improving the welfare of all. But having said this we must remind ourselves that the current level of practice of IT is really primitive. We have come a long way in twenty-five years, but a long road remains to explore and travel.

Acknowledgments

We would like to gratefully acknowledge the assistance of the graduate students at the University of Georgia and the University of Southern California who have read this text and provided feedback and fresh ideas concerning its development.

The help provided by Dolly Freud, Livia Bachtold, Gina Lashley, Ann Shore, and Susan Pollack is especially appreciated. Their editorial and organizational assistance made this text possible.

To Pat Knirk who typed, edited, and retyped so many times—thank you. And to Elaine Gustafson who always believed in the authors and the ideas—we appreciate your support.

We thank all of these individuals, as well as the following colleagues, for sharing their invaluable skills and resources: Robert K. Branson; Alex Cuthbert, Director of Educational Technology, Washington, D.C.; Fred Pula, Boston College; David Salisbury, Florida State University; Margaret Tossia, Millersville University; Walter Wager, Florida State University; and Thomas C. Wilson, Consultant, Educational Design.

F.G.K./K.L.G.

Contents

PART TWO INSTRUCTIONAL DESIGN

PART THREE   INSTRUCTIONAL DEVELOPMENT

APPENDICES

Instructional Technology
A Systematic Approach to Education

1

Antecedents of Instructional Technology

. . . to be optimally effective, undertake at outset the most comprehensive tasks in the most comprehensive and incisively detailed manner.
                                                                    Buckminster Fuller

Objectives

After completing this chapter you should be able to:

1. Discuss the learner orientation of instructional technology and contrast it with the teacher orientation of a "teacher aids" media philosophy.
2. List at least ten major developments which have led to the development of an instructional technology.
3. Discuss the history of instructional technology.

Since the 1950s, three main thought streams have been instrumental in creating the field of instructional technology:

1. The concept of designing instruction directly for the student instead of designing audio-visual (A-V) materials for teachers to use in their presentations.
2. Benchmark developments in learning theory as identified by B. F. Skinner, Sidney L. Pressey, N. A. Crowder, and others.
3. The influence of World War II and later the rapidly advancing hardware technology, which required developing quick task analysis procedures, effective training, and new communication technologies; often labeled the "systems approach."

TEACHING OR LEARNING ORIENTATION?

Learning in formal settings has, since time immemorial, been viewed as resulting from teaching. The teacher has been considered both the storehouse of requisite knowledge and the medium of its transmission. While books, and later other media, greatly increased the ability to store information, the teacher

1

remained the primary channel for relaying it to students. However, advances in information storage and retrieval technology have increased both the amount and type of information directly accessible to learners. Interactive systems have added a dimension to information search and utilization that is unparalleled in history. As a result, the teacher's role as both source and medium of information for learners is being modified. We will see an increasing number of teachers leading students to the information, not just transmitting it. Of course, under many circumstances, the information must still be sequenced or arranged to simplify or clarify learning. However, it is becoming more possible for a teacher to make these instructional decisions and store both the knowledge and a structure for acquiring and using it. This trend toward less teacher-dependent learning will not eliminate teachers. Rather, it will increase teachers' roles in curriculum planning, student guidance, and student evaluation while reducing their role as presenters of knowledge.

DEVELOPMENTS IN LEARNING THEORY

The move toward extended learner control of instruction progresses as more becomes known about how people learn. In the 1950s, B. F. Skinner at Harvard University applied stimulus–response (S–R) psychology principles to human instruction. He also developed a procedure for maintaining the required level of performance through reinforcement "schedules." Based on S–R principles, linear-programmed instructional materials were constructed so that a student would almost always provide the correct answer to questions. Skinner's programs were characterized by short, highly structured "frames" of instruction which required students to "construct" their own responses. The student would then immediately be shown the correct response or how to judge its appropriateness. Skinner's work, like most of the significant developments in instructional technology, focused on techniques or methods to increase learning.

Research indicated that stimulus/response-based programs were usually effective for students with similar backgrounds and for definitional or associative level instructional/training objectives. Norman Crowder in the early 1960s, however, thought the programming method could be improved by using principles of Gestalt psychology. Crowder, who was working for the Air Force in training research, felt that other mechanisms could be used to increase learning effectiveness for a greater variety of students and instructional objectives. He developed "intrinsic" programming, which presented larger amounts of information to the learner (up to a full page) before requiring a response. Also, unlike Skinner's linear programs, Crowder's contained multiple-choice responses. After selecting one alternative, the learner was "branched" to a specific next step based on that response. Hence, the term intrinsic, meaning "guided internally" by the learner (or at least the learner's response). Research has indicated that intrinsic programs can effectively teach a variety of types of objectives to a wider range of students.

DEVELOPMENT OF THE SYSTEMS APPROACH

The "systems approach," as applied to teaching and learning, originated in training programs developed by the military. As weapons systems became more complex and required teams of specialized interacting personnel, the armed services sought new procedures for developing and delivering training. The systems approach draws on concepts from general systems theory as well as from information science, communication, learning theory, and other fields. While a variety of systems models was created, all contained three fundamental steps: defining needs; stating instructional objectives; and developing, evaluating, and implementing the instruction. While the systems approach and its elements will be presented in detail later, it is important at this point to keep in mind its relationship to an overall technology of instruction which includes people, processes, and devices.

A HISTORY OF EDUCATION

We turn now to a general historical review of education as it has developed over the ages. From this review it should become clear that instructional technology is not a totally new and different set of concepts. Rather, it is an evolutionary step as people seek to improve their educational enterprise by making it more effective, efficient, and humane.

The invention or development of tools and language created the need for education and training. Word of mouth, demonstration, and limited written records were the primary media for early training. The Greeks found the Socratic method of carefully structuring questions and answers to be effective. This method, which included short organized units of instruction directed toward specific objectives, was tailored to an individual student's interests and abilities. While we reject Socrates' concept that a person's ideas are present at birth, instructional technology is based on many of his tenets. Socrates' students did not take notes, but another Greek, Aristotle, considered notetaking an essential part of the learning process. Both, however, viewed learning as an active and individual process based on objectives and a structured learning environment.

Eventually, a system of providing instruction to individuals through an apprenticeship system developed, which led to grouped instruction processes. This occurred in response to economic pressures when it became desirable to educate a large percentage of the population. Early forms of hardware technology such as chalkboards and books also made grouped instruction feasible.

Thus, over the centuries we have moved from individualized instruction to highly structured organizations providing group instruction.

Apprenticeships in medicine, art, warfare, business, law, masonry, and the like, for direct transmission of information began more than a thousand years B.C. The professions and business communities relied on apprentices for their support and for the continuation of their "trades."

Guilds were formed by people of similar interests for mutual protection and assistance. In this system, which reached its peak in Europe between 1100 and 1500 A.D., the masters and their paid journeymen trained the new apprentices. The regulations on hours, prices, wages, and tools were similar to those found in labor unions today.

Factory schools were established by industries in the United States in the 1800s. They arose because the apprenticeship system did not provide the necessary number of trained people for the factories. Also, because of increasing job specialization workers did not need to be highly skilled at many tasks; they usually had to know how to do only a single operation. Because the workers needed little general education, the training program could be tailored to the specific tasks to be accomplished. During that period, industrial progress was not so rapid that it was necessary to teach principles to permit generalizable understanding and the ability to work in varying or evolving situations.

Elementary and secondary education in the United States was eventually legislated for all children, and it was further legislated that communities be taxed to provide this education at no cost to the student. This decision meant that the skills needed in business and the professions could now be provided by the "public school" system. Children's right to public education now meant that schools had the primary responsibility for their training.

Initially, colleges and universities provided training for only the wealthy in politics, law, religion, and the liberal arts. Vocational training for teachers, farmers, home economists, and industrial workers evolved later because of federal legislation (for example, the Smith-Hughes Act of 1917) and various social pressures. During the early twentieth century much federal money was spent to educate as many adults as would avail themselves of the opportunity.

While economic factors and the shortage of trained teachers once forced abandonment of one-to-one or one-to-a-few instruction in favor of group instruction, advancements in instructional technology are now permitting a return to individualized instruction. The preparation of evaluated and revised instructional materials is initially expensive (like the design of any new product such as cars or computers), but replication of that design for many learners can reduce the cost of individualized instruction or communication to a level comparable with group instruction. The desirability of providing individual programs for learners with different interests, abilities, learning paces, and study habits will be examined throughout this text with discussion and examples. This should not, however, be taken to mean that instructional technology is applicable only to individualized instruction. Instructional technology makes it possible to design and deliver instruction in a wide variety of formats with the decision on group size based on the characteristics of the learner, the type of learning objectives, and the available resources.

In the nineteenth century the Industrial Revolution began with the invention of machines for power and the direction of that power into spinning and weaving on assembly lines. In education, though, the same revolution did not occur, and the technology of instruction remained largely at its preindustrial level. However, during the latter part of the nineteenth century, some materials were designed and mass produced for educators, such as maps, charts, and textbooks. By the beginning of the twentieth century, industrial technology had become well established with plants and factories oriented to assembly lines and interchangeable parts. What the products of mass-production lines lacked in aesthetic appeal was made up for in lower costs, accessibility, and dependability. Henry Ford was able to "produce any color car you desired—as long as it was black." Today, more advanced technology allows even greater diversity and many options in both cars and education.

The U.S. military services have developed many training devices and instructional development procedures that are useful to both public school and training professionals. For example, one of the first blackboards was used at West Point in 1817 by Claude Crozet. Crozet, a Frenchman who spoke poor English, wanted to draw visuals to help overcome his handicap, so he painted a wall of his classroom black and wrote on it with chalk. During World War II, the army bought 55,000 16mm projectors and spent a billion dollars on training films. Their film units developed many of the techniques still used in producing instructional training films. It is reported that Hitler, when asked in 1939 to name the Third Reich's most important new weapon, replied, "my 60,000 motion picture projectors." Following Germany's surrender in 1945, William Kietel, chief of the German General Staff, said, "We had everything calculated perfectly except the speed with which America was able to train its people. Our major miscalculation was in underestimating their quick and complete mastery of film education." (Olsen and Bass, 1982, 33)

The overhead projector was originally called a "viewgraph" by the Navy when it was developed during World War II to improve map briefings and instruction. It was designed to permit the use of previously prepared visuals or allow instructors to face students and use the device as a substitute for a chalkboard. In the mid-1960s the overhead projector began to appear in many nonmilitary classrooms and is now widely used.

The military also supported much of the work of Skinner and Crowder and others who contributed to the development of linear- and branching-programmed instruction techniques. The military language schools also pioneered work on language laboratories. One of the most significant contributions of the military was the development of instructional design models. In 1968 the Department of Defense asked university faculty and industrial trainers for plans for applying a systems approach in the development and management of training courses on a servicewide basis. A demand existed for training programs that would quickly and effectively train many unskilled individuals to operate or

Prehistoric	
	Cave drawings
	Language
Second Century	
	Paper and ink
Fifth Century	
	Block printing
Ninth Century	
	Books
Fifteenth Century	
	Printing from movable type (Gutenberg)
Eighteenth Century	
1793	Use of interchangeable parts (Whitney)
Nineteenth Century	
1837	Telegraph (magnetic) (Morse)
1867	Typewriter (Sholes)
1876	Telephone (Bell)
1878	Transparent film (Eastman)
1879	Incandescent lamp (Edison)

FIGURE 1.1   Educational Technology Milestones and Their Inventors

maintain sophisticated devices—computers, radar units, high-performance aircraft, communications equipment. This demand continues today with the military remaining a significant force in the continual evolution of instructional technology.

In the late 1970s the information revolution began to accelerate due to a societal emphasis on basic research on information processing, artificial intelligence, computers, and advances in publishing technologies. The fruits of this research made possible the generation and dissemination of information at a rate which is now doubling every ten years. Recently, the microchip has allowed average citizens to own their own computers and to directly obtain and manipulate information. For example, programs like Visicalc allow the manipulation of data in a manner and speed never before possible. Access to data banks such as The Source, Dialog, and CompuServe by telephone permits access to encyclopedias and news networks, for example. The information era is certainly

1887	Record, cylinder (Bell)
	Record, disc (Berlinger)
1892	AC motor (Tesla)
1898	Photographic paper (Baekeland)
1899	Wireless telephone (Collins)

Twentieth Century

1907	Radio tube and amplifier (De Forest)
1909	Mass production techniques (Ford)
1913	Heterodyne radio (Fessenden)
1927	Television (Farnsworth)
	Talking movies (Warner Brothers)
1935	FM radio (Armstrong)
1938	Xerography (Carlson)
1944	Digital computer-automatic (Aiken and others)
1945	Computer memory (Von Neumann)
1946	Electric digital computer (Eckert)
1947	Transistor (Bareen and others)
1948	Cybernetic theory (Weiner)
	Information theory (Shannon)
	LP record (Goldmark)
1954	*The Science of Learning and the Art of Teaching*, Skinner
1962	Communications satellite (Pierce)
1965	NDEA funds for training instructional technologists
1967	Open university planning in Britain
1972	Word processing via computer
1978	Extremely high-speed computer printing
1981	Low-cost personal computer

FIGURE 1.1   (cont.)

upon us. Since teaching is primarily an information-handling profession (transfer of knowledge from "data sources" to receivers with a need for the information), this next decade should be an exciting one for professional educators.

In recent years technology has burgeoned, piling machine upon machine and system upon system, adding fantastically to the control and manipulation of information. Technology has transformed American society, added to its feeling of having a "good life," raised concerns about the ability of various individuals and organizations to obtain "too much" information about an individual, and even modified the fine arts with computer-generated poetry and "painting." And last but not least, it is affecting our educational institution.

Figure 1.1 clearly shows the development of communications hardware, technology, and theory which make possible a comprehensive instructional technology.

During the twentieth century radio, the motion picture, television, computers, and other pieces of communication technology were invented and are now widely used. These media and their accompanying messages are used to create a need for a product or a political candidate, to provide entertainment, or to create educational experiences. American educators, however, have not yet really chosen to use these devices on a large scale in the teaching/learning process.

The development of photographic film and later the transistor, integrated circuits, and the microchip began a technological wave of development which has resulted in less bulky, less expensive, and more reliable training devices. In addition to the book as a medium of instruction, still materials can now be inexpensively presented by slide or microfiche projectors. Motion visuals can be presented using film, videotape, or videodisc equipment. Audio stimuli can be presented alone or with film or videotape equipment in a broad variety of arrangements. The use of computers for instruction now permits educators to store and process an extensive range of data that can be useful in presenting the most desirable sequence of instruction to the learner. While personnel costs have soared, the price of computers has greatly declined. It has been estimated that since 1960, the performance of computers has increased ten thousand times, while the price of "each unit of performance" has declined 100,000 times.

The awesome power of the computer is just beginning to be known by the majority of Americans. You should not find it astonishing when people compare the impact of the computer and microprocessors to that of the Watt steam engine which ushered in the Industrial Revolution more than two hundred years ago. The power of the computer as an information-handling technology will drastically affect formal learning. Indeed, it is already making an impact on learning through "educational toys." Interactive cable systems, satellite communication, lasers, and microstorage devices are also having a profound impact on how information is stored, retrieved, learned, and utilized.

From this brief history of the developments leading to a technology of instruction, we now turn to learning and the development of instruction as two major components of instructional technology.

A TECHNOLOGY OF LEARNING

In the past few decades, developments in learning theory have been remarkable. The development of new information-processing and -transmitting technologies has been multiplying at an ever-increasing rate.

In 1926 at Ohio State University, Sidney L. Pressey developed an early "teaching machine," initially as a test-scoring device which evaluated students' responses and then provided them with the correct responses to the questions. To everyone's amazement, the students learned simply by taking the test.

During that same decade most audio-visual equipment was used as a teacher-aid. Such equipment was usually called audio-visual aids. Some educators began to wonder if direct instruction might be provided by the devices themselves. Could these devices require student involvement by eliciting student responses to questions? Could students be required to answer questions or press buttons to ensure their comprehension before the presentation continued? Could the "programs" be so well designed that the students would generally obtain a challenging and interesting question they would answer correctly and thus be positively reinforced for their learning? These and related questions opened major areas of research on how people learn and how to design effective instruction.

Many research studies were done to compare one approach or medium of instruction with another. Teacher-based systems were usually the referent to which other approaches were compared. The most frequently asked question was, "Did the media work as well as the teacher?" Although some studies favored live teachers and others the mediated approaches, the vast majority of studies resulted in "no significant difference." It is now generally accepted that, for most cognitive objectives, systematically designed mediated presentations will produce about as much learning as a teacher-based system. It is this focus on student learning—and learning principles—rather than on teaching techniques that makes instructional technology stand apart from conventional education and training procedures.

Robert Kilbourn at Wayne State University was the first to change the name of his "audio-visual education" department to "instructional technology." More than just a name change, it reflected a move away from the "aids" concept of assisting teachers to teach and toward the concept of at least some materials being directly used by students without teacher intervention. This philosophy of education was generally championed by James Finn of the University of Southern California, who is usually credited with first defining "instructional technology." Finn was also instrumental in promoting legislation passed by the U.S. Congress in the late 1950s and 1960s that provided funding for research involving instructional technology procedures. Funding also became available for training of instructional technologists through the efforts of Finn and others.

There is a consanguinity between science and technology: advances in learning theory have permitted the development of an instructional technology just as advances in DNA research have resulted in rapidly developing industries using this biogenetic knowledge. Discoveries in management sciences have also resulted in tools useful to educators. Some areas of science that have influenced instructional technology are shown in Figure 1.2.

A TECHNOLOGY OF PROCESS

Complicated problems like designing and manufacturing ships or planning and implementing instruction require handling large amounts of information. The

Behavioral sciences	Management sciences	Physical sciences
Learning theory	Cybernetics	Physics
Perception	Accountability	Chemistry
Communication	Systems theory	Electronics
Motivation	Economic theory	Optics
Measurement	Task analysis	Communications
Programmed instruction	Systems analysis	engineering
Learner analysis	Accountability	
Instructional	Cost-effective analysis	
design	PERT, PPBS	
Test design		
Needs assessment		

FIGURE 1.2   Sciences That Have Contributed to an Instructional Technology

more thoroughly educators understand learners and their perceived and real needs, the easier it is to design instruction. Instructional technology, then, is not only the use of hardware or devices and learning theory in instruction; it is also the use of procedures for structuring learning environments for solving instructional problems. These processes were developed in the behavioral, social, and physical sciences and adapted by instructional technologists for use by trainers and educators. The process element of technology is usually described by using a model or flow chart indicating steps to be taken or functions to be performed. The models serve as guidelines or prescriptions much as road maps aid the motorist. In the next chapter we will present one model of the technology process as it can be applied to instruction.

SUMMARY

More than anything else, in the fifties and sixties educators became aware that a technology of instruction might be possible. *Not* a science of instruction, but a technology of instruction, would increase the probability of achieving desired outcomes. Instructional technology is based on the use of hardware, learning theories, and systematic development processes to help solve teaching/learning problems. The solutions may or may not involve teachers, media, or materials; the only requirement is that the "solutions" really work.

By the 1950s American educators began to have the capability of developing an instructional technology. The hardware (projectors, recorders, amplifiers, computers) and the materials (slides, videotapes, computer software) were available. Knowledge about human learning was rapidly expanding and processes were being discovered that facilitated the development of instruction. To date, the inertia of a large, diversified, and labor-intensive institution like education has restricted its exploration of the potential IT. However, the industrial and military training communities have widely accepted it and sponsor and conduct most of the research in the field. Public educational institutions are only now beginning to examine and adopt IT. Despite the later start and lesser interest in IT shown by schools and colleges, recent events indicate heightened interest. Higher educational institutions and vocational-technical schools in particular are increasingly turning to IT for help in increasing their instructional effectiveness and efficiency. This trend appears to be well established and is expected to grow rapidly during the eighties and nineties.

Suggested Readings

Fuller, B. (1981). *Critical Path*. New York: St. Martin's.

Olsen, J. R., and Bass, V. B. (July/August 1982). The Application of Performance Technology in the Military: 1960–1980. *NSPI Journal*, 32–36.

Percival, F., and Ellington, H. (1984). *A Handbook of Educational Technology*. New York: Nichols.

Saettler, P. (1968). *A History of Instructional Technology*. New York: McGraw-Hill.

Skinner, B. F. (1968). *The Technology of Teaching*. New York: Appleton-Century-Crofts.

Unwin, D., and McAleese, R. (1978). *The Encyclopaedia of Educational Communications and Technology*. Westport, CT: Greenwood Press.

PART ONE

Problem Definition

2

Instructional Technology: Development

The only justification for our concepts and systems of concepts is that they serve to represent the complex of our experiences; beyond this they have not legitimacy.

Albert Einstein

Objectives

After completing this chapter you should be able to:

1. Define instructional technology.
2. List the ways in which an instructional technology process is potentially different from more traditional curriculum and instruction processes or methods.
3. Label each step of the instructional development model on which this text is based.
4. Discuss the impact of instructional technology programs on the learner.
5. List the advantages and disadvantages of instructional technology from an instructor's viewpoint.
6. List the advantages and disadvantages of instructional technology from a curriculum coordinator's or training manager's viewpoint.
7. List the advantages and disadvantages of instructional technology from a learner's viewpoint.

Learning is a complex activity. Thus designing education and training programs is a challenging and exciting professional arena. The emerging field of instructional technology is center stage in the struggle to make education more predictable and rewarding for both the learner and the instructor.

In this chapter definitions for "instructional technology" and "instructional development" are explored. To guide this exploration, several instructional development models are reviewed to alert the reader to the variety of available models. One model, which will be presented in greater detail, serves as the organizing structure for much of this book.

DEFINITION OF INSTRUCTIONAL TECHNOLOGY

Anyone who has begun to think places some portion of the world in jeopardy.

John Dewey

As a student of instructional technology, you will soon realize how difficult it is to define this field. IT reflects a philosophy of education, and philosophies often take a bit of time to explain.

First, we prefer the term *instructional*, as opposed to *educational*, because we are primarily concerned with teaching and learning problems. Education is a broader term that may include everything from administration to maintenance. *Learning* might also be an appropriate term since it better reflects the designing of learning environments for the learner.

Second, it is *technology* rather than the *science*, which some educators might prefer. Practitioners of IT attempt to apply principles developed in the social, psychological, and physical sciences that may be used on instructional problems. By science we mean the process of systematically collecting knowledge derived from observation and study. By technology we mean the application of scientifically gathered knowledge to practical problems. However, the division between science and technology is arbitrary because advances in science depend in part on advances in technology and vice versa. For example, at age seventeen, Galileo discovered the principle of the pendulum; ten years later he began to study the more theoretical behavior of falling bodies to explain and project from his observations. Copernicus could not have progressed in his study of the heavens without the technology of telescopes and lenses. Similarly, inventors (or technologists) like Edison and De Forest paved the way for theoretical work on wave theory and electronic amplification.

The application of knowledge has been labeled in a variety of ways over the years. While business and industry trainers currently use the term technology, educators typically use other descriptors. For example, in a publication by the Association for Educational Communications and Technology, "Graduate Degree Programs in Instructional Technology 1978–79," several different titles for instructional technology appear. Those most frequently used for programs in this field are Educational Media, Instructional Technology, Instructional Media, Educational Media and Technology, Educational Communications, and Educational Technology. Many also have the word "library" in their titles, such as Library and Educational Media. The term instructional technology will be used generally in this book to emphasize our concern not just with the media, but also with the use of techniques or tools developed in the behavioral and physical sciences. We will provide a consistent definition and examples of the field. However, since IT is an evolving and changing area of study, new ideas are emerging that may dramatically alter its structure and direction in the future. The future of IT is discussed in the last chapter of the book.

One aim of IT is to eliminate as much of the menial work of instruction as possible, and to increase the creative and productive capacity of teachers. Thorndike, writing in *Education*, in 1912, said a teacher should not be wasted in doing what forty sheets of paper or two phonographs can do.

A formal definition of IT that has received wide circulation was included in "A Report to the President and the Congress of the United States by the Commission on Instructional Technology" in March 1970. It states:

> Instructional technology can be defined in two ways. In its more familiar sense, it means the media born of the communications revolution which can be used for instructional purposes alongside the teacher, text-book, and blackboard . . . The second definition . . . goes beyond any particular medium or device. In this sense, instructional technology is more than the sum of its parts. It is a systematic way of designing, carrying out, and evaluating the total process of learning and teaching in terms of specific objectives, based on research in human learning and communication, and employing a combination of human and nonhuman resources to bring about more effective instruction. The widespread acceptance and application of this broad definition belongs to the future.

The Association for Educational Communications and Technology has also published a definition of IT (although called educational technology) in its glossary of terms:

> "Educational Technology" is a complex, integrated process involving people, procedures, ideas, devices, and organization for analyzing problems, and devising, implementing, evaluating and managing solutions to those problems, involved in all aspects of human learning. In educational technology, the solutions to problems take the form of all the "Learning Resources" that are designed and/or selected as Messages, People, Materials, Devices, Techniques, and Settings. The processes for analyzing problems and devising, implementing and evaluating solutions are identified by the "Educational Development Functions" of Research-Theory, Design, Production, Evaluation, Selection, Logistics, and Utilization. The processes of directing or coordinating one or more of these functions are identified by the "Educational Management Functions" of Organization Management and Personnel Management.*

As you will see, it is this latter definition that reflects the focus of this book.

TRAINING INSTRUCTIONAL TECHNOLOGISTS

Most programs in IT are offered at the graduate level in schools of education, but there is a trend to offer it as an area of specialization at the baccalaureate

---

*Reprinted from *Educational Technology: Definition and Glossary of Terms*, for Association for Educational Communications and Technology. Copyright 1977.

level. Usually baccalaureate and master's degree programs tend to be more operational (media production, administration or instructional development oriented), whereas doctoral programs are more likely to emphasize research, teaching, and systematic model development.

Instructional technology courses in teacher-training institutions usually differ from other courses in the college by excluding nonresearched practices, or the art-of-education courses. IT is also concerned with both large group and individualized instruction as well as conventional classroom instruction. IT also tends to emphasize the use of materials that researchers say work better than, or at least as well as, alternative techniques of instruction. Furthermore, IT is problem oriented and attempts to use a variety of tools such as needs assessment, task analysis, and formative evaluation, which are defined later in the text. Instructional technology-based teacher education, then, provides teachers with a different set of tools than more traditional programs. In fairness, it should be said that IT overlaps with other fields of study in education. For example, IT draws knowledge from educational psychology, curriculum, and administration, among others.

Audio-visual departments may also be subsumed under an IT division. Instructional technology includes many of the design concerns of the audio-visual specialist, but deemphasizes the need for technologists to become writers, artists, or photographers. Instead, IT emphasizes the need to know where to locate materials, how to recognize the problems, needs, interests, and goals of students, and how to provide a rationale for media selection and instructional evaluation. Instructional technologists must also be able to communicate their design requirements to media production specialists.

Recall that instructional technology involves all three of the major components of any instructional system.

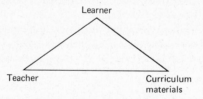

FIGURE 2.1 The Learner, Teacher, Materials Triangle

In IT we are concerned with all three interactions. The focus of the system is on learners and changes in their behavior, that is, learning. However, the curriculum materials and the teacher are essential components of almost all instructional systems because they provide the structure and the environment within which formal learning and its evaluation can take place. Deciding on the appropriate mix of teachers and materials and managing and evaluating the process is the heart of instructional technology.

INSTRUCTIONAL DEVELOPMENT

Experience is the worst teacher; it gives the test before presenting the lesson.

Anonymous

The typical beginning point at which to apply IT occurs when students' current knowledge or behavior does not coincide with that which is needed or desired, that is, when there is a difference between where students are and where the objectives suggest they should be. This difference defines the course of instruction.

What do the students already know? What do they need to learn? What should they be taught? What instructional methods and materials are needed to get the students from where they are now to the point where they can perform at the desired level? These are the four primary questions technologists must consider when developing a curriculum or course of study.

A procedure for answering these kinds of questions has been developed and is called the instructional systems approach. This empirically based approach will vary somewhat depending on the type of instructional problem to be resolved, but its basic elements remain constant. A systematic procedure for solving instructional problems is frequently called an instructional development model. Many models exist, each designed for use in a specific setting for selected types of instructional problems.

This systems approach to problem solving was developed and refined during World War II when Great Britain, the United States, and others had to:

1. Quickly *identify the elements of a problem* (ships are being sunk in the Atlantic);
2. *Gather data* about the problem (too many effective enemy subs—especially at certain times and places);
3. *Choose the best solution* (get more destroyers around the convoys and also change the routing and scheduling of ships). It was determined that the majority of attacks occurred at only a few locations at specific times of day on unprotected vessels.
4. *Develop and implement* the solution (change the routes and schedules to reduce vessel visibility and also build and deploy additional destroyers to protect the convoys).

Similarly, instructional problems often involve defining the problem, deciding on a course of action, obtaining personnel needed to develop objectives, writing scripts, taking photographs, developing graphics, and testing the solution to see if it "works." An instructional development procedure may be employed by a teacher preparing a presentation for a single class, or by a team for a large-scale project such as the training for a space shuttle mission. Specific techniques will vary, but the underlying principles remain the same: gather

---

INDIVIDUALIZED INSTRUCTION AT PIUS X HIGH SCHOOL

In 1972 a Roman Catholic high school in Downey, California, elected to join the Individually Prescribed Instruction (IPI) project designed by J. Lloyd Trump, who was with the National Education Association.

The faculty of the school worked in the summer of 1973 to begin writing the programmed materials they would use with the majority of their students that fall. The students could elect to work in the individualized instruction track or take the traditional "little red schoolhouse" track.

Instructional materials were available in one of several different subject matter resource centers. There were math, language arts, science, and social studies centers. The math materials, for example, were available in the math center, and the students could schedule themselves (with supervision) into the lab at times of their choosing (providing space was available). If they finished a course in algebra in March they could immediately begin the geometry course. Because of this flexibility the average time to complete the high school program became three years rather than four. The students performed far above the mean on the SAT and other "standardized" tests. The individualized school worked and the students liked their school!

---

data, define the problem, develop solutions, and evaluate and modify them as needed.

The quality of these instructional development efforts is reflected in research studies which often indicate that, through their use, students reach a higher level of achievement of their objectives in considerably less time. The more thought and effort that goes into a decision or project, the better the end product is likely to be.

While many school systems are using instructional development models in managing projects, there are a greater number of military and industrial users of these systematic procedures. Increasingly, the industrial training focus is on how to get the best return for the time and money invested.

It is simply good business to get the best return for each dollar spent—even a training dollar. For the military, the concern is training individuals in a broad spectrum of skills ranging from operating and maintaining complex electronic missiles to mechanical and clerical tasks. Their concern is to rapidly train many people to the level specified in the training objectives. Instructional development models, with their analysis, design, and evaluation components, provide a degree of assurance that these training needs are being resolved in the most efficient manner possible.

Instructional System Development (ISD) procedures are used by curriculum developers to ensure the relevance of course content to particular jobs. Orlansky and String (1981) summarized the research on technical courses modified according to ISD procedures and found that the average length of the courses was reduced from 25.3 to 9.6 weeks. The time saving was obviously significant and more than offset the initial development costs. Although these were all military courses, there is no reason to assume time savings would be different in courses developed by ISD procedures for other milieu.

INSTRUCTIONAL DEVELOPMENT MODELS

We must not ask where science and technology are taking us, but rather how we can manage science and technology so that they can take us where we want to go.

René Dubos

The six instructional development models discussed in this chapter have five common elements:

1. Data collection
2. Assessment of learner entry skills
3. Specification of behavioral objectives or performance tests
4. A procedure for selecting presentation methods and media
5. An implementation, evaluation, and revision procedure

In addition, most models also include procedures for:

- Identifying broad instructional goals
- Organizing the management of the project
- Identifying the problem
- Performing a needs assessment
- Identifying constraints imposed by physical facilities
- Identifying a procedure to construct and test prototype instructional materials

Sometimes an instructional development model will also include a method of ensuring that the required support services are accessible.

First we will examine two general instructional development models widely used in education. Then we will examine two military and one industrial model. The discussion concludes with a presentation of our model which guides the organization of the remainder of the text.

Kemp Model

Jerry Kemp of California State University at San Jose developed an early instructional development model for education. The Kemp model guides its user to think about the general problems and purposes of instruction. It also directs

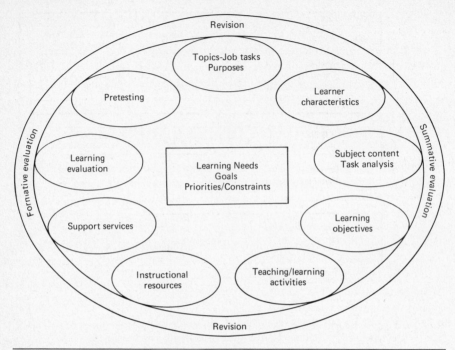

FIGURE 2.2   The Kemp Instructional Development Model *(Used with permission of Jerrold E. Kemp)*

an instructional developer to look at student characteristics and determine appropriate learning objectives. Following this, subject content is specified and a pretest is developed from the objectives. Next, the teaching/learning activities and resources are specified, located, produced, and taught. The components are then evaluated in terms of the objectives. Support services are identified and the revision performed, based on the evaluation.

Instructional Development Institute Model

A second model is the Instructional Development Institute (IDI) model shown in Figure 2.3. The IDI model has three stages divided into a total of nine functions. The first three functions are part of its define stage: identify the problem, analyze the setting, and organize the management.

The second, or develop, stage, also has three functions: identify the objectives, specify the methods, and construct the prototypes. The third, or evaluate, stage involves testing the prototypes, analyzing results, recycling if required, and implementing the system.

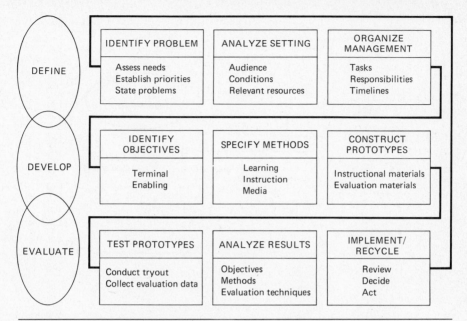

FIGURE 2.3   Instructional Development Institute Model *(Used with permission of the University Consortium for Instructional Development and Technology)*

Interservice Procedures for Instructional Systems Development Model

The Interservice Procedures for Instructional Systems Development (IPISD) was developed by the U.S. Army Combat Arms Training Board at Fort Benning, Georgia, and The Center for Educational Technology at Florida State University. When the U.S. Army training programs were reviewed in the late 1960s, it was decided that the military should follow instructional technology-based procedures. (Logan, 1982) As a result of the study, a comprehensive ISD model was developed to train army personnel. (Branson, 1975) The Interservice Systems model is now used extensively by the U.S. Army. As new items of equipment are ordered, the contractors are required to use this ISD model in developing the operation and maintenance manuals or training courses for the equipment as part of the procurement contract. This model consists of five major phases as shown in Figure 2.4.

This Interservices model begins by requiring analysis of the job to be trained, and then provides detailed information on how to select the tasks or functions to be trained. This model is much like the models described earlier. However, it also includes a detailed management course for instructors to en-

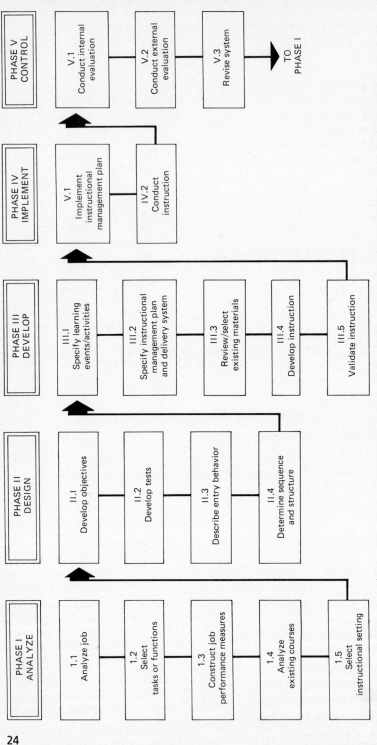

FIGURE 2.4 Interservice Procedures for Instructional Systems Development Model (*TRADOC Pamphlet 340–30*)

**INSTRUCTIONAL SYSTEMS DEVELOPMENT IN
THE UNITED STATES ARMED FORCES**

In the 1960s the Army, Navy and Air Force adopted Instructional Systems Development (ISD) procedures to design and develop their instructional/training materials and programs. This was decided because the ISD approaches had "demonstrated improvements in cost per student, time required to complete, and increased effectiveness."

ISD approaches to instruction differ from traditional approaches in several ways:

"An important difference between ISD and more traditional forms of instruction is that the ISD process, through occupational surveys and job analyses, requires the thoughtful selection of what is to be trained based on solid job data from the field. This practice tends to insure that the training will be provided for (the critical needs).

"A second important difference between traditional schools and ISD procedures is the consideration of how training is to be conducted. The recent past has seen a number of innovations in approaches to training, all of which are either as good or better than traditional methodology.

"A third critical difference between traditional practice and ISD is the ISD use of test data based on absolute standards of performance and the use of that data to grade students and to judge the quality of the instruction.

"Finally, the ISD process requires the application of modern technology to the fullest degree possible in order to optimize training effectiveness, efficiency and costs."

Source: Interservice Procedures for Instructional Systems Development, Executive Summary and Model. TRADOC Pamphlet 340–30, 1 August 1975, 6–7.

---

sure that they know the ins-and-outs of both the instructional system and the materials, as well as a procedure to facilitate the adoption of the newly developed program.

CRI Model

The *Criterion Referenced Instruction* (CRI) model was developed by Robert F. Mager and has been widely used in industrial settings. His procedure specifies a task analysis followed by instructional objective development, selection of a media mix, instructional program development, and evaluation and revision of the materials until they meet the stated criterion. Although the model can be graphically portrayed, it is essentially a verbal model.

UNESCO ISD Model

Under pressure to develop more relevant, higher quality educational programs for developing nations, UNESCO developed a systematic procedure or model.

They felt the systems approach could be used to plan and implement large-scale projects in education. The overall steps of the model are shown in Figure 2.5. (A more detailed discussion of the model is provided by Logan [1982].)

The UNESCO model stresses analysis of the existing educational system and its social implications. This model is also useful for those wanting a model which stresses planning and deemphasizes product development. The UNESCO model places less emphasis on job or task analysis, but does place a great deal of emphasis on specifying the terminal criteria needed for success.

Other Models

A survey and presentation of several instructional development models by Gustafson (1981) has been published by the Educational Resources Information Clearinghouse (ERIC) at Syracuse University. This survey presents and discusses graphic models and provides additional references for individuals interested in a wide variety of instructional development models.

Synthesized Model

The model below contains a synthesis of elements from a variety of specialized models in an attempt to create a more generic model. We believe it has wide application to many types of settings and provides an excellent framework for examining the components of instructional technology. The format for the text itself reflects this synthesized model, and subsequent chapters will amplify and explain its major points. You may wish to study it briefly before continuing. You will note it contains all the principal components common to other models (data collection, problem definition, prototype development and evaluation/revision). Each major component will be discussed in detail and specific techniques for conducting the activity will be provided.

SUMMARY

I question whether we can afford to teach mother macrame when Johnny still can't read.

Jerry Brown (ex-governor of California discussing the need to support community colleges)

In this chapter we have seen that IT includes the application of principles from the behavioral, physical, and social sciences. When systematically applied, these principles allow a learner efficient access to more relevant information than was ever before possible. Most instructional technologists will agree with the philosophy of learning expressed in this chapter: instructional technology should focus on the learner and be oriented toward resolving instructional/

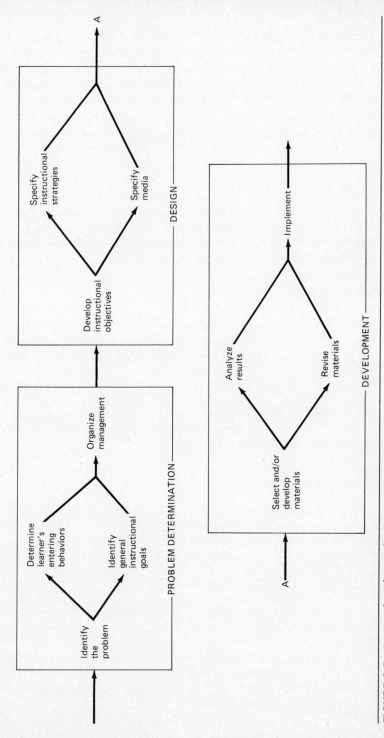

FIGURE 2.5 Instructional Development Model

27

learning problems. The challenge to teachers and administrators is to maximize the benefits of technology and to minimize its undesirable characteristics.

To achieve this goal there is a need for a systematic problem-solving procedure. Several instructional development models from a variety of settings were presented, along with the model used as the framework for this book.

Questions for Consideration and Discussion

1. Does the use of instructional technology make education and training less humane or less desirable or more human and more desirable?
2. What is the impact of an instructional technology-based curriculum on a student?
3. Should all classroom teachers be proficient at using an instructional development model? Should teachers use instructional technology processes or products when they prepare their daily lessons? Who could, or should, use instructional development procedures? Why? When? Where? How?

Suggested Activities

1. Define instructional technology in your own words.
2. List ways in which instructional technology procedures are similar to, and different from, either "teacher preparation" or "curriculum and instruction" courses taught in schools of education.
3. List the key technological developments that encouraged the development of an instructional technology.
4. Compare the instructional development model in this chapter with either the Interservices model or the Kemp model by examining their assumptions about learners, learning, and the instructional environment.

Suggested Readings

Andrews, D., and Goodson, L. (1980). A Comparative Analysis of Models of Instructional Design. *Journal of Instructional Development*, 3(4), 2–16.

Association for Educational Communications and Technology. Task Force on Definition and Terminology. (1977). *Educational Technology: Definition and Glossary of Terms*, vol. 1. Washington, DC.

Branson, R. K., Rayner, G. T., Cox, J. L., Furman, J. P., King, F. J., and Hannum, W. H. (August 1975). *Interservice Procedures for Instructional Systems Development* (5 vols.). (TRADOC Pam 350-30 and NAVEDTRA 106A). Ft. Monroe, VA: U.S. Army Training and Doctrine Command. (NTIS NO. ADA 019-486 through ADA 019-490)

Brown, J. W., and Brown, S. N., eds. *Educational Media Yearbook*. Littleton, CO: Libraries Unlimited. (published annually)

Gage, N. L. (1981). *The Scientific Basis of the Art of Teaching*. New York: Teachers College Press.

Gagne, R. M., and Briggs, L. J. (1979). *Principles of Instructional Design*, 2nd ed. New York: Holt, Rinehart and Winston.

Glaser, R. (1981). *Instructional Psychology: Past, Present and Future*. University of Pittsburgh: Learning Research and Development Center.

Gustafson, K. L. (1981). *Survey of Instructional Development Models*. ERIC Clearinghouse on Information Resources, Syracuse University.

Kemp, J. (1980). *Instructional Design*, 3rd ed. Palo Alto, CA: Fearon Publishers.

Logan, R. S. (1982). *Instructional Systems Development: An International View of Theory and Practice*. New York: Academic Press.

Orlansky, J., and String, J. (1981). Computer-Based Instruction for Military Training. *Defense Management Journal*, 46–54.

Saettler, P. (1968). *History of Instructional Technology*. New York: McGraw-Hill.

Stakenas, R. G., and Kaufman, R. (1981). *Technology in Education: Its Human Potential*. Fastback No. 163. Bloomington, IL: Phi Delta Kappa.

Strauch, R. E. (1981). *Strategic Planning as a Perceptual Process*. P-6595. Santa Monica, CA: Rand Corporation.

Thorndike, E. L. (1912). *Education*. New York: The Macmillan Company.

Tickton, S. G., ed. (1970). *To Improve Learning*. New York: R. R. Bowker.

Unwin, D., and McAlesse, R. (1978). *Encyclopedia of Educational Media Communications and Technology*. Westport, CT: Greenwood Press, Inc.

Wilkinson, G. L. (1980). *Media in Instruction: 60 Years of Research*. Washington, DC: Association for Educational Communications and Technology.

3

Problem Identification

We should ask three questions when we have a problem: (1) What is the problem? (2) What are the alternatives? and (3) What is the best alternative?

John Dewey

Objectives

After completing this chapter you should be able to:

1. List the three steps in conducting a needs assessment.
2. List the key steps in performing a task analysis.
3. List the major sources of data needed to conduct a needs assessment or task analysis.
4. Determine whether a needs assessment or task analysis should be conducted.
5. Perform a short needs assessment or task analysis.
6. Prepare a task hierarchy.

The first step of the instructional development model used in this text involves identifying the problem to be resolved. This step is based on the premise that if you don't know what the real (as opposed to imagined) problem is, you can't solve it. Also, different problems have different solutions and the two require precise matching. For example, employee performance problems are often attributed to a "need for training," but analysis reveals the actual source to be motivational or environmental. All the training in the world will not "solve" an employee motivation problem.

In this chapter needs assessment and task analysis will be examined as two problem-identification procedures. There are other analysis and assessment tools, but these two clarify instructional problems and requirements particularly well.

A problem may be as simple as a teacher feeling there must be a better way to help students understand composition. The problem may be apparent because students do not attend to the instruction, or do poorly in testing situations. In contrast, the problem may be as complex as deciding what to teach an astronaut. However, both simple and complex problems are usually better understood or resolved by performing a needs assessment.

NEEDS ASSESSMENT

Success in solving the problem depends on choosing the right aspect, on attacking the fortress from its accessible side.

George Polya

An instructional technologist, when performing an assessment, should first ask the question, "Are the learners presently capable of doing what they *need* to be able to do?" To make this question relevant we need to determine the discrepancy between what they already know how to do and what we think they should be able to do. Then we can ascertain if it is really important that they be able to perform that behavior, or meet that instructional objective.

Needs assessment is, basically, a process for determining the difference between *what is* and *what is desired.* The gap between the two is the need or problem area. When needs assessment is used, a general question must be posed as the first step. The question asks whether there is some reason to believe the situation can be improved. Steps two and three involve determining whether the behavior is important and if the student already possesses those skills. The instructional technologist must also determine whether the student has the ability to learn the objective and how often the skill will be used. Examining the instructional strategies requires answering the question, "Are there easier ways to teach the objectives than those to which students have been exposed in the past?" If the answer to this question is yes, then the technologist should ask the next question: "What obstacles must be overcome by students before attaining the objective?" Are there negative factors to be overcome? For example, will their friends or family ridicule them for studying? Do they receive attention or reward for *not* learning? Do they feel that being able to perform the objective is rewarding and important? Is the physical environment (noise, light and glare, colors, playground activity) distracting and preventing them from learning? And, has the student already had an opportunity to learn the behaviors under consideration?

Keep in mind that needs assessment is primarily problem rather than solution oriented. We must first thoroughly understand the problem so that a sound solution can be selected or developed. Need statements refer to problems to be resolved, not solutions to be tried. An instructional needs assessment should be learner oriented rather than instruction or teaching oriented. For example, the statement "Students are performing over one full grade level below national average," represents a gap between the observed and what apparently is desired (national average). In contrast, the statement "We need to put a microcomputer in every classroom," is simply an expression of an opinion about a solution and is not based on learners or documented gaps. It is a solution in search of a problem.

Recall that a need is defined as the discrepancy between *what is* and *what is desired*.

Problem Area: Sixth-Grade Reading

1. *What is?* The average reading comprehension grade level of all sixth-grade students in the school is 6.2 at the end of the sixth grade.
2. *What is desired?* The sixth-grade students, at the end of the instructional year should have an average reading comprehension grade score of 7.0 or better.
3. *Discrepancy.* At the end of the year, sixth-grade students are eight months behind the desired reading level.

There are two orientations from which needs assessments can be made: internal and external. An *internal* needs assessment looks at the needs as seen from within the organization. This assessment identifies gaps in achieving organizational goals/objectives. Internal needs assessment should be augmented by external needs assessment data to obtain a holistic view from outside the organization. This latter assessment attempts to identify needs that are important for students once they are outside of the educational environment. An *external* needs assessment considers what students will have to do to be self-sufficient once they exit the educational/training situation. The Sixth-Grade Reading illustration is an example of an internal assessment. An external needs assessment, of what students need to do outside school, might examine their need to read and complete job application forms.

The final step in assessing an education or training problem is to estimate which general avenue of approach will be best for the present situation. This is primarily a design consideration which will be discussed in more detail later. However, the question must be asked at the needs assessment phase because each potential solution will affect the nature of data collected while analyzing the setting. Also, since some solutions may result in undesirable consequences for other parts of the educational system, it is best to examine each potential solution during the initial data analysis. No final decision is made concerning a solution at this time. However, some potential solutions may be discarded or downrated as a result of the analysis.

Needs assessment therefore consists of three phases:

1. Stating a potential problem in terms of a question
2. Documenting the nature and scope of internal and external gaps
3. Developing a tentative description of the solution to the problem

During the *problem identification* phase, people who are involved in, or affected by, the decision-making process are identified and their concerns or goals enumerated. There are generally three groups who can provide information about the problem:

1. Students—select a broad band actually representing the intended student audience
2. Staff—professional, paraprofessional, maintenance, and clerical staff
3. The community—board members, parents, executives, interest groups, and the general public

Members of these groups should be encouraged to state their concerns and goals in specific statements concerning *what* is desired. The resulting list of wishes and wants does not represent actual needs, but provides the basis for further analysis. Also, it does a remarkable job of making visible the attitudes and opinions of these three groups toward the area under investigation. This information can be extremely helpful later when planning and implementing solutions that must be communicated to these groups. After these statements have been developed and collected, it is time to proceed to the next step in the needs assessment.

Formulating realistic goals is a highly creative process. The objectives must be selected from all possible objectives based on "need to know" or relevance to the learner. How can one identify general instructional goals? In schools we can begin by looking at existing school goals and curriculum guides to determine what past analysis has produced. Examination of current textbooks and other materials will also provide useful information. Existing tests are another excellent source of desired objectives. The needs assessment and task analysis will help to refine or specify these goals.

When identifying program goals it is desirable to determine the goals of education with respect to both the individual and society. What goals are appropriate for the person and what for the society? While these goals obviously overlap, some are unique and deserve separate attention. It is also important to determine specifically how the curriculum could contribute to those goals.

Although an instructional technologist may have a voice in creating policy, he or she is primarily responsible for implementing policy decisions. The policies as summarized by the school board, or other appropriate body, should provide the broad goals within which the instructional technologist carries out the role of evaluator, designer, or producer. If the instructional technologist questions the goals, an interpretation should be provided by a representative of the policy-making body.

Once a gap has been identified, for example, the behaviors expected of the student are not being attained, you know you have a problem. That is, if it is agreed that students must know how to operate a computer but don't, a problem exists. Now you must determine whether the discrepancy between the goal and the student's entering behaviors is sufficiently important to warrant the time and money to develop a training program. You must also decide whether education or training is the solution to the problem. Several questions should be asked to determine whether an education or training program will resolve the problem.

- Is the goal, or the more specific restatement of it as an objective, important enough to warrant a training program?
- Could the student perform the desired objectives without an instructional program, that is, by using a job or memory aid?
- Does the student have the mental, physical, and emotional capabilities to attain the training objectives?
- Can the student be encouraged to *want* to learn?
- Is nonperformance or nonlearning rewarded by a peer group, parents, ego?
- Are there specific obstacles to the student's goal attainment such as time, distractions, lack of resources, or lack of prerequisite knowledge?

Lack of knowledge is only one reason people fail to perform as expected. Before jumping to the conclusion that training is needed, we should consider other explanations for the absence of desired behavior. Failure to take this simple step has resulted in the development of many educational and training programs that did not produce the expected results.

We must decide next what should be done. Knowing that a gap or problem exists and that the students are capable of attaining the goals, do we recommend that an instructional development project be started? No! Next we must consider alternative approaches to eliminating the problem or gap. This includes data collection (so the alternative solutions are known) to determine which alternative is best.

Phase two of performing a needs assessment involves collecting additional information about the problem statement. This phase is often called the documentation phase. Information concerning what is desired has to be documented in some quantitative manner. Particular attention should be given to data from outside the organization. When possible, the instructional technologist should collect input, process, product, output, and outcome data that is both current and future oriented. As will be seen later, needs are identified only as they relate to products and outcomes. However, data should also be collected concerning inputs and processes to facilitate the identification of tentative solutions before completing the needs assessment. Below are listed some examples of inputs, processes, products, and outcomes that might be examined.

- *Inputs:* money, facilities, equipment, raw materials, personnel
- *Processes:* instructional strategies, testing and evaluation, diagnosis and placement, performance feedback, reward structure
- *Products:* achievement scores, attitudes, motor skills, product rejection rate, product quality rating, adherence to timelines
- *Outcomes:* personnel placement, customer satisfaction, success on the job, increased sales, reduced personnel grievances

The information is collected, organized, and analyzed to confirm or refute the validity of the statements generated during phase one. During the documentation phase you reexamined the question, "What is?" This documentation may demonstrate that the perceptions collected in phase one are quite accurate, but our experience indicates they are often false. For example, at the beginning of one analysis done for the military, it was reported by instructors that new recruits were failing in school for lack of prerequisite knowledge and skill. However, careful analysis and testing of recruits demonstrated that this view was incorrect. The real problems were within the course structure, particularly with the lack of feedback to recruits on their performance. This example illustrates a point of particular importance. Those involved in an activity—students, instructors, managers—are usually quick to point to "problems" in other parts of the system. They are usually much less able or willing to consider the "problem" as being possibly closer to home.

There are two general sources for documentation data. Internal data from within the organization is usually the easiest to obtain. This information might consist of achievement test scores, characteristics of personnel, facilities, staffing patterns, available funds, availability of validated learning materials, placement data, patient discharge data, number of completed "widgets," number of rejected parts, maintenance information, attendance data, and so on.

On team development projects, a specific individual is usually assigned responsibility for coordinating collection of this information. Procedures might include computer searches, telephone calls, interviews or on-site observation and examination of records and tabulation of data.

The second source of data—external data—is usually not as conveniently or economically assembled as internal data. Sources of external data might include nationwide achievement data from the National Assessment of Educational Progress in Denver, the Educational Testing Service, in Princeton, New Jersey, state education departments, or the Educational Resources Information Clearinghouse (ERIC). A follow-up of graduates and studies of consumers of the agencies' products or services may also provide valuable data.

Once the information has been collected it must be organized and catalogued. The list of what is desired can then be refined, and a series of related "what is?" statements constructed. It may be desirable to organize the instructional goals and objectives into the cognitive, affective, and psychomotor domains. Another pattern is to arrange data so that it corresponds to the various parts of the organization (classroom, media center, and central administration in schools or production, sales and management in a business or industry). Having collected additional data regarding the problem (or problems), it is now possible to proceed to a more precise definition of the "gaps."

In phase three, the *product* phase, we precisely state the discrepancies between what is and what is desired. These statements are the outcome of a needs assessment. If educational goals are being assessed, the result will be a list of educational goals or required activities along with a statement about the perceived status and priority of alternative activities. Direction for subsequent decisions and actions is derived from the type and magnitude of differences and perceived degree of importance of each instructional need.

"Hmm, you say your 'F' in science was because your calculator failed, your 'F' in composition was due your electric typewriter breaking, and your 'F' in your first-hour class, social science, was because of car troubles?"

(S. Bartenstein)

An example of a need (discrepancy) resulting from a training needs assessment would be that of a machine operator who can describe the necessary steps to take in an emergency situation but is unable to recognize the actual warning signals when using the equipment. This type of gap is common when people are taught more about the objective than about how to actually perform it.

An assessment of available personnel and physical resources may be performed concurrently with needs assessment. These data will assist the instructional technologist in developing tentative solutions that appear feasible based on available resources.

Note that not all discrepancies between *what is* and *what is desired* are needs. A need is really a gap in products, outputs, or outcomes. If the gap is related to an input or to a process, you are examining wishes or quasi-needs. You may also have identified your own limitations and those of your system. For example, people may consider a "need" as an additional million dollars to install a new television system. And indeed, they can document that the new system does cost that amount. By our definition, however, such a situation does not describe a need since it does not relate to an output such as a gap in student learning. The world of education and training is so replete with examples of such spurious needs that technologists must be wary. This issue is of great concern because when wants and wishes are expressed as needs they may become an excuse for inaction (since we don't have the money we can't do *anything*). Also, should money become available and then be expended on such nonneeds, the real problems will remain unresolved.

We have been discussing needs which indicate that the solution requires education or training, but keep in mind that many needs that lie outside this domain will be identified. For example, a large manufacturer of office copy machines found, after analysis, that lagging sales of a new line of copiers was not due to lack of knowledge by its sales force. Poor sales performance was due to the existing commission rate structure, which had the unintended effect of reducing the income of sales personnel if the new copier rather than an older line was sold! Simply changing the commission structure caused sales to soar. Technologists must constantly remind themselves that many performance problems are unrelated to lack of knowledge.

The outline for stating a needs assessment is:

Problem Area: _____

1. What is? _____

2. What is desired? _____

3. Discrepancy: _____

A fourth line is sometimes added: tentative solution. Because many alternative approaches to resolving the discrepancy are often available, it may be appropriate to examine all of them in some detail before selecting the approach or solution to follow in any specific instance. It may seem premature to develop tentative solutions at this early stage of the process, but this should be done before final decisions are made on which needs will be attacked first. By having outlined various solutions, it may become evident that some are not feasible considering existing resources. Others may require outside approval before proceeding. Such knowledge will aid selection of feasible solutions and avoid the common error of charging off with little more than good intent, like Don Quixote jousting with windmills. Recall that only an outline of each solution should be developed to specify personnel, time, materials, and other required resources. The instructional technologist is cautioned to remain aware of the fine line between expending too much time and energy specifying details of solutions that will later be discarded, and not considering existing practical parameters before selecting a solution.

Once discrepancies, or needs statements, have been prepared, they should be placed in order of priority. Then a decision can be made as to which of the identified problems are to be resolved. Limited availability of resources will make choices difficult among the identified needs. By publicizing the decision-making process, the various constituencies become aware of the limitations and may, as a result, be more supportive of the ultimate decision than they might otherwise have been. While there are many approaches to establishing priorities among needs and solutions, one of the most desirable is some variation on a point-allocation procedure, which involves giving each participant a number of points (usually 100) to be allocated among the needs or proposed solutions. Participants then allocate their points as they see fit among the alternatives. Totals for each item are tallied and rank ordered. The results can then be accepted as is, or another round of allocations can be made by dropping those categories receiving the fewest points. Naturally, rules governing the procedure should be specified in advance. This procedure creates a sense of involvement on the part of the participants that enhances their commitment to subsequent steps in the development process. A disadvantage is the diffusion of responsibility for the decision, rather than placing it on one or two competent individuals.

TASK ANALYSIS

Great opportunities often come brilliantly disguised as insoluble problems.
John Gardner

Having identified needs, it is often desirable to perform a task analysis in order to specify in greater detail the activities to be accomplished. In other cases, it may be possible to skip this step and proceed directly to writing the instructional objectives. This decision should be based on whether the task is procedural and sequential (using a pay phone) or does not have such an order of performance (recall of symbols for chemical compounds). Obviously the latter does not lend itself to task analysis.

Task analysis helps the instructional designer determine and validate exactly what the learner needs to be able to do. Task analysis examines the process or sequence of actions of a trained or knowledgeable person performing the task. The goal of task analysis is to develop a valid training program with respect to the skills needed by the learner; that is, one that includes all necessary skills and knowledge while ensuring that unnecessary information is not included.

A task is a series of actions leading to a terminal or meaningful outcome, such as taking a test, typing a letter, painting a picture, and writing an essay. These larger tasks can be broken down into "task elements," the smallest units of behavior that can be measured and taught. Examples of the actions taken at a task element level are selecting a question on a test to answer, inserting paper into a typewriter, putting a paintbrush in cleaning solution, picking up a pencil before writing, or outlining an essay. Task analysis, when used on instructional problems, allows an instructional designer to develop objectives from the task elements.

Task analysis "exposes" the tasks and is particularly valuable when prerequi-

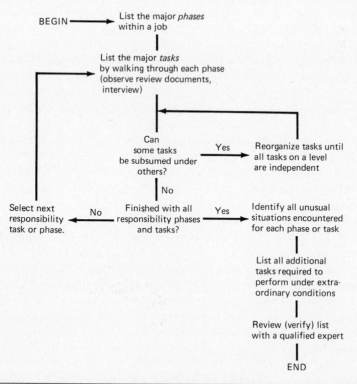

FIGURE 3.1   Flowchart of the Task Analysis Procedure

site content information is not evident. Instructional steps or enabling objectives may also be sequenced as a result of task analysis.

A task description has a formal format. It is a statement beginning with a command verb (press, add, insert, pick up, focus) that reflects the detailed actions involved in accomplishing the goal. Task analysis starts with the task description but focuses on the individual's knowledge, skills, and performance at each step of the task. The task elements are then ordered in a time sequence. "Interaction analysis" is a tool or procedure for analyzing teacher–student interactions. Others include direct observation, interviews, simulations, time-motion studies, content analysis, and information processing analysis. Audio and video recordings may facilitate the analytic process by permitting the technologist and performer to reexamine and recall while reviewing the recording.

A task analysis may be accomplished by 1) observing what a knowledgeable person does; 2) reviewing documents related to the teaching/learning task; 3) interviewing people associated with the task; and 4) performing the task. Task analyses are often done by using a combination of looking, reading, asking, and doing. A task analysis should be sufficiently complete so that the untrained learner could perform the task from the task descriptions. This can be done by writing out in detail, and in order, the specific activities.

The task analysis on using a pay telephone (see Figure 3.2) illustrates how an algorithmic flow chart might depict the process. Note that diamonds designate questions to be answered (yes or no) while squares indicate specific activities. As you will quickly notice, the flow chart could include additional questions or break each action into smaller steps. For example, the sole task of looking up a telephone number requires several skills. In addition, the analysis covers two actions—one requiring the coin to be inserted before dialing, the other after dialing. An analysis could cover only one alternative or perhaps even three or more. If the analysis can yield so many variations, you might ask, "How does it help?" Its value lies only partially in the resulting flow chart.

The process highlights assumptions made about the task and the learner and clarifies the necessary conditions for performing the task. For example, our flow chart assumes the person can make change, find numbers in a phone book, and read and comprehend instructions. (You can probably identify additional assumptions.) Further, notice that we restricted the analysis to using only quarters and to operational phones. If the person you are calling is not home or has a phone that is out of order, you will spend a lot of time in the telephone booth unless you modify the task analysis! As you can see, examining assumptions about the learner, the task, and the environment can highlight decisions about what should be taught. A word of caution, however: do not assume that the order displayed by the task analysis is the optimal order for sequencing instruction. Often the sequence for instruction will be quite different. (We will discuss this important topic later.)

It may be worth constructing a flow chart of the task and its related elements so that each of the specific activities can be graphically seen in relation to the

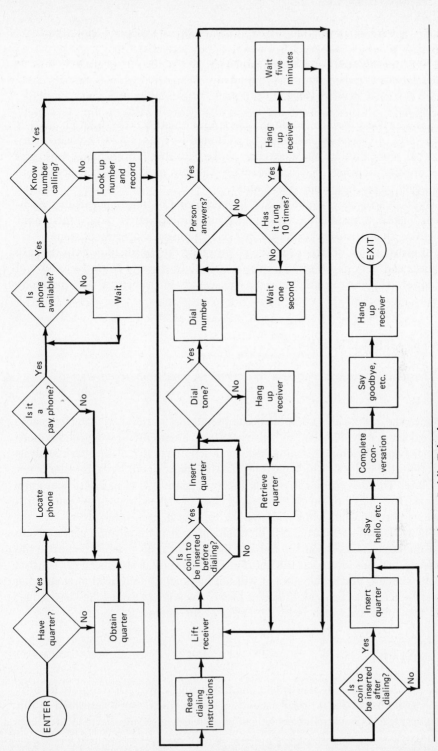

FIGURE 3.2 Task Analysis of Operating a Public Telephone

41

others. A flow chart should allow an instructional designer to determine

1.   Decisions encountered by the performer
2.   Results of making the various decisions
3.   Steps and feedback loops in the system

The flow chart should contain all relevant information collected from analysis of the task. All steps and feedback loops should be connected to indicate every possible route through the flow chart. Take care that no unclosed loops exist that prevent "flowing" through the chart. The flow chart should be a complete reflection of the task from start to finish.

The task analysis procedure may be performed on teaching/learning problems, materials production tasks, or even administrative tasks. Remember however, that it is only useful for tasks containing a sequence of steps.

An instructional designer may be able to take the information from the task analysis and generate the instructional objectives directly from the tasks and activities. However, sometimes it is necessary to prepare a task hierarchy chart.

TASK HIERARCHY

The function of knowledge is to prevent dogma from accumulating.
Jerome Kagan

Once the task analysis has been completed and verified by knowledgeable individuals it may be useful to construct a task hierarchy showing the relationship between teaching/learning tasks and activities. Recall that task analysis describes the order in which parts of a task are performed, but this order is not absolute. The driver-education task listing (Figure 3.3) is in a task hierarchy format. The activities on the bottom of the chart usually are associated with lower-order learning, while those at the top are higher-order tasks.

Figure 3.3 shows a partial task hierarchy for a driver education course. Note that the larger tasks are at the top and the smaller tasks—which comprise the larger tasks—are located at the bottom. Thus the task of steering a car consists of one subtask, which the student will not be taught (identification of steering wheel) since it has been identified as part of the student's entering knowledge, and two subtasks, which must be taught in the course.

SUMMARY

Two procedures, needs assessment and task analysis, which are used to identify and clarify instructional problems and relevant content were described in this chapter. Needs assessment provides a format for ensuring that real problems

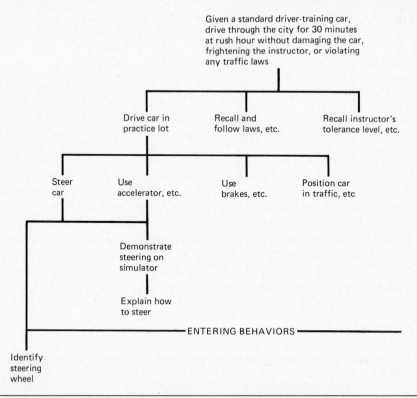

FIGURE 3.3   Driver Education Course Task Hierarchy (Incomplete)

are identified. The difference between *what is* and *what is desired* represents the need, which must then be examined to see if it has an instructional solution.

Some problem statements can then be further refined by using task analysis procedures to isolate and relate specific learner activities. In other situations a task hierarchy may be constructed to determine how the tasks are related. The rationale for devoting time and effort to these analysis procedures is that the more time spent on analyzing problems and designing solutions, the higher the quality of the instructional program. This chapter was limited to problem identification. In later chapters we will consider designing solutions to these problems.

Questions for Consideration and Discussion

1. How can a classroom teacher use the needs assessment procedure?
2. Determine whether each of the following factors is relevant to an internal or an external needs assessment.
   a. Sixth graders are reading at the fourth-grade level.

    b. Forty percent of our dropouts are unemployed because they are not functionally literate.

    c. Twenty-seven percent of the new cars are not welded properly.

    d. Sales of the new widget should increase 60% by June.

    e. There is a shortage of adequate library materials.

    f. The lab periods are too short for completing projects.

    g. Field representatives don't know enough about the company's new product.

    h. Computer literacy has been mandated as a graduate requirement.

3. Which of the following are quasi-need (input or process related) or wish statements rather than a listing of needs?

    a. Use computer managed instruction techniques.

    b. Only five graduates with computer programming skills were hired by a major computer firm.

    c. Forty percent of the instructors want longer lunch breaks.

Answers

Problem 2: Internal: a,c,e,f,h
           External: b,d,g
Problem 3: a and c are quasi-need statements.

Suggested Activities

1. Select a general instructional problem and in a small group, perform a needs assessment of that problem.
2. Perform a task analysis using the problem and needs assessment developed in the above activity.

Suggested Readings

Handy, H., and Hussan, K. (1969). *Network Analysis for Educational Management.* Englewood Cliffs, NJ: Prentice-Hall, Inc.

Herschbach, D. R. (Winter 1979). The Relationship Between Job Tasks and Objectives. *Journal of Industrial Teacher Education,* 27–37.

Kaufman, R. (1982). *Identifying and Solving Problems: A Systems Approach,* 3rd ed. San Diego: University Associates.

Kaufman, R., and English, F. W. (1979). *Needs Assessment: Concept and Application.* Englewood Cliffs, NJ: Educational Technology Publications.

Kaufman, R., Stakenas, R., Wager, J., and Mayer, H. (Summer 1981). Relating Needs Assessment, Program Development, Implementation, and Evaluation. *Journal of Instructional Development,* 4(4), 17–26.

Nager, R. F., and Pipe, P. (1970). *Analyzing Performance Problems or "You Really Oughta Wanna."* Palo Alto: Fearon.

Setsler, H. N. (March 1979). Foreign Language Task Analysis: A Systems Engineering Approach. *Educational Technology,* 35–40.

Tanner, C. K. (1971). *Designs for Educational Planning.* Lexington, MA: Heath-Lexington Books.

4

Analyzing Learner and Organization Characteristics to Identify Goals

The world belongs to he who does his homework.

James Finn, Law Number 1

Objectives

After studying this chapter you should be able to:

1. Outline a procedure for analyzing a potential instructional problem.
2. List the learner, curricular, and organizational components of a problem setting that affect the solution to the problem.
3. List criteria and procedures for examining existing instructional resources relevant to your instructional problem.

Typically a teacher works in a classroom of twenty to forty students with instruction being aimed at the mythical "average student." However, since all students are different, the instruction is not really geared to any one particular person in the class. Books, chalkboards, and the teacher are the primary sources of information available to the students. This teacher-based instructional system is no longer the best available for achieving many objectives.

The products and processes of instructional technology can, when appropriately incorporated, provide instruction aimed at individual learners. The pacing, study time, degree of repetition, and often the examples and curriculum itself may be tailored to a specific student. Instructional technology-based materials provide sufficient sources of information so that students can have their own "teacher." This "mediated teacher" can often ask the student questions and adapt, within limits of the material, to student responses.

Using IT forces an analysis of educational goals and instructional procedures.

INDIANAPOLIS AND ALTERNATIVE INSTRUCTION

Learning Unlimited was a study in North Central High School in Indianapolis, Indiana. Students in a senior government course were selected and assigned to one of three groups. One group was taught using lecture, textbook, discussion methods, and the like. Two other groups used alternative learning approaches including independent study, community-based experiences, and contracts. All groups took the same exams on the same textbook material. The results indicated that students in both the alternative groups scored higher than those in the "traditional" group on ten of the twelve exams they took during the semester. The traditional group scored higher early in the semester, but as time progressed the experimental groups outpaced the control groups. It appears, again, that students can learn the same content in different ways.

It also makes instruction more relevant to the individual learner and increases motivation by individualizing instruction. Teachers, released from the preparation and actual lecturing or presentation of lesson content, may devote more time to additional student counseling and shaping new or more positive student attitudes toward schooling.

Research on the use of alternative instructional methods (ITV, film, programmed instruction, language laboratories, computer-based instruction) is fairly conclusive. These alternative media-based instructional systems generally work about as well as conventional teacher-based presentation systems. The majority of comparative studies have resulted in findings of "no significant difference," but this research is of significant value because it is saying that there are many alternative ways to teach a given set of objectives.

Many questions have been raised concerning both traditional and media-based systems. We are still not sure which method works best for which student, under which conditions, and through which medium. It is also probable that students will learn differently at various times as they work with different types of instructional problems. Aptitude-Treatment-Interaction research is currently being done at many universities and research institutes to better understand this learner-medium-content interaction.

From this general discussion of alternative means of instruction we now return to our instructional-development model. Once the problem has been identified it is necessary to continue to collect data. Two data collection activities can be performed at about the same time (see Figure 4.1). The learners' entering skills must be determined so they can be considered in designing the instruction. At the same time, it is necessary to analyze the instructional goal. The difference between the students' entering knowledge and the instructional goal represents the instructional problem statement.

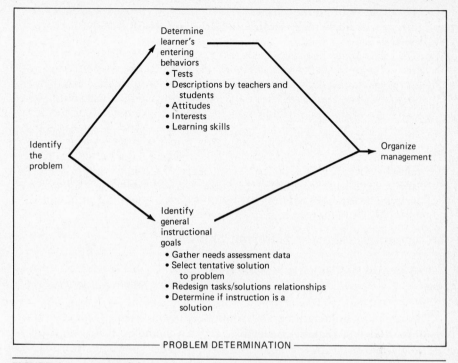

FIGURE 4.1   I.D. Model: Identifying Entering Behaviors and Instructional Goals

ANALYZING THE INSTRUCTIONAL SITUATION: WHERE THE PROGRAM BEGINS

What we want is to see the child in pursuit of knowledge, and not knowledge in pursuit of the child.

George Bernard Shaw

An instructional problem exists only if the learner's knowledge does not coincide with the desired objectives and goals. In order to determine the nature and extent of any gap, you need to know several things:

- The learner's entering abilities, skills, and attitudes.
- The content or objectives to be learned and the characteristics of that content.
- The characteristics of available educational personnel.
- The adequacy of existing materials (texts, references, media, supplies).
- The physical environment (size, location, internal spaces of buildings and other instructional spaces).

- The characteristics of the community: Do they support the school activities? Do they provide study spaces for their children at home and otherwise encourage them to learn?
- The relationships that exist among these factors.

All these factors comprise potential problems. Any one of the variables can inhibit student learning. Data collection on each should be consistent with the needs assessment and task analysis requirements.

A common example of this gap between the learners' entering knowledge and educational goals can be seen in the reading capability of many learners who simply do not read at grade level. For instance, when most new trainees in a company cannot perform essential maintenance or operator tasks it may be because they cannot read the instruction manuals.

Determining Learner Entering Skills

The secret of education is respecting the pupil.
Ralph Waldo Emerson

The school or training program should be student oriented, for in order to improve students' cognitive, affective, and psychomotor skills, we must be aware of what they already know and believe. This knowledge provides the starting point from which to develop the instructional program. It is therefore essential to obtain relevant information concerning the student.

The student's entering behaviors are usually vital to an instructional designer. The instruction must be geared to the student's current level of knowledge and learning ability. If prerequisite information is omitted the student will be unable to comprehend the instruction, and if the program is too redundant the student will be bored.

There are several types of general background information which might be collected:

- Knowledge base—what do they already know about the topic to be learned?
- Communications skills—what is their speaking vocabulary level? What is their listening comprehension level? What is their reading comprehension level? How well do they write?
- Learning style—do they learn better inductively or deductively? In a structured or unstructured situation? By themselves or with others (teacher or peers)? What time of the day do they prefer, or need? Through which senses do they learn best?
- Student affect—what is their attitude toward people, learning, and school? What subjects and activities interest them? Which of their goals can be used to direct their learning activities? Have they any heros or heroines? Who are their friends? What are their favorite activities? What kind and how much reinforcement do they desire or need?

- Physical and mental health—what are their physical limitations? What is their ability to withstand pressure and stress?

This list is so extensive that the instructional technologist will probably not collect all this information. Generally it is necessary to collect data you believe particularly important to the development effort and that is feasible to collect within existing time and resource constraints. One useful rule to follow is, "If you don't know exactly how useful the data will be, don't collect it."

Each learner is obviously unique: backgrounds, abilities, goals, and interests are, to some degree, different in every person, and in some cases, the differences are extreme. Often it is impossible to group students in homogeneous sets so that a single lecture or presentation of sufficient quality and effectiveness can be provided. Under such conditions, individualized instruction is a desirable approach for some objectives. However, this requires access to a collection of instructional materials which may not be available. Thus, techniques of group instruction may be necessary even when they are not the optimum choice. Instructional technology engages in the act of the possible. Instructional technologists must develop the ability to adjust their own, and others', decisions to match existing constraints and available resources. Learner skills will be discussed at length in Chapter 7.

Knowledge of the learners' communications skills is vital to instructional designers who desire to gear the vocabulary of the program to the students' abilities. Hence, instructional designers often collect information concerning the students' verbal and nonverbal communications skills. This data may consist of standardized test scores which already exist and can be easily examined. An assessment of the learners' speaking comprehension level may be gathered informally through teacher assessment or directly through interviews. Vocabulary tests can also be administered to assess learners' existing knowledge of prerequisite vocabulary.

Learners' listening comprehension level may be determined by using formal or informal evaluation instruments. Students may be asked to listen to a story read by the teacher or presented on tape and then be tested on their comprehension of the story's meaning. Commercial programs as well can be used for assessing listening skills. Reading level can similarly be determined except that the student is asked to read one or more paragraphs or short stories and respond to an assessment form. Several reading tests are available for this purpose.

Writing level may be determined by showing students a picture depicting some action and asking them to describe the action in writing. Analysis of the writing can be performed in terms of clarity, technical skill, style, and mechanics. There are several vocabulary lists which can be used to "assign" a reading level if it is appropriate.

Assessment of learning style is difficult because there is little agreement about what constitutes style. Nevertheless, a number of educators and psychologists believe that the manner in which a student approaches and processes information can be identified and used to structure a presentation for maximum learning. For example, does the learner seem to learn best in a structured situation? If the answer is yes, then consider designing highly structured materials and situations for that student. Other students may benefit more from less structured approaches.

Several additional questions might be studied. Do some students learn best by working alone? What types of objectives do they prefer to learn? Some people require visual stimuli (print, graphics, realistic still or motion photos, animation) while others are more auditorily oriented (teacher's voice, tape, or records). Some students rely heavily on tactile contact (braille, handling of objects), and some obtain meaning from kinesthetic stimuli (body gestures, proximity, role playing). Fortunately, research indicates most individuals learn well from a combination of stimuli such as slide-tapes, television, lectures, and demonstrations.

A learner's conceptual tempo and basic disposition to reflect or make impulsive and unconsidered responses also pose design constraints for the instructional technologist. Knowing the learner's styles of learning may permit tailoring the design of instruction to match that style.

The instruction students receive should also be matched to their mental and emotional states if the connection is to be strong enough to last and affect their behavior. A teacher or designer who is observant will infer much by observing students while they are learning. This can also be done by examination of student records or by interviewing individual students and their teachers. Evaluation instruments such as those developed at Oakland Community College near Detroit and Orange Coast Community College near Los Angeles are also useful in assessing how the student learns. However, even when a preferred style is identified, the instructional designer may wish to vary the instructional setting in order to broaden the student's capabilities. In many situations, however, instruction can be presented in a style which is effective.

Attitude and motivation toward learning and school also affect learning. Students with poor attitudes toward schooling might be presented materials intended to help them understand how their in-school activities could be useful to them elsewhere. Instructional designers should also attempt to determine what subjects or activities are of greatest interest to the learners, and, if possible, determine learners' goals, special skills, achievement, and other related attributes. Learners' attitudes toward the subject will also affect the amount of reinforcement and motivational material needed during instruction.

Likewise, the physical, mental, and emotional health of students can affect learning capabilities. Lack of food, high levels of anxiety, or emotional stress outside the classroom have a major influence on learner performance. A good instructional designer must know whether any of these external factors are present, and if so, what measures to take to neutralize their effect.

EIGHT-YEAR STUDY

One of the most significant studies of the twentieth century was the Eight-Year Study. This study (Aikin) was conducted during the 1930s. Thirty high schools agreed to exempt their graduates from the usual college entrance requirements and three hundred colleges participated. These high schools did not have to use grades, required courses, credits, class rankings, and so on. They could experiment with the curriculum any way they wanted. Some 1,500 students from the experimental schools were paired with the same number of students in control schools. The students from the experimental schools did as well or better in college grades, participation, critical thinking, aesthetic judgment, knowledge of contemporary affairs, and other measures. Students from the six *most experimental schools,* when compared with those from the most traditional control schools, were much more successful in college.

Content/Curriculum Characteristics

My idea of education is to unsettle the minds of the young and inflame their intellects.

Robert Maynard Hutchins

In addition to learner characteristics, an instructional designer must be aware of characteristics of the lesson's content which will affect the way a lesson should be developed. One important content characteristic is the degree to which it is possible to predict and verify that the student can function more effectively in the future as a result of the lesson. Is the instruction really needed? Will the student perceive the lesson as relevant? Is the curriculum future-oriented, contemporary, or out-of-date?

A second content characteristic to be considered is how the content relates to the rest of the curriculum. Have the prerequisites for the lesson been met? Is any redundancy in this lesson known and included for a reason? Does the lesson fulfill the requirements for entering succeeding lessons? Does it reflect revisions made throughout the course of instruction?

A third characteristic is related to community values, mores, and folkways. Does the curriculum conflict with community values? This entire question has to do with the issue: Does the school lead or follow the culture and its values? Someone in a policy position needs to make this decision as instruction is being developed.

A fourth question has to do with the method of structuring and presenting the material. A parallel question was asked in the previous section dealing with student characteristics.

Information and opinions regarding the relevance of the content and how it should be structured and presented can be obtained from community records, the mass media, local decision makers (PTA, school board), parents, community surveys, local industry, trade schools, and colleges and universities. There is usually more information available than anyone can use so the problem becomes one of determining which sources should be used in making curriculum decisions.

Fifth, and perhaps most important, is there a systematic plan for continual curriculum revision? Any curricular structure and accompanying instructional methodology must be reexamined at regular intervals, since what is current today may be obsolete in a short time. Application of the principles of instructional technology will guarantee present but not future relevance.

Characteristics of Educational Personnel

Sixty years ago I knew everything; now I know nothing; education is a progressive discovery of our own ignorance.

Will Durant

Teachers, counselors, administrators, and other support personnel employed by schools represent a force that can make or break any instructional program. The characteristics, skills, and attitudes of these educators need to be known and acknowledged when making curriculum decisions.

It is advantageous for an instructional technologist to know about the institution's educational personnel when analyzing the setting. Of particular importance are:

- What are their skills?
- How flexible are they?
- How quickly do they perceive a problem and, thus, a need for any change?
- How well do they work with students?
- How much time do they spend with their students?
- How do teachers' goals affect the instructional program?
- What areas of specialization are represented?
- How do the faculty, staff, and administration interact with one another?

The answers to these questions will suggest how much support is present for any change in the existing program.

It should be remembered that an innovative instructional program, even an excellent one, will fail if teachers and others hinder its implementation. The system cannot work without their support. The acceptance by educators of their role in the system is predicated on their understanding of that system and how it operates. Cooperation is more readily obtained from teachers and others if they have been involved in the decision to develop or adopt the new program. The scheduling process can also dramatically help or hinder a program's chances of success. Many educators feel one reason individualized instruction programs often fail is that they are scheduled into schools where class periods are predetermined. Under fixed schedules, students must drop their investigation (learning) and proceed to something else at a specified time, even though they may be engrossed in their lesson and progressing nicely.

It may be possible to resolve instructional problems even when the faculty and staff resist change, but generally it is desirable to work with them when analyzing an instructional situation (as well as later). The instructional technologist must clearly understand that faculty support in implementing any new program is crucial. Administrators, support staff, and members of boards of education should also be educated and won over, since they are the major gatekeepers. Involving these personnel in the process of analyzing the setting not only keeps them involved, but it may provide extra hands to do the work!

Some sources of information about faculty and staff are:

- Personnel files
- Student opinions
- Academic records
- Student performance
- Opinions of associates and other staff
- Questionnaires
- Direct discussion

Evaluation of Existing Materials

The new electronic independence recreates the world in the image of a global village.

Marshall McLuhan

Just as it is important to know what the students and faculty know and believe, it is also essential that existing materials be evaluated. The purpose of performing an evaluation of existing materials is to facilitate better decision making based on accurate, reliable, and complete information. Evaluation of instructional materials involves the use of several different assessment techniques.

Specific questions can be asked to determine to what degree the objectives can be met by students after using the available materials:

- Do materials appear dated because of dress or language?
- Are they suitable for the age or cultural make-up of the audience?
- Have materials been checked for stereotyping?
- How adequate is the pacing? Is reinforcement provided in the materials?
- Are students motivated to complete the lessons?
- How long does it take students to achieve the desired criterion level?
- Can they be used directly by students, or are they designed for a teacher to use with the students?

Some data may already be available from librarians or media specialists responsible for developing and maintaining collections of instructional materials.
Discussing the desirability of obtaining these data, in his article, "What Do 50 Years of Media Research Tell Us?," William H. Allen concluded:

> And we need to know the efficacy of different media program administrative procedures, the nature of innovative practices, the distinctive roles that media can play in instruction, the cost-effectiveness consideration of media, and other critical but sticky educational problems.*

Allen goes on to suggest that the reason some media "work" is very rational. He thought that if we use IT techniques that provide for 1) a systematic analysis of the problem; 2) active student participation; 3) direction of attention; 4) introductions to learning materials; and 5) repetition of stimuli in a well-thought-out manner, research is likely to show that these techniques work. Materials can be evaluated for their inclusion of these elements even when it is not possible to collect student performance data.

Physical Environment

The physical environment in which the instruction occurs is important to the instructional designer. Since buildings are expensive and usually permanent, some changes may be possible, but the overall physical plant design remains fairly fixed. Studies have shown that color of the learning area, degree of ambient sound, height of tables and chairs, location of water fountains, density of students in a given area, and many other factors affect learning and performance. Variables to consider in an analysis of the physical setting are:

- Is there ample space to house students?
- Is there sufficient administrative, counseling, and storage space?
- Are there enough laboratory areas?
- Is the space for instruction flexible enough to serve both current and anticipated future (five years) activities?
- Is there a communication system in the building that would allow a teacher to contact someone in case of an emergency?
- Are the colors, light levels, and contrasts adequate for the tasks to be performed?
- Are the acoustics appropriate for both instruction and learning?
- Are the furnishings sufficient throughout?
- Is the overall maintenance of the facility adequate?
- What is the proximity of the school to students' homes?
- Is the electrical circuitry adequate?
- Is there cable or conduit for electronic equipment?

*Reprinted from *Audiovisual Instruction*, March 1973, by permission of Association for Educational Communications and Technology. Copyright 1973.

- Does the building design permit thermal control?
- What are the safety and security provisions (stairs, projections, safety closures on outside doors, emergency lighting, outdoor lighting, location of walks, drives, and play areas relative to safety, earthquake, fire)?
- Are there adequate darkening facilities for projected media use?
- Are there sufficient areas for individual, small-group, and large-group activities?

Generally, when a building contains underutilized space it may be possible to remodel to serve a new curriculum or instructional approach. It is thus best to determine to what degree the building is a part of the problem and how it will limit the range of solutions.

The overall size of a school can affect learning as well. Research studies suggest that larger schools are cheaper and more educationally comprehensive. These studies argue that large schools provide more scheduling and staff flexibility and a greater range of curriculum specialists. They also permit sharing of limited resources by many more students. Data suggests that larger schools have a better-prepared staff, as measured by the number of degrees and certificates held and years of experience. On the other hand, there are studies showing that "neighborhood" schools better reflect community values and are more widely supported by parents. A greater percentage of students in small high schools participate in extracurricular activities than do students in larger schools. It is also felt that close instructor–student relationships, a desirable goal, can be achieved in a smaller school. An ERIC report (1981) concluded " . . . the optimum range of high schools in terms of cost effectiveness is probably in the neighborhood of 1,600 to 1,700 students, give or take a hundred." This optimum size is affected by population density. This issue of school plant size, like many other physical environment issues, needs to be considered by educators when designing an instructional program.

Open-type classroom construction facilitates the use of individualized instruction and instructional hardware. Open education is a concept of teaching involving flexible spaces, student choice of activities and learning materials, integration of curriculum content areas, and increased use of individual and small-group instruction. At this time there appears to be no consistent trend toward increased application of open classrooms, although they appear to be as functional as those used in more traditional instruction. Student attitudes toward schooling often seem to improve, but many teachers tend to be frustrated when attempting to implement open classroom instruction. It seems clear that it will only "work" as part of a carefully thought out and well-designed program in an appropriate facility.

Community Characteristics

The general socioeconomic level of the community affects parents' ability to support the school, fund trips, provide home study space, and perhaps most

"What did I learn today? My mother will want to know."

(Button)

importantly, to provide motivation for doing homework. All these things affect the quality of instruction—particularly in more innovative programs. Thus, it is also important to examine the characteristics of the community.

An instructional designer should know about the following community characteristics:

- What are the parents' attitudes toward the school and schooling? Toward learning?
- Is there conflict between the behaviors taught inside the school and behaviors expected of students outside the school?
- What goals or tasks do community members expect the school to perform?
- Are community resources an integral part of the school program (airport, medical center, businesses, libraries, political centers)?
- Do the avocational activities of the faculty and staff differ from those of the community?

This information can be obtained through questionnaires directed at parents and faculty. Interviews are an alternative data-gathering method. Additionally, it may be desirable to determine if there are various groups or "camps" on any issues: Are they at odds about anything? Be specific! Know the problems. Who are the opinion leaders and how do they feel about important issues? How open are the learners, staff, and community to change (in procedures, materials, time, working spaces)?

These relationships have little meaning by themselves, but when examined in conjunction with management concerns and educational goals they can help in specifying instructional content and methods.

SUMMARY

When in trouble, or in doubt, Run in circles, yell and shout.
Robot from Lost in Space

The specification and organization of content begins with an analysis of the instructional setting:

- What does the learner already know? Hence, where should an instructional program begin?
- How will the program's content characteristics affect its transmittal to a potential learner?
- How do the characteristics of the teachers, administrators, and other institutional personnel affect instructional or teaching effectiveness?
- What administrative practices or policies affect the teaching/learning process?
- What physical or environmental considerations might affect the instructional program (existing or projected)?
- What community characteristics affect the solutions being considered?

Questions for Consideration and Discussion

1. How would you analyze an instructional situation with which you are familiar and isolate the specific core of the problem?
2. Which of the instructional activities discussed in the chapter do you consider the most important and why?

Suggested Activities

1. Visit the training department of a local industry and have the department head discuss how they analyze learner and environmental components. Or, invite a trainer to your classroom to discuss these issues.
2. Visit a curriculum or development specialist from a local K–12 school district or college to discuss instructional development.
3. In groups of five to seven, outline how you would approach an analysis of the learner characteristics of this course.
4. Evaluate available instructional material such as a textbook. How should it be revised? How should the revision be done? Who should pay for the revision? How long should it take to do the revision?

Suggested Readings

Aikin, W. (1942). *Story of the Eight-Year Study.* New York: Harper and Brothers.

Allen, W. H. (March 1973). What Do 50 Years of Media Research Tell Us? *Audiovisual Instruction, 18*(3), 48–49.

Coleman, J. S., et al. (1967). *Equality of Educational Opportunity.* Washington, DC: Superintendent of Public Documents.

Dunn, R., et al. (January 1977). Diagnosing Learning Styles: A Prescription for Avoiding Malpractice Suits. *Phi Delta Kappan,* 418–420.

ERIC Clearinghouse on Educational Management. (1981). *School Size: A Reassessment of the Small School. Research Action Brief Number 20.* Eugene, OR: University of Oregon.

Farr, B. (1971). Individual Differences in Learning: Predicting One's More Effective Learning Modality. Ph.D. diss., Catholic University of America.

Jennings, W., and Athan, J. (March 1977). Startling/Disturbing Research on School Program Effectiveness. *Phi Delta Kappan,* 568–572.

Knirk, F. G. (1979). *Designing Productive Learning Environments.* Englewood Cliffs, NJ: Educational Technology Publications.

Marshall, H. H. (Summer 1981). Open Classrooms: Has the Term Outlived Its Usefulness? *Review of Educational Research, 51*(2), 181–192.

Phillips, G., and Faris, R. (October 1977). Learning As Much in Different Ways at an "Action Learning" High School. *Phi Delta Kappan,* 133.

Schramm, W. (1977). *Big Media, Little Media.* Beverly Hills, CA: Sage.

Schramm, W., and Lerner, D. (1976). *Communication and Change: The Last 10 Years and the Next.* Honolulu, HI: An East-West Center Book, University Press of Hawaii.

5

Managing Instructional Development

*A method of solution is perfect if we can foresee from the start, and even
prove, that following that method we shall attain our aim.*
Gottfried von Leibnitz

Objectives

After completing this chapter you should be able to:

1. Define the role of management in instructional technology.
2. List and describe the five principal management functions—
   planning, organizing, coordinating, evaluating, and reporting.
3. Describe essential characteristics of project and organization
   management and differentiate the two.
4. Provide examples of each of the five management principles in
   process and organizational management.
5. Describe the role of public relations and other communications
   modes in developing support of IT activities.

Resolving a problem requires personnel, resources, and time. How the management team is constituted and supported represents the last step in the problem-determination phase of our model. The following management activities are related to designing the instruction.

When developing a program, many activities must be managed by the unit leader. Personnel may have to be located, hired, and trained. Budgeting must be done and the proposed activities funded, which may require developing a proposal. Required materials and equipment must be determined, secured, and managed. The instructional development activity must be administered so that the necessary materials are developed and the supporting systems provided in such a way that the alternative solution has a chance of being adopted and used.

"One of these days we've got to get organized," has taken on a ritual meaning in today's complex world. Everyone talks about getting organized, but all too often it doesn't translate into action. Getting organized is also the common expression for the management functions associated with instructional technology. Organizing, however, is only one element of the management process. We must also ask: Organized for what purpose? Within what line- and staff-reporting relationship? To report what? What other units within the organization will affect the likelihood of our success? And, how should the IT unit relate to them?

While entire texts have been written about general management principles (Hampton 1977; Pavlock 1981), this discussion is limited to the specialized considerations associated with managing instructional technology. Thus, we have excluded general aspects of personnel management, although they are essential to any organization.

Following the model presented in Chapter 1, "Organizing Management," is the third major function of the development process. While management can be limited to a single project, we treat it from both a project (development) and an organizational perspective; that is, not just managing a project, but also managing an IT center. Figure 5.1 shows the management function in our instructional development model.

Perhaps the most critical dimension of IT management is the philosophy of both managers and workers about the role and contribution of the management function. Often, managing is viewed as a negative force or necessary evil to be tolerated in order to get the job done. Under such circumstances, technologists tend to avoid careful planning, documentation, and evaluation of their own managing, while rigorously applying these procedures to the learning system. The lack of evaluation activity in many IT centers, coupled with scant documentation of unsuccessful projects, bears witness to this inconsistency and can be traced to the philosophy that the least amount of management is the best.

Adopting the philosophy that managing is a *facilitative* function enhances interest in its performance. Successful completion and implementation of effective and efficient instructional systems, within time and budget constraints,

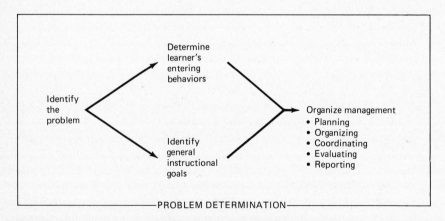

FIGURE 5.1   I.D. Model: A Management Subsystem

creates future demand for the same approach. Also, contrary to popular belief, active management increases rather than decreases the potential for unleashing the creative talents of technologists. The poorly managed project, which fails to reach its objectives, reduces both current and future opportunities for technologists to apply their skills. Many instructional development projects fail to achieve their objectives more because of poor management than because of faulty instructional design. To illustrate, one important ingredient of any development project is the budget, which must be realistically determined and its expenditures monitored as the project progresses. The budget must be taken into account at all stages of the project, particularly in selecting instructional strategies and media delivery systems. Decisions on whether to purchase or develop materials are also affected by the budget. Expending all the funds before completing the project or selecting unaffordable designs which must later be scrapped is not only poor management, it is poor design.

Instructional designers must learn to operate within their resources and should recognize that limited funds must cover all activities to ensure completing the project. This requires preliminary allocation for each step and ensuring that any cost overruns in one area can be offset by reductions elsewhere. Making conscious decisions to reallocate during the project and understanding their consequences is essential to good management. This contrasts sharply with a project that has exhausted all its resources by the time it has developed a prototype and is thus unable to test, revise, and implement the instruction.

Advanced instructional technology makes many assumptions about developing, installing, and monitoring instruction. Probably the most important is that there should be a division of labor. In the one-room schoolhouse of yesteryear, there was no division of labor; the teacher was the principal, custodian, counselor, and whatever other roles were required. As schools became larger and more complex, specialized roles emerged. Similarly, IT started with individuals who were expected to do all the related roles. However, as the process has expanded and become more complex, numerous specialized roles have emerged. Specialized expertise is now found in problem identification, objective specification, message design, and evaluation. The specialized role of project manager is also emerging, and this trend is expected to continue.

Increased specialization creates greater demands for competent management. As each expert becomes more and more specialized in one area of IT, he or she begins to lose sight of the "big picture." Instructional development has now become a team approach with the manager ensuring that *all* team members contribute their unique skills. The concept of an IT team cannot even be implemented without management. Who would think of fielding a basketball team without a manager? Simultaneous activity by different team members must be planned, coordinated, and evaluated to have any expectation of success. There should be both internal and external coordination. As an example of the latter, if a company is planning to manufacture a new piece of equipment such as a word processor, it must simultaneously develop operator-training materials so that both can be delivered at the same time. If the production schedule is accelerated, so must the development of training materials. If a product specification is altered, the training materials must reflect the change, and so it goes. The need for coordination across groups is apparent. Internal coordination must also exist. If graphic artists are needed, they must be scheduled (and rescheduled if target dates change). The availability of a television studio may dictate production schedules. Locating and arranging for access to a population suitable for prototype testing interacts with changes in product specifications, time-lines, and budgets. The list goes on and on. Careful attention to coordination is critical to the success of the project.

This "all at onceness," which characterizes IT, makes managing both a challenge and a necessity. Being able to plan despite many unknowns, and adjusting to constantly changing conditions, requires a systems view of the world. The world will not stand still just to make the management task easier. The ability to cope with simultaneous and often conflicting demands is a necessary characteristic of IT managers. IT is just as much a system as a school or training department. It has interdependent elements which require coordination and accurate communication.

PROJECT VERSUS ORGANIZATION MANAGEMENT

In IT there are at least two distinctly different types of management needs. One type is associated with managing development projects, the other with managing organizational requirements. Project management is dynamic, with activities and assignments changing frequently. Communication needs also change depending on the current stage of development of the project. In contrast, there are organizational management concerns such as long-range planning, building political support, budgeting, and reporting, all of which follow a different externally determined time-line. Five management activities—planning, organizing, coordinating, evaluating, and reporting—will be discussed as they relate to both types of management. While almost all technologists will be directly involved in managing development projects, only a few will be involved with organization maintenance. All technologists, however, should understand the important role of both types.

As you will see, the questions, issues, and tools vary considerably between the two types of management. Strategic planning associated with the future direction and activities of a technology center is qualitatively different from planning a development project for a new course. It is thus desirable to consider them separately. However, keep in mind that many of the managing decisions or actions in one area will affect those in another. Technology is a system!

Project Management

The process of instructional technology is usually depicted as a model with a series of steps. The model may or may not specify a linear lock-step sequence of activities. This becomes a major consideration when managing the development project. The lock-step approach is more common in business, industry, and the military, whereas holistic approaches are more common in educational institutions. Lock-step approaches are somewhat easier to plan since the sequence of steps is clear and time-lines can be projected to indicate at what point specific resources and people will be required. More holistic approaches pose greater management problems since each new step is often decided after completing the current step. This latter situation makes long-range project planning and coordination much more difficult.

We turn now to the principal categories of management activity. First, all five categories will be considered as they relate to managing projects. Then, each will be considered as it relates to organization management needs.

Planning

Probably the most important planning activity of IT projects is establishing goals and objectives. This is typically a joint responsibility of the organization manager and project manager. The goals and objectives may be easily determined (for example, develop a 5–8 hour training session for a new "control valve"), or result from a detailed needs assessment. While a strong case can be made for conducting needs assessments for all projects, time and other resources may prevent such analysis. Managers may be forced to create the development "game plan," including specification of project objectives, time-lines, budget, and other resources in the absence of hard data. Faced with this constraint, the project manager must guard on the one hand against overpromising, and on the other of being unwilling to make a firm commitment.

The project planner must also select a model to follow during development. A general development model may be specified by the organization, but the specific steps and procedures must be tailored to the specific project. For example, instructional technologists in the military are often expected to use the Interservices Procedures for Instructional Systems Development model described in Chapter Two. But, depending on the size, scope, and purpose of the project, many specific decisions remain to be made.

Staff allocation and project time-lines are additional areas of joint concern to project and organization managers. Depending on the availability of design and development talent and the subject-matter expert's schedule, a decision must be made to either organize horizontally or vertically. That is, a single team may carry the project from beginning to end, or it may be transferred to different people at the various stages in the development process. Continuity and designated responsibility for project completion are the principal advantages of the horizontal arrangement. Availability of higher levels of specialized expertise to more projects has an advantage over passing projects from specialist to specialist. For example, evaluation skills are often in short supply. One method of extending this valuable asset is to assign the expert evaluator to several projects for only that activity. However, such an arrangement requires greater attention to preparing precise written specification of goals and objectives by the designers to ensure that the evaluator assesses the original intent of the project. Most agencies using the vertical approach have developed detailed specification forms to reduce miscommunication when the project is transferred from one developer to another.

Organizing

Organizing involves bringing together and arranging all the resources required for a project. Within a project, the manager assigns personnel to specific tasks, often on a day-to-day basis. It may be necessary to reassign or rearrange parts of tasks because of unforeseen personnel difficulties (resignations, illness) or slippage in time-lines.

In forming teams, the manager may assign an experienced developer to work with a new person or provide extra help on a particularly knotty problem. Or, the manager may discover that some staff work best alone while others thrive in mutual collaboration. Judging the individual talents and personalities of team members and organizing to maximize their strengths is one of the most challenging aspects of the manager's role.

Establishing and maintaining communication channels is another vital management activity. Both formal and informal channels must be used to send and receive information. Formal channels serve well for making assignments, providing feedback on performance, and for general announcements. Informal channels tend to work better for increasing motivation, assessing the general level of morale, and squelching rumors. Clear lines of communication in *both* directions are the lifeblood of a development project. Managers must become good listeners as well as good senders of information.

While no hard and fast rules for effective communication exist, Gentry (1980) has developed a set of heuristics for instructional technologists to use if there is no evidence to suggest an alternate strategy. Their consistent use will improve communication between project manager and team members.

Gentry's Heuristics

- Decisions should be based, not only on *what* is said, but *how* it is said, as well.
- Rumors should be attended to, despite their inaccuracy, because they often convey psychological truth as symbolic expressions of feelings.

- You should encourage critics of your project, because they may be the only ones telling the truth.
- When discussing changes in procedures, don't let subject matter concerns interfere with an understanding of the process.
- During your initial contact with a colleague, when providing information about a modification in the ID project proposed, use real examples rather than abstractions.
- Always provide accurate information to colleagues when reporting project concerns or activities.
- Don't let words (jargon) get in the way when communicating with project members.
- Keep the number of intermediaries between the source of information and the destination of the information to a minimum.
- Always proceed from written agreements, with the individuals or groups affected by the project.
- Communication channels should be kept open in both vertical and horizontal directions.
- Communication is more effective if project members are aware of the *frame of reference* of their colleagues (i.e., beliefs, attitudes, values).
- Always set up future meetings of groups during the current meeting.

Coordinating

Coordinating is related to organizing in the sense that it involves establishing and maintaining communication links and orchestrating the work of different people. The principal difference is that organizing deals with relationships and activities within the team, whereas coordinating generally deals with *external* relationships. If the team requires access to subject-matter experts, the manager must coordinate with people in another unit. If the training package for a new copy machine must be ready at the same time the machine is announced, there must be close coordination between the production and training departments. Coordinating quick turnaround of drafts of printed material from a central word processing department is essential to implementation of projects within tight time-lines. As another example, coordinating the data collection requirements of different units can decrease costs, increase the amount of data available, and reduce negative reactions from those being asked to provide the data.

Coordination may also include gaining entree for team members or in other ways alerting the people they will contact. If, for example, developers will be collecting sensitive or potentially embarrassing information, management should do what it can to alert and prepare the contacts and reassure them about the need for, and use of, the data.

Evaluating

Internal evaluation of development projects might also be called project monitoring. This includes monitoring people, time-lines, budgets, and products.

Team-member performance should be evaluated against stated criteria in order to provide objective feedback and make valid personnel decisions. In a performance-based system like instructional technology, tangible results should be rewarded. Gilbert (1978) makes a useful distinction between behavior and performance. He points out that a person can be busy doing nothing, or busy doing it wrong. The evaluation question becomes: Are we rating behavior or results? Only when performance expectations are expressed in performance terms can genuine progress be assessed on a project. Management by objectives (MBO) can contribute to this effort if the manager can write a set of objectives for each team member and each project activity.

Comparing actual progress to stated time-lines is another important monitoring activity. Detailed time-lines with both major and intermediate checkpoints are essential to good management. Any delays or failures to make deadlines will almost certainly lead to later problems, since a delay in completing one activity usually impedes the starting of another. The delay is likely to ripple through all remaining steps in the project. Moreover, the failure to detect missed deadlines may imply to the staff that delays are acceptable. Inadvertently creating such a perception can have devastating consequences for both present and future projects.

Evaluation of the techniques and procedures employed during the project may have immediate and long-term implications. If for example, a particular technique such as information processing analysis yields significant data not otherwise available, this should be noted for future reference. If, on the other hand, a questionnaire does not yield necessary data, an immediate adjustment must be made. Well-organized managers systematically collect information from team members about the utility, advantages, and disadvantages of all techniques and procedures employed during a project.

Reporting

Project managers are usually expected to prepare reports for higher-level management. They should also report to team members under their direction. Both interim and final reports, or at least abstracts, often serve a useful communication role with team members by alleviating concerns about what is being reported "upstairs." Of course, project managers should not rely on written reports alone to communicate to either audience. Lengthy print material is often ignored or skimmed with little attention paid to its detail. Brief executive summaries, short status reports, verbal briefings, and informal encounters may also be employed to deliver important information. Communication experts agree that introducing redundant messages in different channels is one of the best means of ensuring the information is received.

Reports should be written with the audience clearly in mind. Questions to keep in mind about your audience include:

- Do they want detailed information or only an overview?
- Do they want facts, opinions, or both?
- Do they want both sides of the issue or only one?
- Are they familiar with the technical jargon?
- Do they prefer a formal or informal style?

These questions, and perhaps others you can think of, should guide report preparation. If these questions suggest that more than one format may be necessary for the same report, you are correct. If the extra effort sounds unnecessary, keep in mind that the unread report is not only a waste of your time, it can also be hazardous to your professional health.

Organization Management

Having considered management from the perspective of the project manager, we now turn our attention to the instructional technologist as an organization manager. By this, we mean managing an organization responsible for a variety of activities related to instructional technology. These might include, in addition to development projects, operating production and distribution facilities, managing instructional facilities such as computer or autotutorial labs, maintaining a resource collection, or maintaining an equipment pool. All these services are integral to a comprehensive technology of instruction. While different organizations may organize these resources into a variety of configurations, they remain part of the technology.

We shall now examine each of the five areas of management activity as they relate to managing instructional technology organizations. Due to the wide variety of organizational patterns which can exist, this discussion must, of necessity, be general.

Planning

Organization management requires both short- and long-term planning. Probably the most important area deserving attention is continuous reassessment of the missions and objectives of the unit. Given rapid changes in education and training environments, coupled with almost daily advances in the hardware associated with instructional technology, the manager must constantly estimate what shape the future will take. For example, currently microcomputers seem to hold enormous potential for significant changes in how instruction is developed and delivered. Low-cost microprocessors for controlling audio-video devices in interactive modes and interactive cable networks are also likely to have profound effects on education and training. On the behavioral side, it seems likely that new insights into learning, human information processing, and memory will have major implications for designing instruction. The technology man-

"Hello, I'm Billy Bernard . . . part of the mess you inherited from the previous administration."

(Campbell)

ager must thus stay abreast of these developments or risk professional obsolescence.

A second area of planning involves selecting or promoting key content areas as candidates for application of instructional technology. This requires maintaining communication with upper-level managers to detect changes in priorities or missions of the organization. For example, if a university makes major and genuine commitments to distance learning (instruction offered via a variety of media in many locations), what are the implications for IT? Similarly, if the military makes a commitment to basic skills training for recruits, what does this mean for technologists? Instructional technology does not exist in a vacuum: if it expects both financial and psychological support, it must adjust to changes in the organization's direction and priorities.

A powerful means of responding is through the projects selected for systematic instructional improvement. Technologists face a particular dilemma here in that the areas of greatest potential benefit are often staffed by people who are the least interested in, or least able to make, the effort. To illustrate, in a large manufacturing enterprise it is common to find well-developed management and sales training programs. However, many of the real problems that will affect long-term profitability exist elsewhere in the company. These might include poor first-line supervision, inconsistent quality control, or poorly trained workers. While it may be more glamorous and psychologically rewarding to work on refining management and sales training, the greatest contribution of IT is often in these other areas. The parallel case in education is deciding to work with instructors who are already among the best, rather than seeking out the less effective faculty. Gilbert (1978) describes what he calls a Performance Improvement Potential (PIP) ratio to use as a guide in selecting areas for development. His basic concept is that if the difference in performance between the best person and the average or below-average person is small, there is probably little payoff to rigorous development efforts. On the other hand, if the difference is large and a substantial number of people are involved, the benefits can be significant. Projects should also be selected because of the number of persons affected, criticality of the tasks, stability of the content area, and availability of existing instruction and subject-matter expertise.

More sophisticated cost-benefit analysis techniques can also be applied to the initial selection of projects or when deciding which should be continued. Although different approaches to calculating cost benefits have been described (Wilkinson [1973], Doughty [1979]), most contain common elements. The general structure of most cost-benefit analyses uses an input-output model. Inputs about people, facilities, and resources are calculated as "costs." Outputs include learning, attitude change, motor-skill development, or other performances and are calculated as "benefits." The greatest difficulty has occurred in assigning values to outputs. This has been a particularly knotty problem in educational institutions. Becker and Davis (1983) developed a model to help in selecting projects with the greatest potential for benefit from application of systematic development processes. Their approach includes examining how long the course will be, how many people will be affected by the training, and estimating the useful life of the product. Using this tool, they can select from among the alternative proposed projects those which will provide the greatest rate of return on a company's investment.

Annual budget planning must also be completed by managers. Costing for routine services, such as operating a self-instructional lab, is comparatively simple, but developmental activities pose a real challenge. How does one budget for a project in which there are numerous unknowns? Generally, experience within the organization is the best guide. If complete and accurate documentation exists from previous projects, norms can be determined for the time and other costs associated with each step. Care must be taken that these norms or standards be based on experience, not on what someone thinks.

Organizing

Organizing people, work, and resources is another important management activity. Managers need to remember that they accomplish little by themselves. Goals are reached by the people being managed. Creating an organizational structure that facilitates productivity is one of the most critical tasks of a manager. The line-and-staff organizational structure itself communicates an important message to both providers and consumers of IT services. Do you have a single production division or do you have graphics, photography, TV, film, and the like? The former suggests the goal is instructional products, while the latter implies specialized media formats, each having unique characteristics.

The location and reporting relationship of instructional designers will also affect both how they are viewed and how they view themselves. If they are placed in a unit reporting directly to the head of IT, there is a tendency to develop an elitist point of view. But if they are distributed among the other service units, their visibility and credibility to users will probably be reduced. In commercial organizations, instructional designers may be distributed outside the IT center to operating units of the organization such as sales or production. By distributing the designers, the developers tend to become "adopted" by the units and be more readily utilized. On the other hand, much control and coordination may be lost along with the power and influence of the main IT unit. Again, there is no right answer. The manager must make difficult decisions in selecting an organizational structure.

Once the organization is established, the staff must be organized within that structure. Will they work in teams or as individuals? Will they be considered as interchangeable, or be encouraged to develop unique expertise in specialized areas? Will work assignments be based on past success with a particular client or topic, or will they be presented different and more challenging assignments regardless of their past record? This latter issue can be of considerable importance when working with creative, upwardly mobile employees. From the standpoint of project success, it is often desirable to assign personnel based on past success. On the other hand, bright, creative, and talented technologists often prefer new and challenging opportunities to hone their skills and prove their competence.

Identification of competent team leaders and those having first-line supervisory responsibility also has great impact on the success of IT centers. A common dilemma is finding a person with considerable technical competence who lacks the necessary skills to supervise or lead. Often, the only means of rewarding such people is to promote them; but if they lack the necessary interpersonal skills to succeed in their new position, problems will be created both up and down the line.

Establishing a career ladder or path for advancement is critical to recruiting and retaining the best personnel. If they see no opportunities for professional advancement, they may decide to seek a more promising future elsewhere. Given the high demand for IT personnel, this promises to be a chronic problem for many years to come. The problem will be particularly acute for educational institutions because of their lower pay scales and limited opportunities for advancement outside traditional academic career paths.

Communication channels both within and without the unit must also be organized and maintained. As the unit increases in size and diversity of services, the requirements for both formal and informal communication channels also increase. The problem of internal communication can become particularly acute if subunits are located in different facilities or if personnel are assigned to remote locations. When establishing formal communication channels, the manager should keep in mind the informal channels already existing in any organization. These informal channels exist both inside and outside the unit. Being aware of how they operate is essential to successful management.

The manager should attempt to be named or elected to membership on key committees and ad hoc study groups. While few people really enjoy these assignments, they do provide excellent vehicles for collecting and disseminating information. Effective managers ensure that they are on the distribution list for company or institution information circulated to administrators. Although much of the information will not be directly relevant, it does provide an indication of what issues are of current concern. It also aids technologists' credibility in the organization when they are able to demonstrate awareness of issues with which they are not directly concerned.

Coordinating

Internally, coordination among subunits is necessary to ensure prompt, efficient delivery of services. Here again, routine operations such as circulating equipment and materials may require little attention once procedures are well established. In contrast, development and production often require substantial coordination. Workloads tend to be cyclical with periods of high and low demand. Particularly near the end of the budget year, volume tends to pick up as other units attempt to complete work before funds revert. If new products are traditionally announced at some specific time, that date is usually preceded by hectic development and production. Educational institutions are geared to an academic calendar which often significantly affects work flow.

Taking these cycles into account while planning workloads and target dates for projects falls into the category of coordination. If multiple development projects are to be scheduled, they should be planned so as not to require the same resources and facilities at the same time. Each project must be monitored, since any changes in time-lines will affect demand for the facilities. When possible, some IT centers keep a few low-priority projects in their system to level out the workload, the assumption being that it is better to have staff busy on a low-priority project than not working at all.

Careful coordination can greatly reduce overtime and the need for extra staff and facilities. Overtime, in particular, can cause huge cost overruns. Use of outside services may also be considered to level out the workload. Many companies maintain their IT centers at a level which keeps them completely assigned but not to a level requiring extensive overtime salaries for staff. All additional work is contracted to outside agencies. Outside contracting may be limited to one function only or include complete analysis, design, and production for selected projects. Coordination of outside contracts is as critical as inside work and it may be necessary to assign one or more persons specific responsibility for that task.

Relationships with other units in the company or institution are another dimension of coordination. In some situations these units may control resources such as word processing, printing, or material distribution. Obviously, if the IT center is dependent on a print shop to produce its instructional booklets, a high level of coordination is essential. Other units, including purchasing, accounting, and personnel administration, also have an impact on IT operations. Requirements for specialized equipment or materials must be communicated to the purchasing unit and be expeditiously handled. Accounting must be able to provide accurate up-to-date information on the financial status of projects and other accounts. The personnel office must understand the need for, and be able to help recruit, the wide variety of specialized talent required to operate a successful IT center. This list could be expanded, but the idea should be clear. Coordination with other units in the organization is prerequisite to success.

Evaluating

Evaluation can be subdivided into three elements—people, operation, and products, each requiring unique criteria and procedures. Personnel evaluation is probably the most emotionally difficult management function. No doubt the organization will have forms and procedures for personnel evaluation which the manager will be expected to understand and use. Rather than discuss them in general terms, we will limit this discussion to unique evaluation considerations within an IT center.

First, will evaluation be based on output or effort? How do you evaluate an instructional developer if the major project he or she was working on failed? Suppose, for example, one of your developers in a university was assigned to work on a project in a department where there had been no previous projects. As a result of numerous factors, and after considerable effort, the department decides to abandon the project because of faculty resistance. Assume a second developer was assigned to a project with the faculty in another department. This second department has engaged in several previous projects, and in fact, the present project simply involved revising and updating a previously developed and highly successful instructional system. The project went smoothly and everyone was delighted. Now, how do you evaluate your developers? Do you reward success or effort? Or do you reward both, and in essence say there is no difference? If you do not reward risk-takers in your unit, you will soon have none. On the other hand, how do you reward personnel on a project that failed?

A somewhat different evaluation problem occurs with production personnel. Do you reward artistic style or instructional effectiveness achieved at the lowest possible costs? It has been demonstrated that inexpensive, simple line drawings are often as effective as expensive artwork or photography. Production personnel naturally desire to show their skills and often prefer the latter. How do you evaluate and reward an artist who went to great pains to create artistically pleasing visuals which are no more effective than the simple drawings of another artist? If you reward artistic values, you will encourage many aspiring artists. If you reward pedestrian designs, you may lower everyone's sights.

Evaluation of creative instructional design efforts creates a similar problem. How do you compare and evaluate two developers who develop different strategy specifications for a set of modules? Assume one design incorporates all the ideas from a recent book that advances a new, but relatively untested theory of design. The second design uses only time-tested strategies that suggest little creative thought or imagination. Further, you are aware this latter designer has used these same designs exclusively over an extended period of time. Do you reward experimentation and searching or adherence to the proven design? To reward the former is to encourage new approaches—some of which are almost certain to fail. To reward the latter is to promote dogma and perhaps creation of dull but generally effective instruction.

While there are no simple answers to these questions, they suggest the manager should establish a clear set of objectives with accompanying criteria and make them known to the staff. They also suggest that some structure might be created to facilitate risk-taking, artistic expression, and experimentation without destroying the basic integrity of the design-evaluation process.

Evaluating the operation of the IT center is a second area of concern. Any evaluation should be within the context of the missions and objectives developed during planning. Typical objectives in the service area might be to reduce the cost of providing a service by 10 percent, reducing the turnaround time on production by three days, or increasing the volume of users by 5 percent. In the development area, objectives might include adding new clients or courses, decreasing design time, testing new methodology, or showing a "profit." This last item is of increasing importance as companies convert IT centers to cost centers.

An IT center might also evaluate its procedures by comparing different configurations or development techniques for comparable activities. Case studies, observations, and critical-incident techniques borrowed from research methodology could be applied to formal evaluation efforts. Tracking the costs of providing services or performing specific tasks can also help in decision making. Data collected from staff concerning how much time they spend on each assigned task can provide valuable insights into how resources are really expended. Client attitudes and perceptions can be collected and plotted over time to detect trends or sudden changes. Surveys of nonusers may also be desirable to assess their attitudes and level of awareness of the IT center and its services. Identification of their reasons for nonuse might also be identified, but may require interviews or other expensive data collection techniques.

Reporting

As would be expected, IT centers are required to prepare periodic reports on their activities. In addition, the manager should seek opportunities to publicize the center's accomplishments by using newsletters, articles in a company publication, speeches, informational memos, and mediated programs. One popular technique is to assist the top administrators in preparing their major address to management and/or stockholders. Being close at hand often permits including a "plug" for the IT center's activity.

IT centers based in educational institutions have found newsletters and memos to the faculty to be inexpensive channels of communication; for example, describing a successful project with a faculty in a flyer and distributing it campuswide. The publicity is a reward for the faculty and good PR for the center. Company newsletters may serve the same purpose in business or industry settings.

Although reporting implies upward communication, managers should also report to the staff. In small centers this might be done informally or at staff meetings, but larger centers may require more formal arrangements such as memos, abstracts, copies of reports, or briefings.

SUMMARY

Science commits suicide when it adopts a creed.

Thomas Henry Huxley

In this chapter we have examined the important role of management in applying instructional technology. Of particular concern was the challenge of creating an awareness that management has a facilitative function, rather than being a necessary evil. Two types of management were considered: one involving managing development projects, the other dealing with managing the organization. Each management approach has five major activities: planning, organizing, coordinating, evaluating, and reporting.

Project management can be particularly difficult because development always contains an element of the unknown. Management plans must remain flexible and sensitive to changing conditions. Communication channels must be kept open to obtain accurate and current information on the status of the projects. Coordination with other units that control resources needed to complete projects is also necessary. Budgets and time-lines must be carefully monitored to ensure proper expenditures and prompt delivery.

Managing an IT organization involves establishing its goals and missions and communicating them to the staff as well as to the rest of the organization. Both long- and short-range planning must be conducted in addition to designing the line/staff structure of the center or organization, and selecting services or products to be provided. Personnel decisions are of vital importance, since most of the service will be provided by staff rather than the administrator. Reporting to superiors and staff requires a manager's attention. Finally, both formal and informal communications channels are needed to ensure adequate information flows in two directions.

Questions for Consideration and Discussion

1. Specifically, where in your present organization would you locate graphic artists to work on a project you are working on?
2. Where could you obtain funds to work on an instructional problem you would like to solve?
3. How would you resolve the conflict between making the media and materials easily available to teachers (so they will use the equipment) and safeguarding them so they do not get lost or stolen?

Suggested Activities

1. Invite a training officer to your class. Perhaps a recently retired military officer with training experience would be willing to discuss military training problems with the class.
2. Visit an IT center and study its management procedures.
3. List the differences between military training and adult education or university-oriented education that would affect management decisions.
4. List the problems unique to an instructional technologist working in a developing nation that are not present in the United States.

Suggested Readings

Becker, W., and Davis, R. (Winter 1983). An Economic Model of Training in an Industry Setting. *Journal of Instructional Development, 6*(2), 26–32.

Borg, W., and Schuller, C. (Spring 1979). Detail and Background in Audiovisual Lessons and Their Effect on Learners. *Educational Communications and Technology Journal, 27*(1), 31–38.

Brown, J. W., et al. (1977). *Administering Educational Media: Instructional Technology and Library Services.* New York: McGraw-Hill.

Chisholm, M. E., and Ely, D. P. (1976). *Media Personnel in Education: A Competency Approach.* Englewood Cliffs, NJ: Prentice-Hall.

Cook, D. (1971). *Educational Project Management.* Columbus, OH: Charles Merrill.

Doughty, P. (Summer 1979). Cost-Effectiveness Analysis Tradeoffs and Pitfalls for Planning and Evaluating Instructional Programs. *Journal of Instructional Development, 2*(4), 17–25.

Gilbert, T. F. (1978). *Human Competence: Engineering Worthy Performance.* New York: McGraw-Hill.

Hampton, D. R. (1977). *Contemporary Management.* New York: McGraw-Hill.

Levin, H. M. (1975). Cost-Effectiveness Analysis in Evaluation Research. In Guttentag M. Struening, ed., *Handbook of Evaluation Research.* Beverly Hills, CA: Sage.

Pavlock, E., ed. (1981). *Organization Development: Managing Transition.* Washington, DC: American Society for Training and Development.

Pinto, P., and Walker, J. (1978). *A Study of Professional Training and Development Roles and Competencies: A Report to the Professional Development Committee.* Washington, DC: American Society for Training and Development.

Romiszowski, A. J. (1981). *Designing Instructional Systems: Decision Making in Course Planning and Curriculum Design.* New York: Kogan Page.

Spangenberg, R. W., and Smith, E. A. (December 1975). *Handbook for the Design and Implementation of Air Force Learning Center Programs.* AFHRL-TR-75-69. Brooks Air Force Base, TX: Air Force Human Resources Laboratory.

Wilkinson, G. (Spring 1973). Cost Evaluation of Instructional Strategies. *AV Communications Review, 21*(1), 11–30.

PART TWO

Instructional Design

6

Objectives: The Cornerstone of Instructional Technology

The objective of education is to prepare the young to educate themselves throughout their lives.

Robert Maynard Hutchins

Objectives

After completing this chapter you should be able to:

1. Locate or develop and evaluate instructional objectives for any course of instruction. (terminal objective)
2. List at least three reasons why teachers need to be able to develop behavioral objectives. (enabling objective)
3. List the four primary components of behavioral objectives using the ABCD format. (enabling objective)
4. State the source and relevance of two objective data banks. (enabling objective)
5. Recall and list the names of the three general educational taxonomies. (enabling objective)
6. Discuss two uses of instructional objective taxonomies. (enabling objective)

Although some educators consider interest in objectives to be only a recent phenomenon, objectives were used in the Eight-Year Study conducted in the 1930s. The objectives for the instructional programs were written in behavioral terms so that modification of student behaviors could be measured and used in program evaluation. At that time, however, few educators saw a relative advantage to using behavioral objectives, and as World War II began the project terminated with little notice. During the 1950s interest in objective writing was rekindled when Robert Mager published a programmed text describing how to write behavioral objectives. His model continues to be used widely. According to Mager, a well-written objective has three components:

1. A specific objective written in terms that allow a teacher to watch the student and know when the objective has been mastered (for example, "List the steps . . .").
2. The conditions under which the behavior is to occur (such as, "The student can use the textbook in listing the five steps . . .").
3. The criterion or degree to which the learner must perform the behavior (for example, "List four of the five steps in a criterion test following the instructions").

Mager believed it was time for instructional technology to evolve from its "audio-visual aids" roots. Using behavioral objectives to design programs with observable outcomes allowed materials to be revised or "programmed" until specified objectives were attained, which permitted a critical analysis of how well the instruction worked; that is, how the students' behaviors were changed. We believe a useful definition for learning is "a change of behavior."

Today we continue to see interest in objectives at all levels of education from kindergarten to the twelfth grade to higher education as well as in business and industry training programs. While there is no universal definition for the word "objective," there is general recognition of the requirement to state measurable behavior or the products of that behavior. This widespread interest in objectives provides a cornerstone for the growth of instructional technology.

After an instructional problem has been examined, it is then possible to develop a set of objectives that further refine the problem. The broad objectives are called *terminal objectives,* while their subordinate elements are called *enabling objectives.* After the objectives have been written, it is then possible to logically specify instructional strategies and the media to be utilized. Specification of objectives will be discussed in this chapter, while instructional strategies will be considered in Chapter 7.

OBJECTIVE TAXONOMIES

A taxonomy of educational objectives listing skill levels from simple to complex can help educators and trainers determine the appropriate instructional level for students. It is generally accepted that there are three classes of educational objectives: *cognitive, affective,* and *psychomotor.* Each taxonomy has within it a classification scheme, but the three are not arranged in hierarchical order. However, unlike biological classification structures, the three classes tend to overlap. Many objectives contain elements from two or perhaps all three classes. For example, in a swimming class both motor skills and cognitive knowledge are required to learn a new stroke. If the learner has a fear of water, the attitude domain must also be considered. Fortunately, as we shall see later,

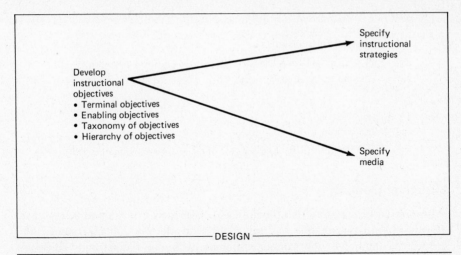

FIGURE 6.1   I.D. Model: An Objectives Subsystem

this overlapping does not limit the usefulness of objectives in planning instruction.

The learning objectives included within each class are ordered so that an instructional developer can specify the level or depth to which the potential learners must be able to "know" the information. Use of a taxonomy also ensures that instruction is focused on "higher-order" as well as "lower-order" objectives.

Cognitive Domain

The cognitive domain is concerned with the intellectual responses of the learner, such as performing mathematical solutions, composing an essay, or solving various kinds of "mental" problems. The most widely used cognitive or knowledge taxonomy was developed by Benjamin Bloom et al. (1956). Their major subclassifications of cognitive domain are:

1.0   Knowledge
    1.1 Knowledge of specifics
    1.2 Knowledge of ways and means of dealing with specifics
    1.3 Knowledge of the universals and abstractions in a field

2.0   Comprehension
    2.1 Translation
    2.2 Interpretation
    2.3 Extrapolation

3.0   Application

4.0 Analysis
    4.1 Analysis of elements
    4.2 Analysis of relationships
    4.3 Analysis of organizational principles

5.0 Synthesis

6.0 Evaluation
    6.1 Judgments in terms of internal evidence
    6.2 Judgments in terms of external criteria*

Affective Domain

The affective taxonomy of Krathwohl et al. (1964) was developed a few years after the cognitive taxonomy was published. The affective domain concerns the attitudinal, emotional, and valuing responses desired of the student. These are also called interests, attitudes, appreciations, and the like.

While most teachers write instructional objectives in the cognitive domain, few have included affective objectives in their lesson plans. Instructors usually consider affective objectives for their students, but these objectives are seldom written out or specifically taught. Some educators feel that the time teachers or technologists spend writing out affective objectives is well spent, since these objectives will jog their memory when planning presentations. Thus, writing down the affective objectives may increase the likelihood of their being achieved.

The major subclassifications in Krathwohl's affective taxonomy of objectives are:

1.0 Receiving (attending)
    1.1 Awareness
    1.2 Willingness to receive
    1.3 Controlled or selected attentions

2.0 Responding
    2.1 Acquiescence in responding
    2.2 Willingness to respond
    2.3 Satisfaction in response

3.0 Valuing
    3.1 Acceptance of a value
    3.2 Preference for a value
    3.3 Commitment

4.0 Organization
    4.1 Conceptualization of a value
    4.2 Organization of a value system

5.0 Characterization of a value or value complex
    5.1 Generalized set
    5.2 Characterization*

In-school social behaviors relate directly to school success and thus are important enough to teach. Behaviors such as attending to instruction, volunteering answers in class, complying with teacher requests, being task-oriented, and interacting with the teacher and other students are correlated with success in learning. The more the learners' affective behaviors reflect these attitudes, the higher their grades tend to become.

A formal instructional plan is usually necessary to effectively teach affective or social objectives. Educators need to be concerned with both in-school and out-of-school social behaviors. The out-of-school behaviors could relate to street crimes, broken windows in a school, or to graduates who register to vote and become productive and informed citizens. The advantages for the social system are obvious. Positive techniques for teaching affective objectives involve differential reinforcement, modeling behavior, and behavior modification techniques.

Psychomotor Domain

The remaining instructional objectives fall into the general area of muscle development and coordination. These objectives are often taught in laboratory classes, athletic programs, and home economics classes. Industrial and military training programs are also often oriented to teaching psychomotor objectives. The most widely used psychomotor objective taxonomy was developed by Elizabeth Simpson (1971), following the general structures created by Bloom, Krathwohl, and others. Her psychomotor hierarchy is presented below:

1.0 Perception (awareness of objects and qualities)
    1.1 Sensory stimulation
    1.2 Cue selection
    1.3 Translation (relating perception to action)

2.0 Set (preparatory adjustment for a particular action)
    2.1 Mental set (knowledge of steps to take in performing a test)
    2.2 Physical set (placing body in position to perform an act)
    2.3 Emotional set (desire to use a tool to perform an act)

*From *Taxonomy of Educational Objectives: Handbook II: Affective Domain* by David R. Krathwohl et al. Copyright 1964 by Longman, Inc. Reprinted by permission of Longman, Inc., New York.

3.0 Guided response (behavior exhibited under instructor guidance)
   3.1 Imitation (performance of an act as previously demonstrated)
   3.2 Trial and error (responding until correct behavior is achieved)

4.0 Mechanism (learned behavior is habitual)

5.0 Complex overt response (behavior is skilled, smooth, efficient, with minimum time and effort)
   5.1 Resolution of uncertainty (performance without hesitation)
   5.2 Automatic performance (coordinated motor skill with ease and muscle control)

6.0 Adapting and originating (modifies performance as conditions change)*

More detailed discussions of the three taxonomies may be found in the materials listed in the Suggested Readings at the end of the chapter.

Several other taxonomies have also been developed and absorbed into the literature. Some have been applied to actual instructional settings, while others remain untested. Robert Gagne's taxonomy of learning has received considerable attention, since he and others have attempted to specify what instructional sequences and strategies are appropriate for different types of objectives. The five major categories of human performance or capabilities of the learner, according to Gagne (1985), are:

1. Intellectual skills
2. Verbal information
3. Cognitive strategies
4. Motor skills
5. Attitude†

Note that Gagne's list also contains the three primary taxonomies previously discussed—cognitive, affective, and psychomotor. However, in Gagne's taxonomy the cognitive category is stressed more than the other two in that three of the five capabilities are in the knowledge domain: intellectual skills, cognitive strategies, and verbal skills. Gagne feels that to find a common ground among the many instances of learning, we must first focus on "what is learned," and then on the conditions appropriate for each of these different varieties of learning.

Instructional designers can use either of these taxonomies (or others we have not presented) as checklists to ensure that the level of instruction planned is

---

*From *Illinois Teacher of Home Economics*, vol. X, no. 4, Winter 1966–67, by E. J. Simpson. Used with permission.

†Abstracted from R. M. Gagne, *Principles of Instructional Design*. Copyright © 1985 by Holt, Rinehart and Winston. Reprinted by permission of Holt, Rinehart and Winston, CBS College Publishing.

comprehensive and at the desired level of difficulty. The taxonomies can also be used to ensure that logical and sequential instruction is planned and implemented. It is our experience that the Bloom taxonomy serves best in curriculum development for classifying content. However, simpler taxonomies, such as Gagne's, appear more useful for actual planning and evaluating instruction. The limitation of the more detailed taxonomies is that, once having made the classification, we cannot describe unique instructional strategies for many of the categories. The issue then becomes whether it is worth the extra effort needed to prepare an extensive classification if the instructional strategies remain the same. Under normal circumstances, we think not.

As you might suspect, it is more difficult to write the higher-order than the lower-order objectives (problem solving versus simple recall). Objectives requiring students to synthesize, generalize, or evaluate are difficult to specify, teach, and test. As a result, teachers often exclude objectives beyond the lower levels of the taxonomies.

OBJECTIVES HIERARCHIES

When designing instruction it is desirable to use a taxonomy of educational objectives ranging from the lowest to the highest. This would result in a sequence where being able to "define terms" is taught before the student uses the terms in making generalizations or inferences. For example, a hierarchical listing of objectives related to exposing film in an industrial camera operation course might appear as in Figure 6.2.

The specific activities in this example would, of course, require further defining and limiting of the content area. The objectives should be classified in a manner ranging from the first enabling objective (defining the relationship be-

		Expose film.			
	Operate camera.			Calculate exposure.	
Load camera.	Focus camera.	Set exposure.		Set film speed.	Obtain light-level reading.
Prepare camera.	Locate focus ring.	Locate exposure ring.			
		Define relationship of exposure speed and lens opening to film exposure.			

FIGURE 6.2   An Objectives Hierarchy

tween speed and exposure) to the second objective (setting the camera) to the terminal objective (exposing the film). A hierarchical analysis will be more beneficial if the content tends to build on prior learning, as in mathematics. However, it may be less beneficial for a "flat" curriculum such as much social studies content.

The hierarchy may be arranged either in tree form or as a list. An example hierarchy in tree format was provided on the process of exposing film as a way to show how this order may be facilitated by using an objectives hierarchy. Figure 6.3 shows a tree hierarchy for constructing a ceramic pot.

While the tree arrangement makes it easier to graphically observe relationships between objectives, it is often space-consuming and also may not lend itself to a specific hierarchy requirement. In Figure 6.4, the same hierarchy is arranged as a list. To save space, the objectives are written in abbreviated form. Note that the terminal objective is at the top of the page. Listed under this terminal objective (finished pot), are its major enabling objectives (form pot, and so on). Listed under these larger enabling objectives is the next level of supporting or enabling objectives. It is common to find that while forming the hierarchy tree, some previously overlooked objectives will become apparent because unless students are taught these prerequisite objectives, they will not be able to complete the higher-level objectives.

A hierarchy in the form of a list always places the terminal, or highest, objective at the top of the list. Numbers are assigned to each objective for easy reference. Each terminal objective is assigned a base number (1.0, 2.0, etc.), followed by the subobjectives numbered 1.1, 1.2, 1.3, and so on. For additional detail, components of, say 1.2, would be assigned numbers such as 1.2.2, 1.2.3, and so on. In this manner it is always possible to precisely place an objective within the hierarchy. Higher and lower objectives can easily be recognized by their numbers. The *base* numbers, however, for terminal objectives do not signify any hierarchical structure.

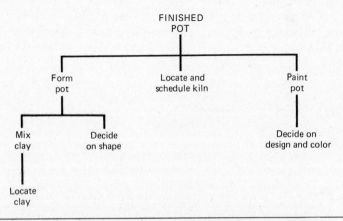

FIGURE 6.3   An Objectives Hierarchy in Tree Format (Incomplete)

Objective Number	Brief Objective Name
1.0	Finished pot
1.1	Form pot
1.1.1	Mix clay
1.1.1.1	Locate clay
1.1.2	Decide on shape
1.2	Locate and schedule kiln
1.3	Paint pot
1.3.1	Decide on design and colors

FIGURE 6.4.   An Objectives Hierarchy in List Format

Developing an objectives hierarchy may appear to be a time-consuming activity but is well worth the effort if the content is cumulative in nature. The hierarchical analysis is often useful for determining the sequence of presentation of instruction. For example, when employing an expository strategy, lower-order content is usually presented first since it is considered prerequisite. Unique conditions, however, may dictate a different sequence. If the learners are already acquainted with some elements of the hierarchy, the order should be adjusted accordingly. Sequencing will be discussed further in the section on instructional strategies. For now, keep in mind that performing the hierarchical analysis yields two important benefits. First, it increases the likelihood that all major elements of the terminal objectives have been identified. Second, it usually has a major positive influence on how the instruction is sequenced.

In some instances it may be necessary to consider the environment within which the problem is to be performed. The development of scenarios may be useful in accomplishing this task. For example, the problems of exposing film indoors or outdoors vary, including the type of film to use and the amount of light. Thus, the instructional problem may be redefined as the environment is described or as alternative approaches to solving the problem emerge. It is a characteristic of systems analysis that solutions are often found in a set of compromises that seek to balance and reconcile conflicting objectives or questions of value.

WRITING OBJECTIVES

The ABCD Method

Once you have decided on the content to include in a lesson by using needs assessment, task analysis, curriculum guides, or other materials, the next step is to develop, write, or select those instructional objectives which will comprise the unit of instruction. The following ABCD format may be useful as you write the objectives.

In the early 1970s the United States Office of Education supported the Instructional Development Institute, which promoted the ABCD approach to writing behavioral objectives. According to the Institute, the four basic components of a written objective are:

1. A is for the *audience* that will perform the objective. (Who is to be doing the learning? What is the entry level of the students expected to perform the objectives? When are they expected to perform?)
2. B is for the expected *behavior* of the performer. (What will be the observable action or product of the action of the learner?)
3. C is for the *conditions* under which the audience will perform when assessed. (What resources will be used? What time limitations or resource limitations will be placed on the students' performance when they are being evaluated to determine if they have achieved the objective?)
4. D is for *degree* of measurement used to determine an acceptable performance level. (Have they mastered the objective satisfactorily? [20 out of 20, 19 out of 20, 5 out of 5, 70% for a minimum grade of C])

Using the mnemonic ABCD, you will be sure to include all four parts in a fully developed objective. It is not always necessary to follow this order in writing an objective. We suggest, however, that you use it while learning to write objectives to ensure that you have a completely stated objective that fully defines the behavior you are describing.

As with an objectives taxonomy, you will usually have a few broad (terminal) objectives, divided into more specific (enabling) objectives. There may be only one terminal objective for several class-hours of instruction, but there will almost always be several enabling objectives per class. In an art class on pottery design, a terminal objective might be: "The student in Art 103 will be able to form, without assistance, a pot six inches high by the tenth week of class. The pot will hold water and its attractiveness will be judged by the teacher." One enabling objective related to this terminal objective might be: "The student in Art 103 will be able to mix potter's clay to a consistency suitable for throwing on a wheel in less than five minutes." There would be several other enabling objectives related to shaping the pot, glazing, firing, and so on.

Art 103 objectives written in the form suggested above might look like this:

Terminal Objective

1. Audience: The student enrolled in Art 103 will be able to . . . (List any required additional or specific requirements such as reading ability, math ability, or motor skill.)
2. Behavior: Design, form, and fire a clay pot six inches high. (Be as specific as possible so there is little question about what is required of the student.)
3. Condition: By the tenth week of class, without assistance, . . . (Identify any specific conditions that should exist when the student performs the behavior, such as using a textbook, notes, or calculator.)

4. Degree: The pot should be able to hold water and be attractive as judged by the teacher (whenever possible use rating scales or other objective measurable statements to support teacher judgments).

Enabling Objective

1. Audience: The student enrolled in Art 103 will be able to . . .
2. Behavior: mix potter's clay . . .
3. Condition: in less than five minutes . . .
4. Degree: to a consistency suitable for throwing on a potter's wheel.

It will not always be necessary to write all your objectives using all four parts. For example, after one terminal objective is written, it is unnecessary to continually state the audience statement. The audience statement, in this case, may be written as a part of the heading, and the rest of the following objectives may then refer to it.

To ensure that the objective is behaviorally measurable and classifiable, the following verbs should be used whenever possible. If the desired behavior involves a *fact* (low-order cognitive domain), use the verbs:

- recall, label, identify, state, request, compute
- recognize
- manipulate, install, replace, respond

If the behavior being specified in the objective is a *concept* (cognitive domain), use these verbs:

- classify
- discriminate, evaluate, recognize, identify, locate, check
- remember
- manipulate, employ, shift, detect, read, receive

If the behavior involves a *rule* (cognitive domain), use the following:

- sequence, analyze, distinguish, identify, compare, detect, generalize, discriminate, classify, describe
- use, apply, relocate, employ, categorize, design, form, calculate, estimate

If the behavior involves a *principle* (high-order cognitive domain), use:

- explain
- interpret
- predict

If the behavior is a *procedure* (psychomotor or cognitive domain), use:

- sequence (the steps from memory), move, shut, mix

- respond, adjust, track, identify, locate, check, shift, connect, join, move, observe, read, scan, survey, fire, disconnect, connect, align, install, evaluate, replace, employ, verify

If the behavior involves an *attitude* (affective domain), use:

- choose, offer, select
- acceptable, approve, volunteer

After the behaviors have been identified, it is necessary to specify the conditions and degree for each objective. *Conditions* are the "givens." They describe the circumstances under which the task is performed. Conditions include, but are not limited to, the following:

- environmental factors (sensory conditions such as space, light, quiet or noise, temperature, weather)
- people factors (alone, part of a team, under supervision)
- equipment factors (available job aids, tools, or equipment)
- information (available relevant information; textbooks, notes, formulas, checklists, charts)
- problem definition (what stimulus is present to initiate the task)
- time (task duration, pacing, and so on)

The *degree* statement should specify to what standards the student should be able to perform: how completely, how accurate, the rate, the time limit, to what degree of quality, and within what safety considerations. These conditions and standards statements will help identify when the student has satisfactorily learned to perform the behavior.

The only way to become proficient at writing objectives is to write some. Remember: a behavioral statement should include statements that can be seen and measured. An objective which states that the student will "reflect democratic ideals" is hardly a behavioral objective. How does a student reflect? What behavior does the student exhibit when reflecting "democratic ideals"? If you want students to listen patiently to others and be respectful of property, then say so and substitute these measurable statements for "democratic ideals."

Nonbehavioral objectives do not provide the communication necessary to effectively design, develop, or evaluate instruction. The more behavioral an objective, the easier it is to communicate its meaning to students, other teachers, parents, and even to another instructional designer.

Occasionally, it will be difficult to develop specific condition or degree statements. In these cases, do the best you can, but do not get stymied by these specific problems. Keep on thinking and writing. Perhaps a clearer idea of what you want the student to do will come to you while you are checking and revising. You can always go back and improve the objective statement. One of the

"Do we need more difficult condition and degree statements in our objectives?"
(S. Bartenstein)

best pieces of advice is to write your objectives in pencil and keep a large eraser handy!

You probably noticed that the objectives at the beginning of each chapter in this text are not stated in the ABCD format. While the behaviors are stated, instructors who use this text will have their own criteria of successful performance. Furthermore, it is usually not necessary (and may be confusing) to state all elements of the objective to the learner. Generally, only the behavior statement is necessary to communicate your instructional intent. The ABCD is more for your benefit in design than it is communication to the learner. Also, since a book can be only a part of the instructional system, it should not control the complete contents of an instructor's course.

Before concluding this discussion of objectives, we again remind you to ask whether the objective is really necessary and appropriate. Although objectives should reflect the task analysis or other information sources which identify the areas in which instruction is required, it is often desirable to reexamine decisions about the appropriateness of instruction. Just because an objective can be taught does not mean it necessarily should be.

Objectives and Testing

An objective can often be converted into a test question, with the verb determining what type of test item to construct. Consider the objective, "The student in Social Science 101 will be able to recall and write, in order, the names of at least eight of the first ten presidents of the United States." It can be rewritten as a test item to read, "List, in order, the first ten presidents of the United States." The verb "list" communicates the type of behavior as well as indicating the type of test item to use in testing the objective. "List," "state," or "recall" objectives require the student to recall and write down the names, so a fill-in type of test item is appropriate. In contrast, the verbs "discriminate," "choose," and "select" would require multiple-choice or matching test items. And finally, if the objective calls for the learner to move a control or manipulate an object, a performance test would be required.

Every aspect of test preparation is greatly enhanced by using the systematic processes of instructional technology for developing instruction. This is often a time-consuming and not altogether pleasant activity for instructors who realize the resulting tests don't measure what they feel is important. By having taken the time to prepare well-stated objectives, test preparation is now much simpler and should more closely reflect the instructor's primary goals in the course.

Measuring a person's ability to perform required behaviors under specified conditions to the appropriate degree should, if possible, be done by examining the behaviors in the actual performance situation. It is often impossible to measure performance under actual conditions. Although you can't create a nuclear accident to test people's responses, realistic simulations can be used to accurately predict behavior in the real situation (predictive validity). But simulations can be very expensive. For example, a flight simulator could cost from two hundred to five hundred dollars per student per hour just to operate! Many measurements must therefore be reduced to paper-and-pencil format (tests, checklists, case studies) or to judging the products of behavior (term papers, analyses of case studies, widgets assembled, welds made). These latter forms are the least expensive to administer, quickest to score, most readily available, and most easily understood by teachers. Hence, they are the most widely used measures of performance. However, their validity must always be examined if they replace a more realistic measure.

Objectives and Instructional Methods

Not only do the verbs used in stating objectives determine the type of test items to be constructed, they also suggest what instructional methods to use. If the objective requires a student to "discriminate," instruction should be oriented toward providing opportunities to make discriminations rather than defining terms, recalling information, or performing some new psychomotor behavior. Thus, behavioral objectives specify the content, instructional methods, and the test format. Objectives are the cornerstone of an instructional technology.

Objectives and Advance Organizers

Research shows that a variety of complex parameters determine whether or not providing the objectives to learners will enhance learning. Each instructional designer must take the responsibility for determining under what conditions behavioral objectives will be made available to the learner.

Advance organizers provide an organizational scheme that assists learners in synthesizing subsequent learning. Ausubel (1968) has suggested two types of advance organizers: expository and comparative. Ausubel recommends using expository organizers when the material is completely unfamiliar. They provide inclusive subsumers that are related to existing ideas in the cognitive structure and to the more detailed material in the learning passage. They also provide the learner with a set of objectives or questions before, during, or after the lesson. On the other hand, he recommends using comparative organizers when the learning material is familiar or can be related to previously learned ideas. In such cases, the organizer provides "ideational scaffolding" for the content by explicitly pointing out similarities and differences. An example of a comparative organizer is drawing an analogy between the elements and functions of the human brain (input, processing, memory, output) and those of a computer.

Melton (1978) concluded the following about behavioral objectives:

- Behavioral objectives might be expected to function as orienting or as reinforcement stimuli according to whether they are placed immediately before or after the related instructional material. For ease of reference we might refer to such objectives as pre- and post-objectives.
- We would expect both pre- and post-objectives to enhance relevant learning. We would, however, expect post-objectives to be more effective than pre-objectives in this respect.
- Pre-objectives might be expected to function as orienting stimuli, enhancing relevant learning but depressing incidental learning.
- The effectiveness of both pre- and post-objective stimuli might be expected to increase if the objectives are spread throughout the text, rather than grouped together at the beginning or end.
- Student performance overall (relevant and incidental learning combined) should be enhanced more by post-objectives than by pre-objectives.
- Although one might expect to observe the above effects in related studies on behavioral objectives, they could well be hidden if the student body concerned is highly motivated. The effects could also be masked by other conditions such as those discussed regarding relevant learning.*

*From R. F. Melton, Resolution of Conflicting Claims Concerning the Effect of Behavioral Objectives on Student Learning, *Review of Educational Research* (Spring 1978), pp. 291–302. Copyright 1978, American Educational Research Association, Washington, DC. Used with permission.

Given Melton's conclusions, it is probably sound practice to include some form of advance organizer in instructional units. They may not help all learners, but are almost certain to do no harm and indeed may help some learners. During field testing, it may be possible to conduct experiments to test the efficacy of including the objectives in your instructional system.

OBJECTIVES DATA BANKS

Preparing a complete set of objectives from scratch can often be dull and time-consuming. Fortunately, several collections of objectives have been developed and are available. These data banks are a smorgasbord from which to choose, add to, or modify. The strength of these data banks is that there are few errors of omission; that is, they include a wide range of objectives. Hence, the instructional designer's creative effort changes from writing objectives to selecting and modifying them to meet local requirements. Moreover, the low cost of purchasing these collected objectives may be more than offset by the saving of much valuable time and effort. Since objectives should reflect the particular needs of the local school or training program, these data banks should not be viewed as providing complete guidance in specifying the program. They are simply a valuable resource to ensure a comprehensive review of the topic.

One of the best-known collections of behavioral objectives is the Instructional Objectives Exchange (IOX). This collection provides objectives in varied subject and skill areas for grades K–12. Every objective from IOX is accompanied by at least one illustrative test item for assessing the skill described in the objective.

Another source of objectives in the reading/language arts and mathematics areas for grades 1–8 is SCORE, distributed by Westinghouse Learning Corporation. Once objectives have been selected from the seventeen hundred-item data bank, corresponding criterion-referenced items are provided by SCORE. SCORE also scores the tests and provides a detailed analysis of the individual learner's answers. Westinghouse also publishes "Learning Objectives for Individualized Instruction" in language arts, science, social science, and mathematics. The cognitive and psychomotor objectives are given level designators, and enabling objectives are listed under their appropriate terminal objective. Other sources of objectives include professional associations, certification agencies, special interest groups, and educational institutions. Although in most cases these statements of objectives will not meet the ABCD format outlined earlier, they can be easily rewritten to meet that format.

Results of needs assessments, study groups, committee reports, curricular outlines, as well as course outlines and tests from previous offerings of the instruction, also provide input for preparing objectives. When ongoing instruction is being reviewed and redeveloped, tests are particularly good indicators of what the instructor's objectives "really are." Tests often contrast sharply with what is stated in course outlines or syllabi. Care must therefore be taken to ensure the validity of the objectives contained in existing tests, since they may have little relation to what the objectives should be or how they should be measured.

EVALUATION, ACCOUNTABILITY, AND OBJECTIVES

Education is what survives when what has been learned has been forgotten.

B. F. Skinner

Behavioral objectives are invaluable tools for evaluating the effectiveness of the teaching method or system. Do students learn what the objectives suggest they are to learn? If, after instruction, students cannot meet the objectives under the specified conditions to the required degree, it generally means the program or materials did not work. Behavioral objectives provide the basis for a technological approach to assessing and designing instruction. Measurable objectives are, as you can see, extremely important.

Robert Glaser (1963) introduced the idea of criterion-referenced testing. His purpose was to obtain test-scoring information to make individual student and programmatic decisions in objective-based instructional programs. As director of the HEW-funded Learning R and D Center in Pittsburgh, he needed measures of how well students were progressing toward their objectives in the Individually Prescribed Instruction (IPI) project. The IPI project was the vehicle for evaluating one form of individualized instruction. The available norm-referenced achievement tests were unable to provide specific progress information needed to individually prescribe instruction for students. Further, Glaser and his staff were unable to evaluate the strengths and weaknesses of their instructional programs. To solve this dilemma, they developed criterion-referenced tests to meet the requirements of their objective-based instructional programs. "Performance-based" and "competency-based" are other terms associated with this evaluation procedure. Criterion-referenced tests determine how well the learner has achieved in relation to specific objectives. Behaviorally-measured objectives with criterion statements are essential for developing these criterion-referenced tests.

One of the more interesting features of criterion-referenced testing is its effect on grading. Under criterion-referenced testing, all students can receive the same grade depending on their performance. Of course, that grade can be an A or an F, but each learner's grade is independent of the others' performance. In contrast, norm-referenced tests compare the learning of a particular student with a national, regional, or other group norm and grade along a curve.

Objectives also provide the basis for most of the statewide minimum competency testing programs. Most of the states have taken some type of action to mandate the setting of minimum competency standards for students in their schools. Competency testing programs are frequently based on objective-referenced or criterion-referenced measures. Tests are devised to measure the objectives identified by the school district or state (depending on legislation). As a general rule, the more specific or behavioral the objective, the closer the test items can be linked or related to it.

In the late 1960s, the United States Office of Education and several individual states considered using objectives in managing the contracts and reports they required from the school districts. The State of California legislated a Program Planning Budgeting System (PPBS) as the reporting system to be implemented by the school districts in the state. As a first step, behavioral objectives were first identified by the individual school districts. These then became the goals/objectives to be used in assessing the school district's expenditure of funds. The current national trend away from using local property taxes for the support of the public elementary and secondary schools increases the importance of this accountability system. Local districts may, in the future, have to account for the use of their funds as never before. Linking expenditures to student performance rather than traditional line-item budgets would have major implications for the way in which instruction is developed and delivered.

While minimum competency testing for students is widely used, California, Georgia, Florida, Texas, and New York are among the few states actively exploring testing for teacher certification. Under these plans, teachers are re-

"Why am I worried about maintaining academic standards? For one thing, this is a class on Chaucer."

(Saltzman)

quired to meet the objectives established by the certification committees and as measured by the criterion tests. There is increased parallel interest in certification (and recertification) of a variety of professional and classified personnel in business and industry. CPAs are an obvious example, but other groups (medicine, dentistry, nuclear industry) are increasingly looking to testing as a vehicle to assure both initial and continued competence of their members. The behavioral criteria and degree statements contained in objectives also have increasing importance in industrial training as accountability and determining the return on training investments are becoming more of a reality.

The judiciary has also provided pressure for minimum competency testing. In Peter Doe vs. San Francisco Unified School District, it was contended that the school district failed to apprehend the student's reading disabilities and permitted him to graduate from high school even though he did not read at the eighth-grade level. Another suit in New Jersey (Robinson vs. Cahill) was concerned with the equalization of educational expenditures. It resulted in the court ordering the establishment of educational goals and instructional programs to produce reasonable levels of proficiency in communications and computational skills. Furthermore, the court ordered an evaluation and monitoring program to assess student progress. Similarly, suits have been filed by police and firefighters (and their widows) on the basis that injuries or deaths resulted from inadequate training. The nuclear mishap at Three Mile Island, which has often been called the "worst civilian nuclear accident in history," has been attributed in part to inadequately trained operators. All these forces suggest that more rigorous and validated assessments will be demanded in the future.

SUMMARY

The education of a man is never completed until he dies.
                                                    Robert E. Lee

As we have seen in this chapter, behavioral objectives can be used to:

- Identify and communicate an instructional program's goals
- Structure the development of materials aimed at teaching those objectives
- Evaluate the effectiveness of an instructional program using criterion-referenced techniques
- Develop test items

Instructional objectives fall into three taxonomies that can be used to develop or select objectives: cognitive, or knowledge-related, objectives; affective, or attitude-related, objectives; and psychomotor, or skills-related, objectives. When terminal objectives are being taught, related enabling objectives will usually be included. The learner should first be taught the enabling objectives and then the terminal objective.

Behavioral objectives have four components: audience, behavior, condition, and degree. This ABCD format helps to develop thoroughly stated objectives, but it is flexible and can be modified.

To save time and avoid duplicating effort, it may be possible to select the desired objectives from established data banks. Modifying or adding to the objectives in the data banks may be necessary, but they will most often provide the majority of the objectives in behavioral form. In addition, the data banks may provide a more extensive range of objectives than would have been identified by the instructional developers. Accountability and competency testing programs will influence interest in behavioral objectives in the future.

Questions for Consideration and Discussion

1. What is the difference between behavioral objectives and goals?
2. Why should educators and trainers be taught how to write behavioral objectives?
3. How are objective taxonomies used in developing instructional programs?
4. Name two educational objective data banks.
5. What are the names of the three general educational taxonomies and how do they differ? Are there any other logical areas within which educational objectives should be written?

Suggested Activities

1. Write at least ten behavioral objectives in a content area of your choice. Write a terminal objective and several enabling objectives. Either exchange papers in a small group and discuss each other's papers or give the papers to the instructor for grading.
2. Identify the objective taxonomy and level for each of the objectives developed in the above activity; for example, Bloom, 2.1.
3. Determine whether the following objectives are fully stated. If they are not, rewrite them as complete objectives.
   a. The student enrolled in Art 102, after viewing a group of five paintings, will be able to identify the artist associated with each work.
   b. The student in Business 201 will understand the difference between a savings account and a checking account after a forty-minute lecture.
   c. Students enrolled in Education 332 will be able to list in their own words at least three ways of directing student perception with no errors.

Suggested Readings

Ausubel, D. P. (1968). *Educational Psychology: A Cognitive View.* New York: Holt, Rinehart and Winston.
Bergan, J. R. (Winter 1980). The Structural Analysis of Behavior: An Alternative to the Learning-Hierarchy Model. *Review of Educational Research,* 625–646.

Bloom, B. S., et al. (1956). *Taxonomy of Educational Objectives; Handbook I: Cognitive Domain*. New York: David McKay.

Gagne, Robert. (1985). Principles of Instructional Design, 4th ed. New York: Holt, Rinehart and Winston.

Glaser, R. (1963). Instructional Technology and the Measurement of Learning Outcomes. *American Psychologist*, 519–521.

Hartley, J., and Davies, I. K. (1976). Preinstructional Strategies: The Role of Pretests, Behavioral Objectives, Overviews, and Advance Organizers. *Review of Educational Research*, 239–265.

Hudgins, B. B. (1977). *Learning and Thinking: A Primer for Teachers*. Tasca, IL: F. E. Peacock.

Luiten, J., et al. (Summer 1980). A Meta-analysis of the Effects of Advanced Organizers on Learning and Retention. *American Educational Research Journal*, 211–218.

Krathwohl, D. R., et al. (1964). *Taxonomy of Educational Objectives; Handbook II: Affective Domain*. New York: David McKay.

Mager, R. (1962). *Preparing Instructional Objectives*. Palo Alto, CA: Fearon.

Mayer, R. E. (Spring 1979). Can Advance Organizers Influence Meaningful Learning? *Review of Educational Research*, 371–383.

Melton, R. F. (Spring 1978). Resolution of Conflicting Claims Concerning the Effect of Behavioral Objectives on Student Learning. *Review of Educational Research*, 291–302.

Seddon, G. M. (Spring 1978). The Properties of Bloom's Taxonomy of Educational Objectives for the Cognitive Domain. *Review of Educational Research*, 303–323.

Simpson, E. (1971). Educational Objectives in the Psychomotor Domain. In M. Kapfer, ed., *Behavioral Objectives in Curriculum Development*. Englewood Cliffs, NJ: Educational Technology Publications.

Simpson, E. J. (Winter 1966–67). The Classification of Educational Objectives, Psychomotor Domain. *Illinois Teacher of Home Economics*, 135–141.

7

Instructional Theories and Development Strategies

If, by a miracle of mechanical ingenuity, a book could be so arranged that only to him who had done what was directed on page one would page two become visible, and so on, much that now requires personal instruction could be managed by print.

E. L. Thorndike

Objectives

After completing this chapter you should be able to:

1. Discuss *instructional strategies* and their use in designing instruction for different types of learning.
2. List several ways in which knowledge concerning learner profiles can be applied to designing effective instruction by an instructional designer.
3. List the ways in which learner characteristics could affect the selection of an instructional method or approach to teaching a given set of objectives.
4. Discuss how instructional objectives and knowledge of learner profiles can be used to determine the instructional or presentation strategies for a lesson or group of lessons.
5. Define and discuss aptitude-treatment-interaction and related research.
6. Discuss when grouped or individualized instruction should be selected and used by an instructional designer.
7. List factors to be considered when deciding to use interactive or linear instructional techniques.

What is the best way to resolve an instructional/learning problem? This is the major focus of, or reason for, instructional development models. These systematic approaches to problem solving are replacing the "teaching as an art" approach of using only one's personal knowledge rather than the combined experiences of others facing similar situations. Instructional development processes are all similar in that they provide procedures, which if followed, will ensure that major questions have been asked and alternative solutions examined before a decision is finally made.

As specified in the model used in this book, after specification of instructional objectives is completed, the next task is indicating appropriate instructional strategies and types of media. Theories of learning will be discussed in this chapter as they directly contribute to our instructional design decisions. Later chapters discuss research-based design principles and media selection.

A central concern of instructional technologists is the management of learning. John Dewey expressed this concern well in *Democracy and Education:*

> We never educate directly, but indirectly by means of the environment. Whether we permit chance environments to do the work, or whether we design environments for the purpose, makes a great difference. And any environment is a chance environment, so far as its educative influence is concerned, unless it has been deliberately regulated with reference to its educative effect . . . every stimulus directs activity. It does not simply excite it, or stir it up, but directs it toward an object.

An instructional technologist designs, implements, and manages instructional programs. In this chapter we will examine a number of considerations in planning instructional strategies. Later on, we will discuss media characteristics and factors to consider in their selection. Both the strategies and media make up the instructional/learning environment, which is critical to learner performance. Instructional technologists have generally adopted the philosophy that it is their professional responsibility to ensure student learning; briefly stated, "the learner doesn't fail, the technologist does." While there are some exceptions, it is generally believed that the instructional technologist should

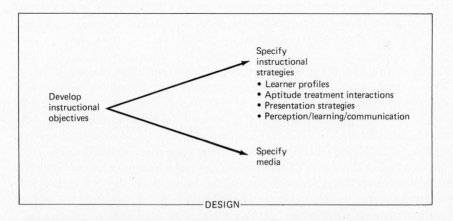

FIGURE 7.1   I.D. Model: An Instructional Strategies Subsystem

select strategies and media which maximize opportunities for learning, independent of their personal preference for some particular approaches. The crucial test is not whether the instruction "looks good" or whether "teachers like it," but whether or not "students learn from it."

Research on learning does provide some guidance for the development of instructional strategies. While we need to know much more about how people learn, we do have some direction. In this chapter we will examine what we already know from existing data.

A primary aspect of any instructional development project involves ascertaining the learners' current status: What do they already know? How do they learn? How do *they* think they learn best? Do they learn some types of objectives better in one way and others in another? It is probable that some individuals learn differently. The design task is to match learner aptitudes with instructional treatments. Ideally, aptitudes and treatments would be matched for each individual learner, yet realistically this is not often possible for a variety of reasons. Nonetheless, it is beneficial to analyze aptitudes and treatments in an attempt to optimize selections, even for group instruction. Also, it may be possible to incorporate more than one treatment (or at least parts of different treatments) into the strategy; for example, using illustrations to promote information processing by holistic thinkers while also listing a sequence of steps for those who think in a more linear manner.

THEORIES OF INSTRUCTION

The perception and learning principles related to instructional design discussed in previous sections were derived from research on how individuals learn. Explanations of how best to interpret these conclusions have resulted in a number of instructional theories that have evolved over the last twenty years or so from primarily behaviorist theories to cognitive theories. It is hoped that these theories will result in a better understanding of learning and in new applications or principles useful to instructional designers.

A general statement of many of these theories is found in *Theories of Learning* by Bower and Hilgard (1981). Some instructional theories try to relate specific instructional events to learning outcomes by prescribing instructional conditions which optimize learning. Instructional design theories are similar to instructional theories but are focused on the broader process of developing instruction. Theories of both instruction and instructional design attempt to relate specific instructional events to learning outcomes. Instructional systems theories are concerned with these same issues but are more concerned with the context within which instruction takes place. Instructional theory can therefore be considered as a subset of instructional design theory, which is a subset of instructional systems theory.

There are many interesting and useful instructional theories, four of which—each different, yet typical—will be discussed here.

Gagne–Briggs

Gagne (1985) made a significant contribution to our thinking about learning as he examined *conditions* for learning. Gagne and Briggs (1979) expanded upon these conditions as they developed a set of principles for instructional design. Their theory tends to ignore traditional factors in learning, such as reinforcement, contiguity, and exercise because they are thought to be too general to be of use in designing instruction. They contend that internal and external conditions must be specified for the learning of verbal information, intellectual skills, and for the other categories of learned capabilities Gagne has identified. The outcome of each learning category requires a different set of conditions for optimizing learning, retention, and transferability.

You will recall from our discussion on objective taxonomies in Chapter 6 that Gagne proposed five types of cognitive learning: verbal information, intellectual skills, cognitive strategy, motor skill, and attitude. The Gagne–Briggs theory provides prescriptions for each of these learning types based partially on an information-processing model of learning and memory similar to that described by Atkinson and Shiffrin (1968). The Gagne–Briggs theory assumes learner reinforcement via information feedback, selective perception, and short- and long-term memory storage and retrieval. It is presented as a comprehensive theory or model that includes all kinds of learning outcomes to which instruction is normally addressed. Their model suggests that instruction can be defined as a set of events external to the learner that support the internal processes of learning. These external events are:

- Gain learner attention.
- Inform the learner of the objective.
- Stimulate recall of prerequisites.
- Present stimulus materials.
- Provide learning guidance.
- Elicit the desired performance.
- Provide feedback.
- Assess the performance.
- Enhance retention and transfer.

Merrill–Reigeluth

The Elaboration Theory of instruction (Reigeluth, Merrill, Bunderson 1978; Reigeluth 1979; Reigeluth and Rogers 1980; Merrill 1984) deals with macrostrategies for organizing instruction, such as interrelating topics within a course and sequencing instruction. Their theory focuses on concepts, principles, procedures, and recall of factual information. In general, the theory looks at instruction as a process that gradually presents details or refinements to previous instruction. According to the Merrill–Reigeluth theory, an instructional sequence is designed by following these steps:

- Select all operations to be taught (by performing a task analysis).
- Decide which operation to teach first.
- Sequence remaining operations.
- Identify supporting content.
- Allocate all content to lessons and sequence the lessons.
- Sequence the instruction within the lessons.
- Design instruction for each lesson.

This prescriptive model uses task analysis to identify the content to be taught. While Gagne and Briggs emphasize relevant prior learning as a basis for sequencing instruction, Merrill and Reigeluth stress beginning instruction with large, general, unifying ideas before proceeding to more detailed or concrete ideas.

Merrill (1984) is currently working on a Component Display Theory, which deals only on a microlevel (aspects of instruction related to teaching a single concept or principle) within the cognitive domain. The theory attempts to integrate knowledge about learning and instruction from behavioral, cognitive, and humanistic perspectives. In exchange for the narrowness of his theory, Merrill provides a level of prescription lacking in other theories which permits its direct application to designing instruction within its sphere.

Case

Case (1978) suggests that the sequence of behavior during each major stage of intellectual development depends on the appearance of increasingly complex cognitive strategies. A learner is thought to use more complex strategies because of both increased experience (including instruction) and a gradual increase in the size of working memory.

Case's instructional design sequence involves identifying the goal of the task to be performed (learned); mapping out operations to assist the learner in reaching that goal; comparing the learner's performance (or reported thoughts) with that of skilled individuals; assessing the student's level of functioning (by clinical questioning); designing exercises to demonstrate to the learner the inadequacies of the current strategy (if any) and explaining why the correct strategy works better; and finally, presenting additional examples using the new strategy.

This model resembles Piaget's work by suggesting that existing cognitive strategies of uninstructed students can be uncovered and used as a basis for sequencing instruction and planning instructional events. Rothkopf (1981) expands on Case's model by providing a theoretical rationale for the inclusion of factors he feels promote learning.

Landa

A separate model for designing instruction using algorithms has been advocated and refined by Landa (1974). His decision trees are especially useful for problem solving or procedure objectives. A number of training programs have been developed around an algorithm of the task that requires the learner to follow the procedures outlined in the training manual. In order to use Landa's design procedure, it is necessary to have previously identified all of the activities and operations the learner must perform so they can be included in the algorithm.

In contrast to what one might call a psychological approach to planning instruction, curriculum specialists tend to focus on the structure of the content based on its application. They often organize learning into: 1) cognitive content; 2) vocational skills; 3) social or cultural learning; and 4) learning oriented toward individual or personal needs. Usually they hold the view that all types of learning may be best taught by using an individual-needs approach; that is, when individuals feel a need for vocational or social instruction, then they will be more motivated than when the content is judged as not relevant. Under conditions of higher learner motivation, instruction is usually easier to design. If a school is individual-oriented, as it must be for this type of personal instruction, then the instructional design process and instructional strategies and media may be simplified.

Jack Frymier (1977) developed a set of curriculum characteristics which, he feels, if included in the design of instructional materials, maximize learning. Frymier identifies six characteristics (experience, intelligence, motivation, emotion-personality, creativity, and social behavior) and suggests that if a learner is classified according to these attributes as being positive (highly motivated), then he or she will require minimal curriculum development and materials support. For example, a student who has had many experiences (traveled widely, read a lot, and the like), is motivated, and has high intelligence would need fewer examples and might be able to use a more specialized and abstract terminology than students having limited experience, lower intelligence, and low achievement. A student characterized as having low motivation (indifferent, lazy, easily discouraged, lacks initiative, present-oriented, demands instant gratification) must be presented with a "charged" curriculum to overcome this problem. This would require a set of relatively more extensive and expensive motivational characteristics (attractive, stimulating, avocative, provocative examples; marked contrasts, compelling, immediate feedback; activity-oriented exercises). Highly-motivated students would not require these types of materials, although they might find them interesting. Frymier's other five characteristics also have a series of variables describing learner attributes and curriculum requirements.

These and other theories of instruction are needed as a part of the research process in organizing information about human learning. However, there is still a long way to go before any of these theories will adequately prescribe a process for consistently designing effective instruction for individuals or groups of students. At the present time they serve principally as useful guides or frameworks within which instructional design can take place. Due to this limitation of current theories, the design process places great emphasis on testing a prototype of the instruction before disseminating it for general use.

LEARNER-PROFILE DETERMINATION

A man must not swallow more theories than he can digest.
Brooks Adams

A learner's existing knowledge, as it relates to deciding where a new instructional program should be started, was discussed in Chapter 4. In this chapter learners' information processing skills will be related to designing their learning environments.

We must remind ourselves that all learning is individual. Each person must perceive, respond, process, store, and retrieve his or her own information, attitudes, and motor routines. Even in the largest lecture hall or TV audience, it all boils down to the impact of the environment on each individual.

Learners, as well, are all unique. They differ physically and intellectually, and in their rate of acquiring new information, perceiving and reacting to stimuli, and so on. At whom should an instructional program be aimed? If the instruction is aimed at "average" individuals, slower students will become lost and brighter students will become bored. Should the vocabulary be simplified and the redundancy levels raised so that, potentially at least, more students will succeed (and more become bored)? Should several parallel programs be developed for the major clusterings of students? Should an instructional program be managed by a computer which could tailor an instructional program to each student? The degree to which instructional objectives and strategies can be tailored to individual learners depends on the educational policy, available resources, and the sensitivity and flexibility of the instructional development model employed.

Individualized instruction is usually thought to be so expensive as to be impractical. While we can order a new car to meet our physical needs and taste, some educators feel we cannot customize our teaching/learning systems for individual learner differences to any significant degree. Others disagree. Progress is being made in tailoring instruction to students' backgrounds, felt needs, learning styles, and goals. We are learning how to identify relevant information from learners' past experiences in order to determine their needs. Perhaps more importantly, we are beginning to know how to diagnose learning styles so we can then prescribe appropriate instructional strategies. These are the "decision points" which make individualized instruction a worthy goal.

Computer programs are being developed to aid in assessing students' progress by examining their responses and the time it takes to make them. It then becomes possible to direct them to the proper learning experiences. This degree of individualized instruction is being done today!

Diagnostic procedures or tools useful in constructing a "learner profile" include IQ data, motivation assessment, achievement data, personality profile data, and directly stated student-preference data. Much of this profile data is already being used by schools to make decisions concerning placement of individuals in different instructional environments. What is still needed is a formal learner profile that can reliably relate this data to instructional treatments. The profile must be a diagnostic tool capable of reflecting student learning styles— the best way they learn. This predictive profile must include data on learners' physical, social, and emotional needs, their way of interacting with people (teachers, peers, aides, parents, administrators), the manner in which they process information, and their use of the senses. Do they prefer to learn from visual stimuli (television), audio stimuli (lectures), or print stimuli (textbooks)?

There are many types of information about learners which instructional designers need for constructing individualized instructional situations, and the interactions are complex. Ideally, designers should possess data on the following to provide relevant individualized instruction:

1. *Information-processing style*
   Learns best from inductive presentations
   Prefers and/or learns best with a high degree of redundancy
   Prefers to have lots of positive reinforcement in the training materials
   Prefers continuous and active involvement with the training materials
   Prefers to learn through tactile and "hands-on" activities
   Prefers to pace own learning progress

2. *Use of senses for perception or reception of stimuli*
   Learns best from motion visual stimuli (ITV, films)
   Prefers to learn from auditory stimuli (lectures, audiotapes)
   Prefers to learn from print material
   Prefers to learn from several simultaneous stimuli

3. *Emotional needs*
   Needs frequent expressions of love and encouragement
   Is self-motivated
   Is persistent
   Is responsible

4. *Social needs*
   Prefers to learn with peers
   Requires frequent peer approval
   Likes to learn from peers

5. *Physical and emotional needs (real or felt)*
   Prefers quiet
   Desires background noise or music
   Prefers a low light and contrast level
   Prefers a certain room temperature
   Prefers frequent access to food
   Likes to be able to move around
   Prefers visual isolation, as in a carrel
   Prefers to study at a particular time of day or night
   Likes to sleep or rest frequently
   Likes access to a smoking area
   Prefers a particular type of chair for studying

Matching learning styles with instruction may be the most important way to affect academic achievement and the most promising development in curriculum and instruction in a generation. Once we have determined a student's learning profile, instructional designers can use these preferences to prescribe instruction for the individual. It may also be possible to modify or expand a student's profile if necessary. While this approach makes intuitive sense, research does not consistently validate this position. Studies involving college students and adults do show some positive results, but studies of younger individuals indicate they do not benefit as much from these approaches (Kulik, Kulik, and Cohen, 1979; Bangert, Kulik, and Kulik, 1983). However, much more research is needed.

Traditional methods of instruction which make the assumption that students are pretty much homogeneous are almost always based on audio stimuli supported by print materials. This instructional system works well for some students (who are easily recognized since they usually get the As). However, to best match the learning profiles of the other students with their learning environment requires a wide variety of audio- and visual-based materials. And of course, these materials must be available to teachers who are trained to use them.

A study of gifted junior-high-school students revealed that they have unique learning styles when compared to their peers (Dunn, Dunn, and Price, 1981). The variables corresponded well with the Lorge-Thorndike Test of Mental Ability and the Stanford Achievement Tests. Gifted students, compared to those nongifted, were less teacher-motivated and more self-motivated; more persistent; preferred some amount of background sound rather than quiet while studying; preferred learning through visual, tactile, or kinesthetic means rather than through auditory means; and preferred to learn alone rather than with peers or adults. Knowing these students' characteristics makes it possible to tailor instructional materials for them.

The language or languages an individual speaks also appear to affect learning. Speaking two or more languages requires that the language systems be kept separate by the student. For the bilingual, every linguistic situation involves a choice. Bilinguals may use the brain's right hemisphere to make decisions related to which language system to process by the left hemisphere. They seem to have a greater ability to distinguish figure from ground, that is, to pick out an object in a picture from its background. These individuals also appear to be more field-independent than monolinguals. Young children who acquire a second language are generally believed to differ in their method of processing information from individuals who learn additional languages in later life. The very early bilinguals take a more semantic—a more left-hemisphere—approach to understanding. Older bilinguals seem to judge more on the basis of the physical features of the words, such as melody or sound combinations. Again, knowledge about a learner's language(s) may assist in designing their instructional materials.

Diagnosis of learning profiles and some prescription of instruction is being used in a few schools today. In some cases teachers "intuitively" make the diagnosis and prescription when they feel they know their students well enough and if alternative approaches and materials are available.

Unfortunately, there is currently too little research which supports the use of these diagnostic and prescriptive instruments. According to Arter and Jenkins (1979) most ability-assessment devices have inadequate reliability and suspect validity. In addition, abilities resist training. Research shows a low correlation between ability and reading achievement, which further confuses this assessment and prescription "technology." To make this process a predictable instructional technology requires much more research and development. It is, however, generally believed that major breakthroughs will occur in the next few years. What we now have in the form of guidance is better than nothing, but caution should be used. Fortunately, formative evaluation techniques can be used after strategies have been selected to test their effectiveness and can be revised if necessary. Perhaps someday prescriptions can be written without this subsequent testing. Today's state of the art, however, mandates tryout and revision.

APTITUDE–TREATMENT–INTERACTION

Science is nothing but developed perception, integrated intent, common sense rounded out and minutely articulated.

George Santayana

Aptitude–Treatment–Interaction (ATI) has been advocated by some IT researchers as the ultimate method of investigating the interaction of individual differences and instructional treatments. ATI research investigates the relationships among learner variables, instructional-method variables, content variables, and instructional-mode or media variables; in other words, it seeks to determine which student learns which types of objectives best, under which circumstances, using which sensory modes.

There is little question that ATI interactions do exist. On the other hand, the effects of various treatments are not fully understood, and various studies seem to contradict each other. This is often due to inadequate research design, confounding of subject content, and uncontrolled implementation procedures. Hence, there is not much reliable research in ATI. Unfortunately then, ATI does not as yet provide many guidelines upon which to build a more stable instructional technology. The problem of studying large numbers of variables is almost overwhelming. Cronbach and Snow (1977, 193) describe this problem thus:

The substantive problem before us is to learn which characteristics of the person interact dependably with which features of instructional methods. This is a question of awesome breadth. In principle, it calls for a survey of all the ways in which people differ. It requires that individuality be abstracted into categories or dimensions. Likewise, it calls for abstractions that describe instructional events in one classroom after another. The constructs descriptive of persons and instructional treatments pair up to form literally innumerable ATI hypotheses. It is impossible to search systematically for ATI when the swarm of hypothesis is without order.

In the future, ATI instruments may be available which will let instructional technologists or students make highly valid instructional decisions about the teaching/learning system. This is an area in which graduate students in instructional technology may wish to devote their research time and energies.

PRESENTATION STRATEGIES

Anything scarce is valuable: praise, for example!

Anonymous

In Chapter 6 it was urged that objectives be written as behavioral statements so that each objective can then be examined to determine the instructional stimuli's organization.

Before students can perform an objective at a higher taxonomic level, as when analyzing or synthesizing information, they must have been trained at the lower levels on the relevant facts. It is for this reason that an objective hierarchy should be developed to ensure that each terminal objective has been supported by the necessary enabling objectives.

If the objective primarily involves *facts*, then it will usually be necessary to design instruction that provides a complete presentation of the facts or data. In addition, a fact objective will generally require students to practice remembering, recalling, or recognizing the data. Extensive drills and practice are often required for young learners and for large amounts of information that must be recalled from memory.

If the objective is a *concept*, students must be presented with all of the critical characteristics of that concept. Concept learning should enable learners to correctly classify objects or symbols into members of a specific class. Students may also be required to recall the concept's definition. They will then be given several divergent examples showing the critical characteristics required for inclusion in that concept classification. They may also be given nonexamples that show the absence of the critical characteristics of the concept. Next, they may be required to practice using the concept by classifying both examples and nonexamples of the concept. Graphic or pictorial representations may be presented for concepts having concrete referents. If the examples are complex, it is necessary to distinguish the relevant attributes of the example. Generally, it is desirable to first present easy or clear examples and nonexamples of the concept. Later, more difficult discriminations can be introduced.

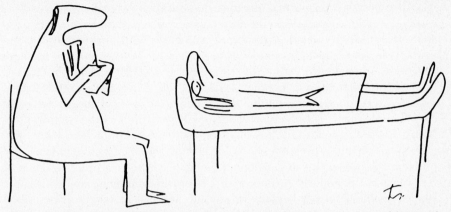

"Your feelings of insecurity seem to have started when Mary Lou Gurnblatt said, 'Maybe I don't have a learning disability—maybe you have a teaching disability.'"

(Saltzman)

If the objective involves a *procedure,* a presentation of all of the steps in correct order must be provided. Any subordinate facts and concepts should also be taught or their earlier acquisition confirmed. Students should practice remembering by recalling all of the steps in correct order. They can then apply the procedure in several example situations. The procedure should always be performed in the correct order. A simulation must sometimes be developed in order to allow the student to practice using the procedure. It is often necessary to divide lengthy procedures into segments, which are learned separately, followed by the important step of linking them together in correct order.

In some cases, a strategy termed "backward chaining" may be employed. Following this approach, the last step in the procedure is presented first. When it is mastered, the next-to-last step is introduced—but in correct sequence with the last step. Next, the third-from-the-last step is introduced, and so on, back to the beginning. Note that all steps are always practiced in correct relationship to each other: only their order of introduction is backward. Backward chaining has the advantage of permitting the learner to complete the task each time it is practiced, which may increase motivation and reduce inhibitions. It has been found to be successful for both physical skills, such as gymnastics, and for mental skills, such as learning to play a musical score. It dramatically illustrates that the sequence of introduction of elements for procedure does not necessarily follow the order of performance in the real world.

Rule objectives will usually be taught using a sequence of instructional steps that begins with a statement or a presentation of all of the steps and the branching decisions within the rule; for example, using proper grammar. Prerequisite facts, concepts, and procedures should be taught or confirmed. The student may then be asked to practice remembering the rule by recalling all the steps and the branching decisions in the correct order. The student should be able to apply the steps or branching decisions to examples of the rule. Finally, the instruction should include some practice in using the rule in new problem situations. Adequate feedback to the learner is essential throughout the instruction. Of particular importance when teaching a rule is to clarify its applicability, which may be done concurrently with teaching the rule, or taught before or after the rule itself. This decision will generally be based on the complexity of the rule and its applications as well as on the learner's prior knowledge.

Problem solving is probably the most difficult type of objective to teach. By problem solving, we mean developing the ability to solve a problem or set of conditions not previously encountered. Under this definition, much of what is labeled problem solving is really rule using, and can be taught as described above. By its very nature, problem solving is difficult to teach because the behaviors must all reside within the learner. Generally, the best approach is to first identify all prerequisite facts, concepts, procedures, and rules or those that are subsumed within the problem-solving task. These should all be taught if the student does not already know them. Then the learner is given the structure of the problem along with specific criteria for determining when the problem is solved. The learner must also be told what resources are available and how he or she is to interact with the instructor and other learners. Of particular importance is varying the time for different learners.

The instructor's role then becomes that of motivator, guide, and evaluator. Care must be taken not to "overguide" the learner. If the instructor observes a learner proceeding on the wrong track, it is generally best to let the learner discover this without direct assistance. Extensive trial and error may be required before the learner finds the correct path. However, being able to discriminate between fruitful and unfruitful behavior is an essential ingredient of real problem solving. Obviously, the instructor cannot allow students to become completely frustrated and quit, but more often the tendency is to be too helpful. Providing a model or heuristic device for problem solving may be done before or during the learning activity. For example, when learners become stymied, the instructor might remind them of the heuristic, "When you seem to be at a dead end, back up and look for another approach." Referring them to a problem-solving model may also provide the necessary guidance to get them back on track.

If the above description suggests that few objectives represent real problem solving, you are correct! In an introductory course on instructional technology, there is likely to be only one problem-solving objective. A final course project which requires learners to prepare a plan for implementing all steps of the IDI model around a single problem would be an example of problem-solving activity. All other course content would most likely be classified as facts, concepts, procedures, or rules. We would expect any instructor to have seen that all prerequisite content was learned before presenting a problem-solving project.

If the objective primarily involves *attitudes*, the use of human modeling is often appropriate and effective. Attitude learning often involves the imitation of a respected human model, which may be presented live, in still or motion visuals, or in print. Attitude changes are enhanced if the models are rewarded or punished based on the appropriateness of the behaviors they are portraying. Attitude learning is associated with almost every other type of learning and is often complex and difficult to teach. Graphic signs without models, like "Keep off the grass," have little effect on changing attitudes, but they may serve as a reminder. Simulations and games, group discussions, open-ended vignettes, and active participation in role playing or real situations can also produce attitude changes. For example, prospective teachers of the blind or handicapped are often required to role-play those conditions for extended periods to "feel" what it is like to be blind or deaf. Many individuals' attitudes toward the environment have been shaped by films showing the destruction of our natural lakes and rivers. In contrast, research has consistently shown that simply providing objective information to people almost never changes their attitudes. The success of the tobacco industry in promoting smoking via attractive role models more than offsets the grim statistics and warnings on packages that state its dangers.

Psychomotor-skill learning usually involves three phases: 1) the early or cognitive phase; 2) the intermediate or associative phase; and 3) the final or autonomous phase. The three are sequential over time, but the exact point of delineation among them is arbitrary.

In the cognitive phase, the learner attempts to understand the task and evaluate the required skills. The instructor can provide guidance and direct the student's attention to the cognitive elements and sequence of actions. During this stage, previously acquired skills are identified and integrated into the required procedure. In the second, or associative, phase, two types of changes typically occur. First, part-task skills not previously brought to a sufficiently high degree of smoothness and timing are practiced and perfected. Second, specific subskills are integrated into the overall skill, and competing alternative/incorrect responses are eliminated. In the third phase of motor-skill learning, the procedure becomes autonomous. The procedural steps no longer need to be initiated by separate cues supplied by the student and the student no longer needs to think about the next step. The motor skill becomes less subject to interference from external influences, so that additional activities may be performed at the same time.

Psychomotor activities may be practiced by themselves or interrelated with cognitive activities in real-life situations (on the basketball court, in an airplane, in the chemistry lab) or in a simulator where only selected aspects of the environment are included. Simulators provide a safer and cheaper environment on which to focus the needed practice. For example, a small basketball court with a single net would permit shooting practice, and an aircraft simulator would permit landing practice without spending a lot of time flying. Feedback is essential to motor-skill acquisition. The more rapid, accurate, and complete the feedback, the more the student will benefit from the practice. Feedback should always relate the actual performance to the performance standard identified in the degree portion of the training objective.

Before concluding this discussion of motor learning, it is necessary to consider how it interacts with the cognitive and affective domains. If cognitive content is associated with the task, it should be introduced early, if not before, motor instruction. If forgetting occurs or seems likely, it may be desirable to review cognitive material as motor instruction continues.

Attitudes play a vital role in motor-skill acquisition. The person who is deathly afraid of water must overcome this fear before real progress in swimming can be expected. Negative self-images can also inhibit learning. Boys or girls who believe themselves clumsy or uncoordinated must overcome this self-consciousness before they can be expected to achieve any real success in learning new motor skills. This suggests that preinstructional activity might be used to reduce fears or improve self-image. Have students who believe themselves incapable of remembering names well repeat over and over to themselves that they really are good at remembering names, and reward positive steps toward that skill. These learners will require individual encouragement, moral support, and positive feedback.

GROUP VERSUS INDIVIDUAL INSTRUCTION

Whether to develop group or individual instructional programs is a key decision of an instructional developer. An ERIC (1980) summary of research studies on individualized instruction suggests that in the right settings, individualized instruction does affect learning. It apparently has particular value for students from poor backgrounds and for delinquent male adolescents. The ERIC study concluded, "It appears that students who are not well served by traditional instructional methods are the best candidates for individualized approaches."

We do not assume that all systematically designed instruction should be planned for individual use. Social interaction is both desirable and often necessary to achieve desired goals. It is often logistically difficult or unwise to offer individualized instruction. Furthermore, only at the expense of other students can a program be tailored to maximize one type of student's learning. Although some IT professionals feel that the ultimate goal of a well-designed program is individualized instruction, with any other approach being less desirable, we do not share that view. In our opinion, the decision on group size (from one to several thousand) should be based on numerous local conditions. We feel instructional design should generally include a variety of instructional strategies and group sizes.

To facilitate individualized systems, administrative, grading, and record-keeping systems must also be supportive. Bells going off in the middle of an interesting individualized module help defeat the instructional program. Individualized programs are made possible by the many alternative communication or instructional channels found in books, films, and other media. A continuous progress program (which individualized instruction permits) allows students to progress at their own rate but it does not mean that students are free to do their "own thing." Together, the teacher and student identify the learner's objectives and the means for attaining them. One particular advantage of the continuous progress program is that it accommodates a broad range of curriculum structures.

Under a continuous progress plan, students are promoted when they are ready. If a student is ready for a new course of study he or she can then begin. There need be no failures, since the units of instruction are typically small and learners can progress from one unit to the next as they attain each set of objectives. We must keep in mind, however, that not all students work well in an individual or in a grouped presentation situation. Students' assignments in a continuous progress program should be made only when a teacher feels they have the motivation and ability to work in the programs at their own pace. In some cases, continuous progress plans attempt to have pairs of students work together as a team.

As the grade designations disappear, there is a need for detailed record-keeping of student progress. For perhaps the 25 percent of the students who do not work well in individualized systems, alternative group-based presentation should be made available in the same or in neighboring schools. The earlier students start learning on their own, the greater the number who can accept the responsibility for their own pacing. Additionally, since many individualized industrial and military training programs are becoming available, learners will need to be able to function more independently in the future. As we approach the twenty-first century and the era of high information technology, it is clear that numbers of adults will require frequent training and retraining. Obviously, the ability to learn independently is an increasingly valuable competitive asset to adults. It seems clear they should be exposed to independent learning environments as children, rather than waiting until adulthood to acquire this competence.

INTERACTIVE INSTRUCTION

Another design consideration involves determining to what degree the instructional environment will be interactive or linear. Interactive instruction involves adapting the instruction according to the learner's error rate, speed, interest, or some other variable. Linear instruction, usually found in classrooms oriented toward groups of students, commonly results from a teacher-based lesson plan. While the plan will vary with overall class response, the instructional pattern is modeled after a hypothesized "typical student" and progresses independently of a specific learner's knowledge or need for practice.

Until recently, interactive instructional environments generally required an instructor who could interpret responses and adjust them to the learner. However, recent developments in artificial intelligence theory, computers, and information storage and retrieval devices make possible a high degree of learner-machine interaction. An example of interactive instruction is found in high-fidelity simulators such as those used in pilot and astronaut training. Low-cost microprocessor and videodisc systems can also provide interactive instruction for more common tasks such as finding the lowest common denominator of a fraction or identifying an unknown chemical substance via a series of tests. Computer-controlled instructional programs can be written to analyze the learner's response to each problem and adjust the level of difficulty based on the student's pattern of responses or interactions. Thus, if a student provides a wrong response after five correct ones at a given level, the program responds differently than if three of the last five answers had been wrong. By tracking the student's responses, the difficulty level of instruction can be maintained low enough to prevent frustration due to high error rate but high enough to provide a constant challenge.

In a chemistry lab, students can run a series of tests and obtain feedback via a computer-controlled videodisc rather than by using actual chemicals. Each test the student "conducts" may reduce the range of possibilities until the chemical's correct identification is made. Of course, students may run unnecessary tests by duplicating the same tests due to poor recordkeeping, or fail to observe critical data when presented. They can be allowed considerable freedom to explore physical phenomena through experiments and backtracking, if needed, much as a scientist does. Other advantages of the interactive environment are quicker test results, reduced hazard, and reduced need for chemicals and laboratory facilities. Additionally, students can be allowed to widely vary the amount of time spent on each exercise, as well as perform the identification activity on many more chemicals than is generally possible in an actual laboratory. Naturally, at some point the student should also work with real chemicals. Experience with the interactive-instructional laboratory, however, reduces total lab time while increasing its value.

These two examples of interactive instruction are but a small sample of what can be done in a variety of subject areas. As designers become more familiar with the new hardware and its interactive capabilities, we will see much more interactive instruction. For more detailed descriptions of interactive instruction and its design, see Bork (1981) or DeBloois (1982).

Problem-solving tasks can often be taught using flowcharts similar to the ones used throughout this text. These are an alternative to written instructions. They can be just as helpful to the student in understanding and performing a specific task. Krohn (1983) measured the number of incorrect solutions to problems, the time taken to view the problem formats, and the time taken to solve problems. He found that the graphic structure of flowcharts aided problem solving. Performance was optimal when the flowchart was consistent with reading patterns (from left to right and from top to bottom), and the complexity of the flowchart as measured by the number of alternatives leading from decision boxes had no effect on performance.

SUMMARY

Instructional development strategies focus on students' entering knowledge or behaviors and their methods of learning; characteristics of the content to be taught; and selection of effective instructional strategies since each individual differs in background, goals, attitudes, and learning style. Instructional content (objectives) may require the student to deduce, manipulate, or define. The instructional strategies selected must be based on the learner, the content, and the available resources. Then a prototype of the instruction must be developed and tested. Only when all these steps have been performed and the instruction proven to be effective can the designer label the program a success. Like the engineer responsible for creating a bridge, the instructional designer must collect and analyze data, select a design, test that design, make revisions, and finally, build the product.

This chapter has dealt with a number of factors related to the learner and to the content that can be considered when designing instruction. Many of the issues raised in this chapter require much more research to permit educators and trainers the confidence they would like when making curriculum decisions.

Questions for Consideration and Discussion

1. Can the Gagne–Briggs model of instruction (the nine external events) be used in teaching attitudes? Why or why not?
2. If we agree that all learners are unique, should all instruction be individualized?
3. Review the list of possible considerations of individual characteristics. If you have only limited time and resources, which types of data would you collect? Why?
4. Would you recommend continuing or abandoning research activity on aptitude–treatment–interaction (ATI)?
5. For what types of content would you recommend using interactive or adaptive instruction?

Suggested Activities

1. Write, in a paragraph or two, on the current status of either "learner profiles" in instruction or "aptitude–treatment–interaction." Use the library as your primary source of information. Periodicals will provide the most current sources.
2. Discuss when and why color illustrations should be used in instructional materials. Then list the ways in which color can be used to facilitate learning without considering graphics.
3. Plan a short lesson on facts, concepts, procedures, or rules using the guidelines in this chapter.

Suggested Readings

Andre, T. (1979). Does Answering Higher-level Questions While Reading Facilitate Productive Learning? *Review of Educational Research, 49,* 280–318.

Arter, J. A., and Jenkins, J. R. (Fall 1979). Differential Diagnosis—Prescriptive Teaching: A Critical Approach. *Review of Educational Research, 49,* 517–555.

Atkinson, R. C., and Shiffrin, R. M. (1968). Human Memory: A Proposed System and Its Control Processes. In *The Psychology of Learning and Motivation,* K. W. Spence and J. T. Spence, eds. New York: Academic Press, pp. 89–195.

Ausubel, D. P. (1978). In Defense of Advance Organizers: A Reply to the Critics. *Review of Educational Research, 48,* 251–257.

Bates, J. A. (Fall 1979). Extrinsic Reward and Intrinsic Motivation: A Review with Implications for the Classroom. *Review of Educational Research, 79,* 557–576.

Bangert, R. L., Kulik, J. A., and Kulik, C. C. (1983). Individualized Systems of Instruction in Secondary Schools. *Review of Educational Research, 53*(2), 143–158.

Bellezza, F. S. (Summer 1981). Mnemonic Devices: Classification, Characteristics, and Criteria. *Review of Educational Research, 51*(2), 247–275.

Bork, A. (1981). *Learning with Computers.* Bedford, MA: Digital Press.

Bower, G. H., and Hilgard, E. R. (1981). *Theories of Learning,* 5th ed. Englewood Cliffs, NJ: Prentice-Hall.

Brown, B., and Saks, D. (1981). The Microeconomics of Schooling. In *Review of Research in Education,* David Berliner, ed. Washington, DC: American Educational Research Association.

Case, R. (1978). Piaget and Beyond: Toward a Developmentally Based Theory and Technology of Instruction. In *Advances in Instructional Psychology, vol. 1,* R. Glaser, ed. Hillsdale, NJ: Erlbaum, pp. 167–228.

Cronbach, L. J., and Snow, R. E. (1977). *Aptitudes and Instructional Methods.* New York: Irvington.

DeBloois, M., ed. (1982). *Videodisc/Microcomputer Courseware Design.* Englewood Cliffs, NJ: Educational Technology.

Dunn, R., Dunn, K., and Price, G. (May 1981). Learning Styles: Research vs. Opinion. *Phi Delta Kappan, 62,* 645–646.

Ellis, J. A., Wulfeck, W. H., and Montague, W. E. (Winter 1980). The Effect of Adjunct and Test Question Similarity on Study Behavior and Learning in a Training Course. *American Educational Research Journal,* 499–557.

ERIC Clearinghouse on Educational Management. (December 1980). *Research Action Brief: Individualized Instruction.* Eugene, OR: University of Oregon.

Frymier, J. (1977). *Annehurst Curriculum Classification System.* West Lafayette, IN: Kappa Delta Pi.

Gagne, R. M. (1985). *The Conditions of Learning,* 4th ed. New York: Holt, Rinehart and Winston.

Gagne, R. M., and Briggs, L. J. (1979). *Principles of Instructional Design,* 2nd ed. New York: Holt, Rinehart and Winston.

Klatzky, R. L. (1980). *Human Memory: Structures and Processes,* 2nd ed. San Francisco: Freeman.

Krohn, G. S. (1983). Flowcharts Used for Procedural Instructions. *Human Factors, 25*(5), 573–581.

Levie, W. H., and Dickie, K. E. (1973). The Analysis and Application of Media. In *Second Handbook of Research on Teaching*, R. M. W. Travers, ed. Chicago: Rand McNally.

Mayer, R. E. (Spring 1979). Can Advance Organizers Influence Meaningful Learning? *Review of Educational Research, 49*, 371–383.

Merrill, M. D. (1984). Component Display Theory. In *Instructional Design: Theories and Models*, C. Reigeluth, ed. Hillsdale, NJ: Lawrence Erlbaum Associates.

Reigeluth, C. M. (1979). In Search of a Better Way to Organize Instruction: The Elaboration Theory. *Journal of Instructional Development, 2*, 8–15.

Reigeluth, C. M., Merrill, M. D., and Bunderson, C. V. (1978). The Structure of Subject Matter Content and Its Instructional Design Implications. *Instructional Science, 7*, 107–126.

Reigeluth, C. M., and Rogers, C. A. (1980). The Elaboration Theory of Instruction: Prescriptions for Task Analysis and Design. *National Society for Performance and Instructional Journal, 19*, 16–26.

Rothkopf, E. C. (1981). A Macroscopic Model of Instruction and Purposive Learning: An Overview. *Instructional Science, 10*, 105–122.

Singer, R. N. (Summer 1977). To Err or Not to Err: A Question for the Instruction of Psychomotor Skills. *Review of Educational Research, 47*(3), 475–498.

Snow, R. E., and Federico, P., eds. (1980). *Aptitude, Learning and Instruction* (2 vols.). Hillsdale, NJ: Lawrence Erlbaum.

Stallings, J. (December 1980). Allocated Academic Learning Time Revisited, or Beyond Time on Task. *Educational Researcher*, 11–16.

Stipek, D., and Weisz, J. (Spring 1981). Perceived Personal Control and Academic Achievement. *Review of Educational Research, 51*, 101–137.

Walker, D. F., and Hess, R. D. (1984). *Instructional Software: Principles and Perspectives for Design and Use*. Belmont, CA: Wadsworth.

Witkin, H. A., Moore, C. A., Goodenough, D. R., and Cox, P. W. (Winter 1977). Field-Dependent and Field-Independent Cognitive Styles and Their Educational Implications. *Review of Educational Research, 47*, 1–64.

8

Learning Research-Based Design Principles

Practice does not make perfect; perfect practice makes perfect.

Vince Lombardi

Objectives

After completing this chapter you should be able to:

1. Discuss the impact of learning theories and research on instructional design.
2. Describe how individuals tend to change with regard to how they learn as they become older.
3. Describe how color facilitates or hinders learning.
4. Describe how speech compression techniques affect a learner.
5. Describe which nonverbal communication techniques are useful in instruction.
6. Define theories of instruction and discuss how they differ from learning theories.

While much has been written about perception, learning, instruction, and communications theories as they apply to instruction, too little has actually been concluded. Instructional technologists need sound research that supports those theories to analyze problems and design answers to the problems. This learning-related research would allow educators to predictably affect a learner's behavior. The problems inherent with the ATI research discussed earlier occur throughout learning theory and go back to basic psychology. Experimental psychologists have produced good results related to teaching lower-order skills to pigeons or people, but have not had the same success working on the higher-order, or more complex, skills over any time period. A number of variables need further understanding before there can be a sound basis for applying these theories.

Differences among individuals, and the way in which these differences are assessed, are changing as our scientific knowledge increases. As in all fields of knowledge, researchers' attitudes and values determine which questions to ask.

The answers to these questions then form the basis of our scientific knowledge about an issue such as how individuals learn. Scientific investigations of how individuals differ in mental ability began about a century ago. Yet, we still do not have an extensive database from which to draw our knowledge about how humans are similar or different in their perceptual or learning capacities or processing.

There are also many inadequacies in our measurement of mental skills and abilities, and attempts now underway are focusing on these problems. However, these efforts are complicated by the fact that there is currently less emphasis on selecting individuals to receive education and more on helping all individuals work to their ability levels. Furthermore, this emphasis poses problems for test and measurement specialists, since most tests were designed to make selection and assignment decisions rather than to guide individual progress. For example, IQ tests identify those who are likely to be successful performers, but do not identify individual characteristics useful in designing instruction. We now turn our attention to a number of theories that have significant implications for designing instruction.

COMMUNICATIONS CONSIDERATIONS

Teachers need to be communicators in order to be educators. A brief discussion of basic communication theory may help educators to focus on communication as a necessary competency. The primary components to consider when studying communications theory can be included in a basic communications model:

$$SENDER \longrightarrow CHANNEL \longrightarrow RECEIVER$$

The *sender* is the teacher or instructional designer who attempts to encode a message appropriate to the channel. The *channel,* or medium of instruction (voice, TV, film), is selected because it can transmit the stimuli required to "communicate" the message. The *receiver* (student) must share with the sender a common set of definitions for the symbols in order to decode the communication. The receiver must also be sufficiently motivated to attend to and have physical access to the channel. In addition, the entire communications chain must be relatively noise-free, noise being defined as any environmental factor interfering with communication. If the channel cannot deliver the message (there is too much background noise in the classroom or the TV antenna is broken), the student may not learn; likewise, if the receiver does not attend to the channel because he or she is tired or worried about a friend, is too hot, or is seated in the last row of seats without needed glasses, then noise will have interfered with the communication.

Advertising firms have reams of data which are invaluable to educators. Unfortunately, however, much of their information on perception, motivation, and modifying behavior (purchasing patterns) is not disseminated because it is considered proprietary confidential information which they attempt to keep from competitors.

Let us consider an average TV ad that has 30 seconds in which to communicate its message, or a billboard or a magazine ad, which may have even less time. These ads must be effective in communicating the desired messages and increasing sales, or the millions of dollars they cost would not be expended.

Usually we are not aware that our behavior patterns are affected by these ads. The "learning"—defined here as a change of purchasing behavior—is so effort-free and attractive that children and adults tend to stay glued to their TV sets during commercials. As educators come to understand and use these communications techniques, it may be possible to overcome the problems evidenced in many unmotivated learners.

All commercials must do four things to be effective: (1) identify the item; (2) identify its value; (3) show how the value applies to the viewer; and (4) show how to identify the item when the viewer becomes a purchaser. With an effective magazine ad, this must all be done in less than a second.

In general, effective ads use visuals which are simple and easy to understand. Cartoons are often used to distill complex concepts into characters having simple actions (like the antacid characters). Concepts like happiness, macho, etc., are often translated into visuals in cigarette and alcohol commercials. Key words or phrases are often superimposed on a visual to highlight the key point. Attitudes are shaped by presenting strong behavior models that either add to, or detract from, the credibility of the visual. A doctor is an older, glasses-wearing, slightly overweight male, or more recently, a trim, glasses-wearing, modern-appearing female. Split-screen techniques are used to show before and after comparisons. Repetition is employed over and over . . .

INSTRUCTIONAL DESIGN PRINCIPLES

While research results do not provide the degree of guidance instructional designers might desire, several general principles can be derived from them. Unless there is some specific reason for excluding these principles, each should be included in every unit of instruction. The five most universal principles are:

- Prepare the learner.
- Direct the learner's attention.
- Provide learner participation.
- Provide feedback to the learner.
- Provide repetition.

Several guides to designing instructional/training programs have been identified by educational research. One of the first of these guides involves the principle of readiness, which states that when students feel ready, they can ignore distracting stimuli and learn the material more effectively. In fact, when they are ready to learn and master the objectives set forth, they are likely to feel annoyed if prevented from doing so. Preparing the learner might include stating the objectives, indicating how or why they are important, arousing curiosity, presenting new vocabulary, providing instructions to indicate what will follow the instruction (test, field trip, discussion), or stating what tools the learner will require during the unit (pencil, dictionary, ruler, and the like).

Educators have several tools to use for directing attention to the desired stimuli or channel. Simply changing the stimuli attracts attention and is consistently shown to result in improved learning. Using various cueing techniques such as highlighting, color, underscoring, repetition, arrows, or spots on visuals also directs attention. For audio material, pauses, change of narrator, and changes in pitch and pace all serve to direct attention to critical parts of a message.

While adequate research is not available to confirm how much individuals learn from each of their senses for any given type of learning objective, it is often said that students remember 10 percent of what they hear, 20 percent of what they read, 30 percent of what they see, and 70 percent of what they do. This suggests that instructional designers should attempt to graphically illustrate the instruction and have students perform the act themselves if possible.

John Dewey stressed that learning by doing is important to a learner. Directing students to perform the desired behavior under supervision can provide immediate feedback on the appropriateness of their responses. Hands-on learning provides more rapid learning of many tasks than is normally obtained from a lecture or group discussion. When it is possible to have students learn by manipulating the key attributes in their learning environment, use this method of instruction. Practice can be included by inserting questions into the lesson, stopping for discussion, demonstrating a step and having learners imitate, or using worksheets or problem exercises. As we mentioned earlier, practice without feedback is generally ineffective. If possible, feedback should be given after each question, problem, or step. Latent-image answer sheets, pull-tab cards, and punch cards all provide immediate feedback for multiple-choice-type activities.

In audio-visual materials, feedback can be provided by showing the completed step, describing how the product should now look, or answering questions posed earlier. Feedback may be given verbally by an instructor as to the appropriateness of a student response, or it may be programmed into the presentation. Computers can diagnose the response and, within limits, tailor the response to the student's input. In large-group situations electronic feedback systems may be employed. With these systems, each student can select from several buttons his or her response to multiple-choice questions. Usually an indicator lets the respondents know whether their answers were correct. The system may be hooked into a computer, which can then record each response

"Complimentary verbalization is nice, Mom, but I'd prefer the compensatory approach."

(Campbell)

for grading. It may also provide the instructor with a percentage readout of the number of responses to the alternatives selected by the student, so the presentation can be adapted based on the student's responses.

Repetition is required for many types of learning, but the designer must know *how much* to repeat. Further complicating the matter is the fact that the amount of repetition necessary for mastery varies widely with learners. A good rule of thumb is to include a limited amount of practice in the prototype, but be prepared to add more based on tryout data. Ideally, learners can practice until, and only until, they master the objective. However, this is difficult to arrange with group-based instruction. Simulators, as discussed in the psychomotor section earlier, are often safe, cost-effective, and time-efficient ways to provide repetition when instruction can be individualized.

The principle of exercise or repetition suggests that the more often a set of facts is repeated, the more likely they are to be learned. Presentation through various senses, as well as providing relevant, meaningful activities, also helps. If the repetitions vary somewhat, but are much alike, the probability increases that the students' behavior will change; that is, they will learn. Do not assume that merely presenting information to students means that they will learn it. Perhaps this old saw best tells the tale:

Tell 'em what you are gonna tell 'em.
Tell 'em.
Tell 'em what you told 'em.

Furthermore, do not assume that once students have successfully demonstrated their knowledge or skill, they have mastered it. Require them to repeat it—to "overlearn." This overlearning is especially appropriate for behaviors that students must be able to immediately perform in stress-related situations such as fires or other emergencies. Delayed repetition may also be desirable to offset forgetting.

PERCEPTION CONSIDERATIONS

Some behaviors can be learned, or remembered, through mental rehearsal, which may involve visual and/or verbal activity. For example, basketball players, both professional and amateur, are often asked by their coaches to sit down, close their eyes, and imagine repeatedly shooting perfect baskets. Concentrating on how it feels to perform correctly often improves actual performance on the court. Mental rehearsal has been used by bedridden patients to learn how to touch-type by having only a picture of the keyboard with home-key information. Once out of the hospital, they demonstrated remarkably accurate and fast typing. Many automobile drivers mentally envision accident-related situations, such as a child running out in front of the car, and attempt to "learn" appropriate responses to such a situation. Likewise, pilots are often required to practice accident-avoidance behaviors in simulators. Most of us, however, will only have mental rehearsal to learn and practice such reactions.

Mental rehearsal usually begins by relaxing the body: sitting, closing one's eyes, taking a deep breath, and exhaling slowly. Imagining oneself in the place where the activity is to occur is also desirable. If the learning activity involves an abstract concept such as a name, the learner may imagine writing that name on the person's forehead, or otherwise associate the name with some visually real object by mentally writing the individual's name in vivid red nail polish which runs down onto an eyebrow, or by making some other enjoyable image which can be "seen" and remembered later. Verbally repeating the person's name right away and then a little later may also improve retention. Many memory-improvement books describing these techniques can be found in bookstores. However, seldom are teachers, or their students, taught how to improve their memorization skills.

There is some indication that very young children can learn better from audio rather than visual stimuli. It also appears that as they grow older, to about age seven to nine, they learn more effectively from simple black-and-white and still stick-figure graphics than from more complex visuals with color and detail. Apparently, they have not yet learned to decode complex visuals. Photographs and graphics require decoding skills that develop later than audio-decoding skills. Travers (1982) studied children whose ages ranged from four to twelve and found many of them to be incapable of recognizing unified wholes before the age of nine or ten.

Line drawings seem to be highly effective in instruction for all age groups. In terms of economy of production effort and instructional effectiveness, abstract-line presentation is relatively more efficient in promoting student achievement than the more complex visuals. The simplicity of line drawings succeeds in directing attention to, rather than diverting it from, the object in question.

Realism in visuals does not seem to be nearly as important as the outline or boundaries of the shapes. Cartoons can be an effective means for presenting visual material because they tend to omit all except the essential detail and often exaggerate the crucial characteristics. The rate at which visuals are presented seems to be more important than their technical quality. However, if the technical quality is very poor, or if the audience has learned to assess visual quality, then a lack of visual quality may be distracting.

Motion is seldom required. Many research studies have examined what happens when still frames are taken from motion pictures and presented to students along with tape recordings obtained from the soundtrack of the film. In many studies, students learned and retained as much from the still visuals as from the motion visuals. As would be expected, the cost was much lower for the slides and audio-tape system of instruction. Even when the content is motion related, very little motion is generally necessary from a design or learning standpoint. Motion is only required if the critical attributes of a concept require motion for adequate understanding, such as the action of a water pump, or if instruction involves extensive psychomotor activity.

Color doesn't seem to be as important as many designers assumed. Realistic color photographs do not even seem to make a significant difference even where it might be expected. Color television, for example, has not been found to be as effective as black and white for teaching surgery to medical students. Students, as typical TV viewers, prefer to watch the color visuals, but the color seems to add little to cognitive learning. For younger viewers, the color may actually interfere with learning. Color may be "noise" to six- and seven-year-olds. If learners do watch color television at home, however, by the age of nine, they seem to learn as well from color as from black-and-white television. The question might then be raised: If elementary students learn less well from color photographs than from black-and-white photographs, why then do so many preschool and elementary textbooks and instructional materials use color? The answer probably lies in who selects the textbooks and what they like.

Several researchers have examined the effectiveness of instruction from black-and-white and color television and found that there does not seem to be any improvement for most kinds of learning from color systems. The students almost always indicate they like color television better than black and white presentations, but except in a few cases where color was a part of the objective recognition requirement, color had very little effect on student learning. Artificial color coding to direct attention, a form of cueing, has also been shown to be effective under some conditions.

PREPARING THE LEARNER

An advance organizer may be used when designing instruction to increase the probability of student retention. An advance organizer is presented to learners before they are given new instructional information. An advance organizer generally has these characteristics:

- Consists of short statements written at a more general and abstract level than the learning passages to which it pertains
- May contain verbal or visual information relative to the particular learner and subject matter
- Designed to influence the learner's encoding process
- Stated at a language level familiar to the learner
- Contains no specific content from the information to be learned
- Provides a means of generating the logical relationships among the various elements of the information

David Ausubel, the major advocate of the advance organizer, believes that elementary-aged students learn more rapidly when advance organizers are used with instruction designed to move them from the level of preoperation to that of concrete operation. Organizers are probably more effective with learning passages that are factual instead of conceptual because conceptual material, by definition, is organized. In general, the less well organized the learning passage, the greater the impact of the advance organizer. Mayer (1979) concluded a review of the research on advance organizers by saying, "These tests clearly favor an assimilation encoding theory, and provide consistent evidence that advance organizers can influence the outcome of learning if used in appropriate situations and measured properly."

An examination of the research involving advance organizers is often frustrating because of the difficulty in specifying what comprises an acceptable advance organizer. This lack of a single common definition may be the source of conflicting results and conclusions found in the literature. Among the findings are that organizers are often too time-consuming to be efficient as adjuncts to

1. a text; organizers do not consistently facilitate learning; organizers show greater effects with unfamiliar or technical material that is difficult to relate
2. existing knowledge; organizers are more effective with college-age students
3. younger students; organizers provide little help for lower-ability students, especially educable mentally retarded; expository organizers appear to be useful with younger and lower-ability students

Given these conflicting findings, the best advice for technologists would be that if there is some reason for including them, do so, but study the effect. Also, use a variety of styles, formats, and placements to determine under what conditions they make a contribution to your presentation of materials.

STRUCTURING THE PRESENTATION

The use of interspersed questions will usually enhance learning and recall of specific text segments by requiring an immediate review of the information necessary for answering those questions. Thus, only ask questions of primary importance. Questions inserted into the text should parallel, but generally not duplicate, the test items if maximum retention of the key points is desired. If the intent of the instruction is to promote the transfer of learning to new situations, practice items should parallel the test items. As stated before, feedback to the students as to the appropriateness of their responses should be provided as soon as possible.

Time on task has become an area of much investigation in recent years. Not surprisingly, results indicate that the more time spent on the learning activities or tasks, the higher the achievement. Time spent on textbooks and in small groups (as opposed to one-on-one instruction) is particularly correlated to reading- and math-related achievement.

Class discussion and review are also positively associated with learner achievement. A high degree of teacher–student interaction has been found to be a good use of learner time. A well-designed instructional system which makes good use of learner time as measured by student achievement is characterized by having more content instruction, more discussion, more learner participation, more review, and more supportive corrective feedback to the learner.

The use of speech rate compression techniques can be useful in instruction. Speed-reading techniques allow an individual to maintain comprehension while decreasing study time. It appears that as learners become more able to receive and process information, their ability to focus attention increases. Environmental distractions apparently become less disturbing to learners when receiving and processing information. It is also possible that the speech compression reduces an individual's ability to analyze the stimuli for a match with existing beliefs, and hence can be used to change attitudes.

Speech compression also makes better use of teaching/learning time. Many studies have concluded that students learn more when using speech compression techniques than when listening to audio tapes played at normal speed. These students also learned the material about one-third faster than other students. This technique, however, has not proved successful with all students in all curriculum areas.

Techniques for memorizing large amounts of information have been known for years. The early Greek orators and mnemonists demonstrated that large amounts of information could be accurately recalled by an individual. These are useful techniques today when teaching drama or anything that should be memorized. Mnemonics should be considered when selecting instructional strategies. Most of us can probably still recall ROY G. BIV (red, orange, yellow, green, blue, indigo, violet) from art class, or "every good boy does fine" (EGBDF) from music class. Mnemonics are particularly helpful for an ordered recall of a set of facts or sequence of steps. Keep in mind that there are at least two common types of mnemonics—those using key letters to form another real or nonsense word (Roy G. Biv), and those using a sentence or phrase to jog the memory (every good boy does fine). An additional example of the former, POCER, recalls five management functions—planning, organizing, coordinating, evaluating, and recording. The latter type is illustrated by the phrase, "A Rat In Tommy's House Might Eat Tommy's Ice Cream," for spelling the word "arithmetic," which often gives children trouble.

For some types of objectives, job aids should be considered to both facilitate learning and improve job performance. They are particularly useful in training environments, where they can reduce the amount of classroom time, while increasing recall on the job. A pilot's checklist is really a job aid. Simple flow-charts or algorithms can serve the same function, as well as trouble-shooting or problem-solving matrices. Teaching the learner *when and how* to use these aids has generally been shown to reduce errors and increase the speed of finding and solving problems. Although instructional psychology purists might argue that job aids do not constitute part of an instructional strategy, these aids should be considered before finalizing decisions on what strategies to employ.

Increased motivation may increase effective learning if properly focused. Instructional designers and instructors can influence motivation with extrinsic rewards, because humans often engage in activities for the purpose of receiving tangible rewards. When appropriate, students should be shown how their education or training will reward them now or in the future. Intrinsic motivation, however, is generally the desired goal. This may result as much from environmental considerations as from more formal instructional designs. Instructional designers usually hope that extrinsic rewards will eventually result in intrinsic motivation, but there is little evidence to support this transfer (Bates 1979).

An attractive and pleasing instructional environment will "catch" more students than an unpleasant one. People generally learn better in pleasant surroundings. In contrast, high levels of fear or negative feedback will interfere with learning. Actual objects or realistic color with motion visuals can add interest and can serve to increase motivation.

The carrot-and-stick reward and punishment approach to motivation is still used by many managers: dangle the carrot in front of learners to help them progress, or inflict mild punishment as necessary. When using this approach, be generous with the praise and other positive motivators, but be stingy with the punishment. Praise in front of groups is especially effective in changing behavior, but indiscreet punishment can produce negative results.

The principle of recency suggests that the fresher and more recent a subject, the more a student tends to remember it. A learner leaves a class session or a course with a lot of "information." Yet as time passes, the learner's memory grows dimmer, and after weeks, months, and years, only a small portion of what was learned can be recalled. It is important to repeat instruction occasionally in later classes. Again, planned repetition over time is an important aspect of instructional design. Recall will be enhanced and the level of retention will tend to increase. Review is particularly important if learners will be expected to recall or apply previously learned material. Since forgetting is common to us all, the designer should incorporate at least a minimal review even during the lesson if it has been some time since the prerequisite knowledge was acquired.

The principle of intensity suggests that the more vividly a subject is presented, the better it will be learned. A dramatic chemistry classroom demonstration involving explosions or changes of color will indeed be remembered years later. High-involvement situations and role playing can produce similar results.

The rate at which material is presented (including response time) should be deliberately selected by the designer. Rates that are too rapid confuse learners, and often lead to inattention. Rates that are too slow lead to boredom and can also result in inattention. The capacity for attending to auditory stimuli seems to be about 400 words a minute for a sustained period of time. Research using speech compressors is currently questioning this figure, which may be too low for some types of low-information-density material. The rate at which moderately complex visuals can be assimilated seems to be one every ten seconds. This rate will vary depending on the familiarity of the content, the required decoding or mental activity that must occur, the density of the information in the accompanying auditory channel, and the learner's interest level. Because learners have different capabilities, some lessons need to be speeded up and others slowed down to improve the effectiveness and efficiency of learning.

Nonverbal communication is an effective means for transmitting information in teacher-presented instruction. The messages are transmitted by body movements, facial expressions, eye contact, vocal intonation, gestures, touching, and the use of "personal" space. Even an instructor of slight build can cause a large unhappy student to move away by knowing and using information about the student's personal space requirement. In American culture, we are accustomed to a lot of space around us and generally do not feel comfortable with someone physically close to us except in intimate relationships. Facial expressions can be powerful negative or positive reinforcers. Teachers can effectively use facial expressions to convey a sense of excitement about the content being taught. The use of eye contact is also important when trying to impress upon a person a belief or emotion.

Perceived locus of control of learning events is a motivational variable that affects academic achievement. People control the events around them to varying degrees. For many learners, increasing their control over the instructional environment raises their level of motivation. However, some students prefer others to control the environment and may perform poorly in situations requiring self-structure and discipline. This is particularly true for individualized instruction programs. It has been found that some students require careful monitoring and guidance to keep them moving, whereas others will move rapidly through the material on their own. How much control the learner has over selecting either the objectives or the instructional strategies should be a conscious decision of the designer. The prototype must then be tested to examine the consequences of the design decision.

GUIDELINES FOR DESIGNERS

The instructional design should reflect the objectives, student abilities, and instructional media available. Instructional design is concerned with the way the instructional message is manipulated in the design and production process to influence learners' behaviors. There are some fairly consistent guidelines to help instructional designers plan instructional programs. These guidelines are just that—guidelines. From reading this chapter, you must certainly realize that there are few, if any, hard and fast rules for designing instruction. At least for now, given our current state of knowledge, it is only possible to present a set of guidelines to consider. To us, a guideline suggests what to think about or do if some other course of action doesn't seem appropriate. Once a prototype has been developed, it can then be subjected to the hard test of reality on actual learners. If the decisions were "good," the data will confirm them. If they were "bad," the data will make it painfully obvious. By observing the guidelines, you will avoid much repetition of the latter, unhappy event! The guidelines below are presented in areas of perception, motivation, repetition and practice, and transfer. Concluding axioms are also presented.

Perception

1. An organizing structure in an introductory presentation may enhance perception and learning. Lower-ability students may benefit more from advance organizers than higher-ability students.

2. The organization of stimuli increases reception speed; don't arbitrarily randomize your instructional presentation. Lower-ability students especially benefit from order.

3. Separate the figure from the background; have simple line drawings or visuals if possible—especially for younger learners.

4. If you want a student to compare or contrast two visual stimuli, put them within close proximity to each other—perhaps side by side.

5. Reality is personal and varies with each individual. A teacher should be cautious when being subjective (telling learners what is beautiful, and the like).

6. Attention is drawn to the comfortable and relaxing, to the novel, and to the shocking.

7. Color affects our attitudes and thus our behaviors. It can also be used to attract or direct attention.

8. Eliciting active responses from learners by asking questions during the instruction will tend to keep their attention on the learning tasks.

9. Providing feedback to learners on the appropriateness of their responses will increase learning and keep their attention on the learning task (especially for low-ability students).

10. "Insights" result by grouping perceptions into meaningful wholes.

11. Bulletin boards, unless they relate directly to the topic being taught, detract from the current lesson. Similarly, windows are a source of distraction that interferes with the reception of more relevant stimuli.

12. Learning takes place faster if multiple senses are used. Repeat the learning material in a variety of ways and use those media that seem most appropriate to the content stimuli requirements (need for motion visuals, audio).

13. Learners can attend to multiple channels as long as the channels are related and/or if their content density is low. Visuals and verbal treatments should reinforce and enhance each other.

Motivation

1. Reinforce desired behaviors immediately after their occurrence.

2. Use positive reinforcement wherever possible.

3. The more highly motivated the learner, the greater the learning.

4. A learner who finds satisfaction in learning learns best.

5. The rate of learning increases when students are aware of their progress.

6. The learning task needs to be at the proper level of difficulty (not too simple nor too complex for the individual learner).

7. The activity or learning task needs to be proved meaningful to the student.

8. The use of humor in training materials has little effect on cognitive learning, but can increase student interest to a minor degree.

9. Interest is higher when the students are involved in planning and selecting activities.

10. Training periods should be short enough to avoid fatigue. They should be based on the students' interests and should not be terminated until students become restive.

11. Active student involvement facilitates attention.

12. Physical comfort is important to motivation (an uncomfortable student will attend to the discomfort as much as to the desired stimuli presentation).

Repetition and Practice

1. Repetition or redundancy in the presentation and the use of various examples will increase learning and the transfer of learning.
2. Learner control of pacing by an on/off switch or speech compressor will enhance learning, especially if there are deadlines for completion of instructional events.
3. Reducing the load on the learner's working memory by (a) reducing the amount of information to be considered at any point in time, (b) relating new information to familiar information, (c) presenting relatively small frames or blocks of information at one time, and (d) helping the student to see that the relevance of the instruction will promote learning.
4. The more time, within reason, students spend on learning tasks, the higher will be their cognitive and affective learning.
5. Adjunct questions consistently benefit recall of information when given after short passages of instruction, but are less consistent in increasing transfer of information to new situations when given before the presentation.
6. Use mnemonic devices or systems to improve the memorization and recall of specific items of information.
7. Delayed recall reduces forgetting.

Transfer or Concept Formation

1. Students learn from their peers; provide instructional systems for small groups, large groups, and individual study.
2. Present the new concept to be taught in numerous and varied situations with contrasting experiences.
3. If transfer of learning is expected, require transfer during instruction.

Axioms

1. No two people have precisely the same response to a given learning situation.
2. Slumps or plateaus in learning are normal and must be expected from even the best students.
3. The trial-and-error approach to learning can be more time-effective if the learner has some supervision.
4. Job aids may reduce learning time and improve on-the-job performance.

SUMMARY

To teach is to learn.

Japanese Proverb

Our theories of instruction, perception, and learning are not yet adequate, and though there is much room for refinement, there are many useful guidelines an instructional designer can use in designing instruction. The most consistent research findings involving learning variables include the following:

1. Active student response is required on a frequent and regular basis for effective learning.
2. Feedback should follow practice within a short period of time and must be easily understood.
3. Repetition in either identical or varied form improves learning
4. When attention is directed to the material by advance organizers, color coding, or whatever, students focus on the more appropriate stimuli.

Questions for Consideration and Discussion

1. What are some examples of "noise" in your current learning environment?
2. How are the five instructional design principles in this chapter different from Gagne and Briggs' nine events of instruction in the previous chapter?
3. Would you consider incorporating mental rehearsal in an instructional lesson? Why or why not?
4. What color would you paint a classroom? A lab? A gym? Why?
5. What factors might affect the amount of feedback you provide to learners?

Suggested Activities

1. Each member of the class will list those perception- and learning-related tools, cues, or theories which seem to be useful in assisting a teacher to do the job. List only those tools relating to reinforcement, use of colors, and so on, that an instructor can use to promote or ensure student perception of relevant stimuli and then the retention of those stimuli. Have the class members discuss each list and then rewrite their own.
2. Discuss the utility of one or more of the other theories presented in the chapter. How do they help or hinder us as instructional technologists?

Suggested Readings

Bower, G. H., and Hilgard, E. R. (1981). *Theories of Learning*, 5th ed. Englewood Cliffs, NJ: Prentice-Hall.

Gagne, R. M. (1977). *The Conditions of Learning*, 3rd ed. New York: Holt, Rinehart and Winston.

Gagne, R. M., and Dick, W. (1983). Instructional Psychology. *Annual Review of Psychology, 34*, 261–295.

Kulik, J. A., Kulik, C. C., and Cohen, P. A. (1976). Research on Audio-tutorial Instruction: A Meta-analysis of Comparative Studies. *Research in Higher Education, 13*, 23–30.

Landa, L. (1974). *Algorithmization in Learning and Instruction*. Englewood Cliffs, NJ: Educational Technology Publications.

Merrill, P., and Bunderson, C. V. (Summer 1981). Preliminary Guidelines for Employing Graphics in Instruction. *Journal of Instructional Development, 4*(4), 2–9.

O'Neil, H. F., Jr., ed. (1978). *Learning Strategies*. New York: Academic Press.

9

Projected, Print, and Computer Media

A human being should not be wasted in doing what forty sheets of paper or two phonographs can do. Just because personal teaching is precious and can do what books and apparatus cannot, it should be saved for its peculiar work.

E. L. Thorndike

Objectives

After completing this chapter you should be able to:

1. List four characteristics and four limitations for eight different instructional media.
2. Define the difference between computer-assisted instruction and computer-managed instruction, listing the functions, strengths, and limitations of both uses.
3. Compare the process of programmed instruction with that of programming a computer.
4. List four sources of instructional media equipment using the appendices as a reference source.

Having progressed in the instructional development process through the problem-determination phase into the design phase, it is now possible to examine media characteristics and media selection and how they affect learning. In Chapter 10 we will examine audio media and simulation and games, as well as media-selection models.

The influence of media on learning has been studied for many years. Thorndike (1912) discussed the use of phonograph records and pictures as alternatives to the lecture. Marshall McLuhan and Quentin Fiore (1967) went so far as to say the medium is the message. That is to say, each new medium by its very invention and use changes us both as individuals and as a society. We have learned that reinforcement, the amount of information in a block of instruction, the use of positive feedback, and other design variables do have a consistent impact on learning. Research data involving media, however, have generally resulted in findings of No Significant Difference (NSD); that is, one medium usually does about as well as another. However, these results are significant. They demonstrate that, given multiple channels of communication, the instructional designer can select the medium that is least expensive, most convenient, most exciting or motivating to the learner, and that is acceptable to the instructor or manager. For example, given the NSD results, common sense will mandate the use of an audio tape recorder to teach trouble shooting of an automobile engine by listening to engine sounds rather than by using an overhead projector or a lecture.

Although research indicates that the design or structure of the content is usually far more important than the selection of specific instructional media, the communications channel or medium does permit, or restrict, the types of stimuli which can be transmitted to, or received from, the learner. Having access to alternative instructional channels or media enables a learner to, at least vicariously, experience stimuli which might otherwise be impossible or impractical to encounter if only a limited selection of media were available. For example, without still pictures in some form, teachers could not expect their students to recognize Einstein, or Mount Rushmore. Distant places and objects can be brought to the class via the media. Media make it possible for learners to see otherwise expensive, fragile, or dangerous demonstrations safely and repeatedly. The novelty of using various media seems to promote excitement. Media can recreate the past, portray the present, and help learners speculate about the future through drawings, animation, simulations, and so on.

Media selection should be done only after the designer has developed the instructional objectives and examined the characteristics of the available media. Media selection is often done concurrently with specification of instructional strategies. Decisions on instructional strategy and media selection are interrelated, so a change in one may dictate a change in the other. For example, if excellent videotapes are available, it might not make sense to reject them just because they do not follow the projected instructional strategy. It may be possible to change the strategy to accommodate the videotapes, while achieving the stated objectives at less cost. Given the other options of lecturing or making your own film or videotape to teach the set of objectives, it may be much more desirable to modify the instructional strategy.

The procedure for specifying instructional strategies was discussed in Chapter 8. Some of these strategy decisions will again be examined and their interrelationships with media explored. Their parallel placement in the model is our way of showing that strategy and media selection usually occur simultaneously. Before choosing an instructional medium, it is a good idea to examine each medium in detail. An instructional medium should present instructional stimuli in an efficient, straightforward manner with only the necessary degree of complexity utilized. Complex media tend to be costly, inefficient, and unreliable. The teacher should therefore choose the least expensive instructional medium that results in attainment of the desired objectives.

Despite numerous NSD findings, a review of media research does help the

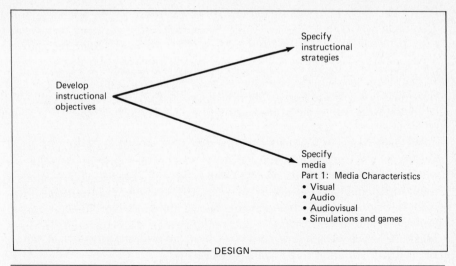

FIGURE 9.1   I.D. Model: Media Characteristics

instructional designer. Many researchers have examined the use of multiple channels for simultaneous stimuli presentation. It appears that if the information density is equal to or greater than a person's ability to process information, there is no advantage to using two channels for presenting it. Learners cannot attend to more than one stimuli simultaneously. If, however, the rate of the presented material is slower than the learner's capacity to process the information, there may be some advantage to using two modalities at the same time. As the complexity of the learning task increases, the advantage of employing a visual medium of instruction also seems to increase. Moreover, the use of visual rather than audio media seems to result in more reliable retention and recall, although learners appear to take longer to process visual stimuli. Specific research involving a particular medium will be presented when that medium is described and discussed.

STILL VISUAL MEDIA

The effectiveness of still visuals in the form of photographs, slides, filmstrips, overhead transparencies, charts, and others, has been extensively investigated. The research related to learning from still visuals generally indicates that:

- Appropriate pictures or drawings help learners understand and recall the content of verbal or printed materials.
- Pictures can increase learner affect.
- Simple graphics are usually more effective than more complex drawings or photographs (apparently, the contextual stimuli often confuse the learner).

- When visuals are used as part of a multiimage presentation that is too rapid, the student is forced to choose between the two channels.
- Highlighting or cueing through the use of arrows, color, or shading can clarify some pictures.
- When attempting to teach concepts involving motion, either a series of still visuals or motion pictures is more effective than a single still visual.
- Color may increase learner affect, but in many cases it contributes little to cognitive retention unless the concept being taught involves color.

Our discussion in Chapter 8 revealed that color visuals are generally more pleasing to a learner than black and white visuals, and thus are desirable in some situations. Yet the use of color often results in confusion and becomes a source of "communications noise." In terms of economy and instructional effectiveness, black and white line drawings are highly desirable. There are times, however, when the instructional task requires color discrimination. In these cases, use of color is advantageous. Colors can also be used constructively to cue or direct attention to part of an illustration.

In different cultures, colors have different meanings. The following figure shows the association of typical emotions to various colors in the United States.

Color is used symbolically throughout all cultures. At college graduations, white stands for arts and letters, blue for philosophy, purple for law, and so on. Black is often used to indicate evil, such as the evil genius of *Star Wars*, Darth Vader, or the proverbial "bad guys" or "black sheep" of the westerns. White, on the other hand, is used to clothe Luke Skywalker, the Lone Ranger, and the "girl next door." These are culturally learned associations. In some countries, purple is the traditional color of mourning, whereas in others it is white. Hence, colors for visuals should be carefully chosen and be consistent with their affective association for the intended audience.

Multiimage presentations may be employed to increase understanding and retention of objectives that require learners to compare or discriminate between visual stimuli. Discrimination may be enhanced by showing two pictures simultaneously, or using two adjacent pictures in a textbook. This arrangement

Color	Affective Associations
Red	Fire, hot, love, active, exciting, danger, excitement
Orange	Warm, autumn, jovial, energetic, lively, Halloween, Thanksgiving
Yellow	Sunlight, vital, cheerful, inspiring, caution, coward
Green	Cool, nature, restful, quiet, peace
Blue	Sky, water, ice, cold, subdue, sober
Purple	Cool, darkness, mourning, mystic, dignified, Easter
White	Cool, snow, good, pure, clean, mourning
Black	Night, empty, dead, depressing, mourning

FIGURE 9.2. Color and Affective Associations

permits learners to note similarities, differences, or changes in people, places, or events. Often, simultaneous multiimage presentations result in high affect, but the density of information may prove to be confusing to receivers, and thus reduce their rate of cognitive learning.

There are several types of media that can present still visuals to learners. These include 2 × 2-inch slides, overhead transparencies, filmstrips, textbooks, pictures or other paper-based materials, microfilm or microfiche, and holograms. Still visuals can be stored on film, paper, or magnetic tape. The images are then viewed either directly, as with the paper-based materials, or projected, as with the film-based materials (except for some holograms, which you look through). Some can be amplified and presented on a cathode ray tube (CRT), as with the images from computers or videodiscs. Still media tend to be easier to prepare and less expensive than motion visuals, but they also tend to be less motivational than motion visuals.

We now turn our attention to several specific media and their instructional applications.

Overhead Projectors

The overhead projector is normally used to project 10-by-10-inch transparencies. It is probably the simplest and most effective single device a teacher can use to present information in a traditional lecture-based system. Because it is used at the front of the room, it permits the instructor to face the students and obtain feedback from them while maintaining visual control. Teachers can also develop ideas and concepts at the front of the class as they would with a chalkboard. Teachers can prepare their own transparencies using any of the methods shown in Figure 9.3, or use commercial transparencies, which are available from many sources. The latter can be modified or supplemented to reflect local instructional requirements.

Commercial transparencies are often prepared with overlays, which allow the basic visual to be developed by overlaying it with additional transparencies. One can thus begin with a simple visual and gradually develop it into a relatively complex one.

Educators who wish to prepare their own transparencies should use letters three-sixteenths of an inch or higher, if they are to be read in a conventional-sized classroom. Direct copies of materials from textbooks or other printed or typed originals are almost always too small to be read when projected. Transparencies may also be hand drawn on clear acetate with colored markers and grease pencils. Press-on letters and other opaque or translucent materials can be placed directly on the acetate.

The overhead projector, slide projector, motion picture projector, filmstrip projector, and the microfilm projector all use an efficient light-through system, in which light passes directly through the film or transparency to a lens system that focuses the light. On the other hand, opaque projector and microcard

Method	Equipment Required	Cost (per Frame)	Production Time	Remarks
felt pen	none	.10	short	fast, poor quality
press-on	none	.75	medium	for charts and graphs
spirit duplicator	duplicator	.50	medium	good for many copies
diazo film	diazo printer	.75	medium	needs translucent original; good color
heat-sensitive film	infrared copy machine	.50	short	needs carbon-based original, one color
photocopy	xerographic or electrostatic machine	.75	short	needs special film; one color usually
pressure, heat, or glue	laminator, dry-mount	.75	short to medium	needs clay-coated color original
photography	camera equipment, darkroom	3.00+	long	high quality, expensive

FIGURE 9.3.   Methods of Preparing Overhead Transparencies

projection systems use a reflected light system that is much less efficient and requires relatively more energy and a darker room. It is for this reason that the overhead projector has generally replaced the opaque projector and that the microfilm systems have replaced the microcard storage systems.

Slide and Filmstrip Projectors

Slide projectors use 2-by-2-inch framed film, usually the inexpensive 35mm color film widely used by vacationers and professional photographers. Originally, slide projectors used 3¼-by-4-inch slides (called "lantern slides") which were hand-drawn, glass-mounted slides. These large-sized slides are seldom found outside of museums today because of their cost, size, and expense of the equipment involved.

Slides are often used in conjunction with audiotapes. Slide-tape packages allow inexpensive presentation of both audio and visual stimuli. An instructor can easily modify these packages by deleting, rearranging, or adding slides. By renarrating a tape, a teacher may be able to use the program to attain objectives different from those intended by the producer. Many slide-tape presentations are synchronized by a tone placed on a second channel of the tape or by an audible tone on the voice channel. This tone automatically advances the slide projector. Synchronized systems such as this are used throughout industry and the military for individualized instruction.

Filmstrips are used instead of slides when lower cost and/or a fixed sequence of visuals is desired. Yet, unlike slides, the order of visuals in a filmstrip cannot be easily changed. Filmstrips are relatively compact, easy to handle, inexpensive when reproduced in quantity, and can be projected with simple lightweight equipment. Compared to slides, filmstrips are relatively difficult to prepare locally since film-laboratory service is necessary for converting slides to filmstrip format. Many commercially available materials are distributed in filmstrip/audiotape format because of its simple and low-cost distribution system.

Microform Projectors

There are two basic types of microform storage-projection systems in use today: microcard and microfilm. These systems are used to store still materials such as photographs, or charts of printed materials. As stated earlier, unlike the microtransparency systems, the microcard employs a reflected light system that is not energy efficient. It is thus losing ground to microfiche, microfilm, and similar light-through storage-presentation systems. Some ultrastorage systems can reduce a three thousand-page text onto one 2 × 2-inch card. These microimage systems require special projectors to enlarge the microimages to readable size and because of this inconvenience (who wants to carry a projector on the bus to the beach to read the latest thriller?), microforms are used mainly to store reference materials rather than materials learners are expected to read.

The most common microform systems store up to a hundred pages of text on a 5-by-7-inch piece of microfilm. These systems, called microfiche, are very common in research-oriented libraries, and many industries use them in lieu of catalogs because of their durability, easy handling, and low cost. Sears Roebuck, Volkswagen, and many other companies use microfiches to reduce their information storage and retrieval files. Educators who are also in the information-handling and transmission business could similarly use these systems to reduce their paperwork storage and handling problems. The cards contain from twenty to a hundred visuals and can be viewed with hand-held viewers. Since they can also be duplicated for very little cost it becomes economically feasible for each student to have a copy to take home to study. Some medical schools are experimenting with having students purchase sets of the color fiche cards for reference, to supplement conventional textbooks. High-quality, locally prepared (or modified) visuals can therefore be available to all students within reasonable cost.

Holograms

Holograms are photographic plates that produce three-dimensional images by first recording and then projecting interference patterns created by a laser beam. The use of holography should expand rapidly, but it may be several years before sufficient materials have been developed for general classroom use. Some graphs and other interrelating parameters may be made easier to comprehend in 3-D because of their ability to show the relationships "in depth." Also, the learner (in medicine, for example) can walk around the image and observe spatial relationships from different perspectives.

Chalkboard

The original blackboard is becoming a thing of the past. Slate is very heavy and expensive and the glare and contrast of the chalk on the black slate often makes viewing difficult. Chalkboards are now available in dull greens, brown, or almost any color. They are less durable than the old slate boards, but are enough so to last until a room is remodeled, at which time they are also replaced. Some may also serve as magnetic boards to assist lecturers who want to spontaneously reinforce the discussion with written words or freehand illustrations. Materials for use on magnetic boards must be prepared in advance and attached to small magnets that will adhere to the board.

Print/Textbook

Print is the most widely used medium in education and training and, in the form of texts, remains the primary information storage and delivery tool. Print media are used for presenting information related to most types of objectives including factual information, principles, concepts and rules, some procedures, and, to some extent, the development of attitudes and opinions. However, they may be less useful in learning situations whose objectives require interpretation of visual cues or stimuli, or when motor skills are to be developed.

The limitations of print media are known by all instructors. In addition to a text's limited ability to create student interaction, there can be problems with outdated material and sex, racial, and other biases. Moreover, it can take from one to three years before an instructor's ideas are realized in print. The author must formulate the concept, find a publisher, finalize the manuscript, review the editor's comments, proofread the galleys, and so on, until the book is published.

Although printing on paper is the established technology in the United States, some developing countries may rely much more heavily on microfiche. Even in the United States, we will see some change in information storage and retrieval as electronic devices including computers, satellites, and cable TV are interconnected.

"Don't you think your Holt, Rinehart and Winston would go well with your Calvins and your Nikes?"

(Campbell)

(Ford Button)

Several questions must be considered when evaluating a textbook. In fact, these same questions can be applied to all other media as well.

- Is the *organization* of the text acceptable? Does the text contain a table of contents, an introduction, summaries, questions to consider, a bibliography, and an index?
- Does the textbook *meet the objectives* better than any other text? *How well does the textbook serve the identified instructional goals?* (The answers to these questions are probably more important than the answers to the other questions in this list.)
- What is the *readability level* of the text? Will students understand the language? (There are several readability formulas or lists that help determine the difficulty of a text. You could also have a representative sample of the intended population use the text and report to you on the level of difficulty.)
- Do the *visuals* adequately support the text? Are they likely to be effective for the learners? Do they reflect a bias?
- Is the *pacing* of the materials appropriate? Are there enough or too many examples and illustrations in the text?
- Is the *sequencing* of the content done in such a way that it will be easy to teach

and to comprehend? (Sometimes an otherwise acceptable text is rejected for use because of the order in which the content is presented. An inductively-oriented teacher, for example, may reject a deductively-oriented textbook.)

- Does the text contain any feedback mechanism for students to help them maintain awareness of their progress? (Questions with answers in a textbook are often desirable, since knowledge of results has been shown to enhance retention and to increase motivation for some students.)
- Does the text have an attractive *design?* Is the typeface large enough to be readable for the intended audience?

There are also print-related readability research issues: type size, interlinear spaces, paper and print color, headings, underlining, highlighting, tables, diagrams, and similar "appropriate" design decisions which need to be evaluated. Hartley (1974) provided a list of research reports on these topics describing the relevance of design decisions on student learning. When selecting a book, examine its characteristics in relation to the levels or types of objectives taught. Coyle and Steinmetz (1977) examined the relationship of levels of objectives, which they call learning factors, to characteristics of the print medium. Their summary is presented in Figure 9.4.

Nationwide surveys on how textbooks are used show that in some subject areas, at least 50 percent of elementary teachers rely almost exclusively on textbooks for content and instructional methodology. Thus, what many students learn depends almost entirely on the textbook they use. In elementary-level mathematics, for example, one publishing house has a large percentage of its texts dealing with conceptual understanding and application. Another publisher, however, emphasizes basic computation and minimal competencies. The selection of a math textbook thus makes a significant difference as to what mathematics skills are acquired. Motivational studies indicate some learners find reading books less intrinsically motivating than watching television or films and tend to resist reading more than they would resist watching a lesson on some other instructional medium. Other textbook selection factors will be considered in the next chapter under media selection.

Many who teach in areas subject to rapid change use current articles with their students to reduce the time between an idea being discovered and its consideration by students. Using a copy machine is a quick way to duplicate materials for class use. Instructors should be aware, however, that copyright laws were rewritten (effective January 1978) to protect both the author and the user (Sinofsky 1984). These new laws strengthen the right of the person who originates and develops an idea to be reimbursed for the time and effort invested. Instructors who reproduce copyrighted material must therefore pay attention to the copyright notice that accompanies the material. Specific guidelines on copyright are found elsewhere in this text.

	Learning factors					
Print characteristics	Motivation and attention maintenance	Attention direction	Accessibility	Comprehension	Retention	Transfer
Advance organizers		X		X	X	
Readability	X			X		
Language style	X			X		
Information density	X			X	X	
Accessory material	X			X	X	X
Graphic cues		X			X	
Illustrations	X	X		X	X	X
Programming	X			X		
Sequencing			X	X	X	
Questions					X	
Feedback	X			X	X	
Summaries				X	X	
Indexes			X			
Type faces	X	X	X		X	
Use of color	X	X	X			
Layout		X		X	X	
Physical characteristics			X			

Source: "How to Choose a Good Book." *Audiovisual Instruction*. Reprinted by permission of Association for Educational Communications and Technology. Copyright 1977.

FIGURE 9.4   Book-Selection Criteria

Programmed Texts

Programmed textbooks or teaching machines were an important step in the development of an instructional technology. They represent a procedure for designing materials for any medium. A programmed unit of instruction will normally have the following characteristics:

- Short "frames" or blocks of information. A single term might be presented, for example, and then another frame might be used to reinforce the term.
- Active student involvement. Individual students are asked to answer questions directly related to the presentation.
- Positive reinforcement is continually provided. The questions used to keep the student involved and alert should be difficult enough to be challenging but simple enough that the student will usually get the correct answer. The student's correct response is then verified by providing the correct answer which, in turn, enhances the student's self-concept and retention of the subject matter.

- The entire content is directly related to an objective; that is, the information presented is there for a well-thought-out reason—to teach an objective. Affective as well as cognitive and psychomotor objectives may be included in the list of objectives for any lesson.
- There should be constant formative evaluation of the materials as they are developed and summative evaluations at the end to determine the validity of the program. Revision of the materials should continue until the objectives are adequately attained by the users.

Programmed materials can be very effective. After eliminating research studies that involved (1) fewer than two months' duration, (2) fewer than thirty students in the experimental group, (3) sponsorship by the producer or distributor of the program, or (4) inappropriate research designs or statistics, some consistent trends were found from programmed instruction research. It appears that programmed presentations take, on the average, only two-thirds the time of a nonprogrammed presentation. Quite possibly the time spent planning and developing programmed materials weeds out nonsignificant content. Generally, as programmed materials are refined, the mean score on criterion tests increases and the standard deviation dramatically decreases. This procedure results in instruction that is effective in terms of both learning time and learner retention.

There are two primary approaches to the development of programmed texts. B. F. Skinner felt that the "linear" procedure with very short frames and fill-in questions was the most desirable. (See Figure 9.5 for an example.) Norman Crowder, more of a field theorist than the stimulus-response-oriented Skinner, developed the branch program format that requires individuals to examine a longer frame and then discriminate between multiple-choice items. (See Figure 9.6 for an example in chemistry.)

Answers to questions at right	
20	There are 10 decimeters in a meter, just as there are 12 inches in a foot. There are _____ decimeters in two meters.
100	Just as there are 10 decimeters in a meter, there are 10 centimeters in a decimeter. In one meter there are _____ centimeters.
1000	We know there are 100 centimeters in a meter. Appendix C tells us that there are 10 millimeters in a centimeter. There are _____ millimeters in 100 centimeters.

Source: Frederick G. Knirk, *The Metric System.*

FIGURE 9.5. Linear Program

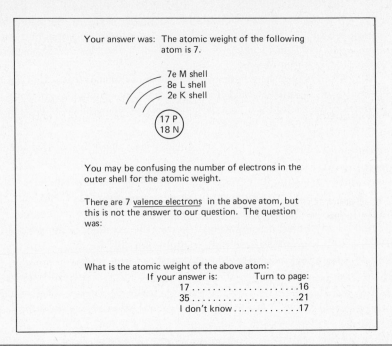

Your answer was: The atomic weight of the following atom is 7.

7e M shell
8e L shell
2e K shell
17 P
18 N

You may be confusing the number of electrons in the outer shell for the atomic weight.

There are 7 <u>valence electrons</u> in the above atom, but this is not the answer to our question. The question was:

What is the atomic weight of the above atom:

If your answer is:	Turn to page:
17	16
35	21
I don't know	17

FIGURE 9.6   A Branch Program (From Frederick G. Knirk, *The Halogen Family*)

Today most programmers will use both techniques at various times. The use of larger frames is logical if students are involved with a "deduction" objective, are familiar with the subject area, or are older. As with tests developed from behavioral objectives, programs usually contain recall questions if the objective requires students to recall or to name something. If students are to discriminate between things, multiple-choice questions may be a better way to monitor their progress.

Programmed texts have explicit course and lesson objectives; therefore, instruction can be standardized. Students learn at their own rate, which allows them to progress according to their own capabilities. They may be able to ignore information they already know or take more time, as required. Teachers can spend time with students who need personal help instead of preparing and presenting lesson plans. Programmed materials are especially useful in the following situations:

- Broad geographical spread of students (the development costs are offset by reduced travel expenses).
- Large numbers of students (the amortized costs per learner can be reduced).
- Subject matter is stable over time (this increases the possible number of users and reduces costs per student).
- Standardized performance is desirable (PI reduces problems caused by unpredictable performance).

- Training occurs randomly rather than in batches (PI avoids the costs of untrained employees waiting for training, and low teacher–pupil ratios, which are expensive).

The primary disadvantage of programmed materials is their high initial cost. Programming also requires that educators become increasingly specialized in program development, evaluation, writing, or individual instruction management.

Computers

In a few minutes a computer can make a mistake so great that it would take many men many months to equal it.

M. L. Mecham

Computers have been used for administrative applications in schools and industry for years. Applications include student records, faculty and staff accounting, and payroll. Computers have also been used on a limited basis for presenting instruction, student testing, and prescription of instruction based on test results.

Some schools use computers to process and store information on student progress and achievement, but not for instructional purposes. In Computer-Managed Instruction (CMI), students are tested by the computer. The results are then analyzed and the appropriate learning experiences are prescribed in textbooks, films, or other instructional media. After the students have utilized these information sources, they return to the computer for evaluation. In both CMI and CAI the computer records student progress so the effectiveness of the instructional materials can be assessed and the progress of each student monitored.

Both large mainframe and small personal computer systems are used for instruction. Large time-sharing computers, such as PLATO and TICCIT, allow several users to work on various programs at the same time and from different locations. Small computers such as those produced by Apple, IBM, and Radio Shack are invading classrooms as their costs decrease. With small computers, it is comforting to an instructor to know that if one computer goes down, the rest of the class can continue working. However, if a large, time-shared computer goes down, the entire class must be reorganized to continue. Also, microcomputers do not tie up telephone lines like the larger time-sharing computers. Moreover, many teachers feel it is much more convenient to have the computers in the classroom under their control, rather than in another location.

CAI has all the advantages of programmed instruction. In addition, it can provide more varied stimuli to the learner. Multiple tracks, which allow individual students to progress differently through the program, are possible and may occur as a result of student responses.

On the other hand, CAI is expensive to develop and distribute. As with programmed instruction, there are high initial costs for the equipment and software. The continuing telephone line charges (on time-shared systems), terminal costs, and computer time further boost the cost of using computers for instruction.

As mentioned earlier, two examples of time-share mainframe computer systems are PLATO and TICCIT. PLATO (Programmed Logic for Automatic Teaching Operation) was developed in the early sixties by Donald Bitzer at the University of Illinois. The current version is available through Control Data Corporation. PLATO uses large central computers and has many computers and terminal locations throughout the United States connected by telephone lines. The PLATO terminal may contain a touch-sensitive display panel and a keyboard. This system provides tutorial, inquiry, and dialogue modes of instruction. Dynamic simulations and many types of computational services and games are also available on PLATO. Extensive management data is also made available to instructors concerning the progress and performance of individual students.

The TICCIT (Time-Shared, Interactive, Computer-Controlled, Information Television) computer system was developed by the MITRE Corporation in 1971. Brigham Young University did much of the early evaluation of this system using freshman-level mathematics and English. Hazeltine Corporation currently sells TICCIT. This system includes user-owned computers with color TV receivers, teletypewriter keyboards, function keys, and light pens. The present cost for a TICCIT system with 128 terminals is about $500,000.

The efficiency of computers in instruction seems to be well established. A study by Orlansky and String (1981) concludes: "The median value of student time saved in military studies is about 25 percent . . . Student achievement and attrition with CAI and CMI are about the same as with conventional instruction. Students prefer CAI and CMI to conventional instruction while instructors prefer conventional instruction." Recent meta-analyses of time and achievement studies involving CAI suggest that computers save from 30 to 50 percent of learning time over conventional instruction (Kulik, Kulik, and Cohen 1980a, 1980b; Kulik, Bangert, and Williams 1983). Other studies also support the view that computers can be used to reduce instructional time without reducing instructional effectiveness. A review of fifty-four studies showed that in thirty-seven cases the use of computers resulted in superior examination performance. In all the studies, the computer produced substantial savings in instructional time (Kulik, Kulik, and Cohen 1980a). Computer-aided instruction may cost more, but it does teach and it saves a significant amount of time.

With the time savings on the one hand, and the increased cost of instruction on the other, it will take some serious investigation by most educational/training institutions before they adopt a computer-based instructional system. CMI systems are generally more cost-effective for schools than CAI systems because they perform student testing only. Thus, many more students can use the system. Industrial training programs are finding both CMI and CAI to be cost-effective, primarily because of reduced training time. Unlike public-school students, industrial trainees are paid while they learn. Hence, any reduction in training time represents a concrete savings in payroll. Quite the opposite is true in schools, for if learners complete a course too quickly, the problem arises as to how to utilize the time which has become available. If schools move from a time-based model to a competency-based model of instruction, the time savings of CAI may become more meaningful.

The concept of embedded training is another rapidly growing area of computer-based instruction. Since many high-technology devices now contain microprocessors, training programs can be installed directly in the devices. Novices can then learn how to operate the equipment using a contrived instructional-operational routine. Examples include learning how to use a word processor or an automated typesetter. By integrating training in the device itself, numerous problems of transfer of learning from the instructional to the real environment are eliminated.

Bulletin Boards, Displays, Models, Charts, and Maps

Bulletin boards, displays, and exhibits are among the least expensive and most extensively used instructional media. Bulletin boards have these functions:

- To stimulate student interest: students may display their homework or desk work on the bulletin board for other students, other teachers, administrators, and parents to see. This can be an excellent use of the medium if the materials are taken down as soon as they have served their purpose. In too many instances a display is left up just to "look pretty" and unfortunately this display, if it is attractive, will distract the students from the then more relevant stimuli being presented in class.
- To present a single copy of a visual: when a single copy of a visual is all that is available, the use of a bulletin board is a practical way to display it. A display case exhibits an object and keeps it relatively secure and clean. Again, it is important to keep the items on display only during the time they are being directly used.

Bulletin boards and other display media can make a classroom attractive and lively, but they must be changed constantly. There are many ways to make a learning area attractive. Form, color, and texture can all be used to provide depth and contrast without being distracting. The design of learning environments will be discussed in more detail in the next chapter.

A few tips for designing a bulletin board or display are:

- Select a theme or key idea which can be presented visually and which reflects the curriculum or objectives. Never put up a bulletin-board display without a specific educational goal.

- Always consider alternatives to accomplish the goal. Many of these may be faster to develop and more effective than the bulletin board or display.
- Plan the display ahead of time on paper. Construct it in the simplest manner possible, consuming the least amount of teacher and student time. In an art class, a teacher may wish to take more time in developing a display to demonstrate to students the design considerations which go into the development of a graphic presentation. Always keep in mind the intended audience and their interests.
- Take the bulletin board or display down as soon as it has accomplished its purpose. If it doesn't make its point immediately, it probably never will.

Models, charts, maps, globes, and similar instructional devices should be removed from the students' sight when not in use. Instead of wall charts and maps, many teachers today buy commercially developed maps and charts on overhead transparencies. These maps, because of their relatively low price, can be replaced frequently. They can also be easily stored because of their small size.

MOTION VISUAL MEDIA

There are two media which can easily present stimuli that appear to move. Television and motion pictures are very similar in their impact on the viewer. A magnetic storage medium, television requires no processing delay as does motion picture film, although the acetate base of film permits a sharper, more detailed image than television. However, the availability of electronic distribution systems allows films to be shown via television.

Research has shown that visual media providing motion stimuli are often overused. Several research studies found that a script or soundtrack and still visuals taken from a film resulted in cognitive learning equal to that from the viewing of the original motion presentation. Affectively, however, students prefer motion presentations. The cost of the motion presentation versus the increased affect that results from its use may make the choice of medium a difficult one for instructional designers.

Motion Picture

Some of the earliest films were produced for Henry Ford and Thomas Edison to teach the operation of the steel furnace and other manufacturing operations. Many of the early films were developed on 35mm film, but today the standard for most instructional films in the United States is 16mm. Recent technical developments in projectors and improved film quality have permitted smaller-sized films on 8mm to become the standard for many developing nations. Super 8 format is more common today than "regular 8" format because it makes better use of the film stock, thus permitting sharper visuals. There is, however, considerable speculation that videotape, videodisc, and other video formats still in the experimental stage will make film obsolete as a motion recording/playback medium.

Most teachers should not be involved with the development of a film any more than they should write their own textbooks. The procedure of developing a storyboard and scripts, shooting and editing the film, and distributing it to enough users to reduce the cost per use requires specialists.

Interestingly, research has shown that a storyboard teaches almost as well as the finished film. Viewers, however, do not like the presentation as well. Motion is not as necessary for cognitive or psychomotor objectives as was once believed. However, affective objectives are met more regularly with motion pictures than with still-visual media. When examining the research on films in instruction, many conflicting conclusions are drawn. It seems safe to say, however, that filmed presentations work about as well as lectures, television presentations, or most other instructional modes as information transmitters. Films often result in higher affect than conventional presentations, and color films can result in a higher student affect toward content and instructional method than black-and-white presentations. Also, the more animated and programmed a filmed presentation, the more students seem to like it.

Television

> *There can no longer be any doubt that children and adults learn a great amount from instructional television, just as they do from any other experience that can be made to seem relevant to them—experiences as different as watching someone rotate a hula hoop or reading the encyclopedia. The effectiveness of television has now been demonstrated in well over 100 experiments, and several hundred separate comparisons, performed in many parts of the world, in developing as well as industrialized countries, at every level from pre-school through adult education, and with a great variety of subject matter and method.*
>
> G. C. Chu and W. Schramm

Television has been used widely throughout the world for education and training. In the United States alone, there are over one hundred fifty authorized educational television stations. It is a very powerful medium in that it can present audio along with still or motion visuals in either black and white or color. A distinction should be made between "educational television," which refers to any type of program intended to inform or develop broad cultural understanding, and "instructional television" (ITV), which refers to programming designed to teach *specific* subject matter as part of a course.

There are approximately 750,000 elementary and secondary school teachers (1 out of 3) in the United States who use ITV. Local public television stations provide most of the programming for these teachers. Unfortunately, only about

17 percent of the teachers have been trained to use ITV effectively. Teachers report using ITV for four reasons:

1. It brings new resources to the classroom.
2. It provides different approaches to presenting materials.
3. It presents new material.
4. It reinforces material taught in other lessons.

The major disadvantage of instructional television is that there is no easy way to provide feedback to the student. Some feedback, however, can be provided by way of a telephone line.

If the students can call the ITV teacher following the broadcast and have their questions answered, it is possible to overcome this potential limitation of instructional television. Nonetheless, handling of feedback can be a real problem in a mass-oriented ITV program.

ITV has several notable characteristics: it provides good quality audio and visual stimuli, is nonpunitive, and can attract and hold the viewer's attention. Furthermore it is nonanalytical, continuous, and often immediately and intrinsically gratifying to the viewer.

Videodisc and videotape recorders can be used to store ITV presentations for future use. Videotapes can be made locally by using a camera to record the presentation or they can directly record broadcast TV presentations. A video-

---

CHICAGO TV COLLEGE

In 1956, the Ford Foundation funded a three-year experiment to see how well community colleges could succeed in attracting students to television courses. The TV College is an extension of the City College of Chicago. Since the program began, over 200,000 course registrations have been completed by over 150,000 students. More than 400 of these students have graduated with an Associate in Arts degree acquired entirely by television. An average of six thousand students enroll every year. The average age is between 29 and 33. Approximately two-thirds of the students are in penal institutions or are disabled persons at home or in hospitals.

When students register, they usually elect a TV College Center in which to take examinations and have conferences. Each course involves a midterm and final examination. Those students confined to their homes, hospitals, or penal institutions are given exams by proctor. The television presentations generally consist of a series of two programs per week for 15 weeks. Most lessons run for about 45 minutes and are broadcast repeatedly. Printed materials and activities which actively engage the student are felt to be essential to maintaining a high level of student interest and success. Frequently a programmed learning booklet is used to increase student participation. The completion rate is between 70 and 80 percent. The TV College reported a cost per credit hour of between 40 and 50 dollars.

disc player cannot record a locally produced or received program, so the recording must be purchased from a videodisc distributor. The videodisc will become increasingly important to trainers because of the following advantages.

- Instructional materials can be presented in a full-color, full-motion format or in a still visual with sound format. Almost any set of instructional materials, regardless of the format of the original materials, can be distributed on videodiscs. A videodisc may contain over 50,000 separate frames and may access any one of them within seconds. Up to 50 hours of digitized stereo music or 30 minutes of motion visuals with audio can be placed on one disc.
- When associated with a microcomputer, the videodisc can be used to store the instructional content, and the computer can evaluate the student input and decide which content to present next.
- Because of the relatively small size of the discs compared to other instructional materials, storage requirements and distribution costs by mail are minimized.
- Duplication costs (once the master has been prepared) are minimal compared to other media.
- In the laser models, the laser beam never touches the disc, so the disc will never wear out.
- Individual frame access is possible at a very rapid rate.
- Total control of the presentation can be achieved locally by the individual trainer or by the student in an individualized system. Pacing and the inclusion of feedback to users about their progress are also possible.

There are some problems with using the videodisc in education and training situations:

- The production of a limited number of copies of a disc is expensive because of the necessity of producing a master from which the copies are made. Once the master is developed, however, a large number of duplicates can be produced at low cost.
- Revising the instructional materials requires remastering the entire disc.
- Most videodisc players cannot record locally produced programs.

Many inferior television programs have been imposed on students. Television has, however, produced Sesame Street, Electric Company, and the Open University project in Great Britain. ITV has also been used in many other countries: American Samoa, Colombia, Nigeria, Niger, El Salvador, the Ivory Coast, and many others. According to Arnove (1976) the costs for ITV range upward from as little as seven cents per student hour. Per-student costs depend on the number of users and the refinements of the system.

What does research say about the effectiveness of ITV? A great deal of research has been done on this medium with the general finding that it teaches about as well as the traditional teacher-based system. Specific findings have been summarized by Chu and Schramm (1967) and Barbatsis (1978).

Specific conclusions about the effectiveness of instructional television are:

- The use of active student response in ITV design improves learning.
- Teacher follow-up of an ITV lesson increases learning more than viewing a lesson twice or with no follow-up.
- There is little evidence to suggest that color will improve learning from ITV.
- Subtitles will improve learning from ITV especially when the original program was not well designed.
- There is no evidence to prove that either visual magnification or large-sized screens will improve learning from television.
- ITV appears to be equally effective with any size group.
- Notetaking while viewing ITV is likely to interfere with learning unless time is provided for notetaking.
- Liking television is seldom correlated with learning from ITV.
- Most students would prefer a live teacher to a television teacher for most subjects.

The conclusions concerning research on ITV are very similar to those drawn from film research. The major difference is that television has a poor-quality picture compared to film. The impact of noninstructional television on children has been studied for years. It appears that children's eyes are not affected, but children's social behavior can be dramatically affected by watching television presentations. Studies by the London School of Economics Survey Research Center and by George Gerbner and Larry Gross of the University of Pennsylvania Annenberg School of Communications indicate that children who watch violence on television tend to become increasingly aggressive. Watching television may raise low-intelligence students' reading level due to the printing shown on television advertisements but, in general, it seems to reduce literacy. Three- or four-year-old youngsters who are heavy television viewers tend to make up fewer games and imaginary playmates. Both adults and children seem to spend a lot of time watching television in an alpha brainwave state, which indicates that television may be conditioning viewers to be inattentive and passive, since alpha surface brainwaves indicate a relaxed, nonattending state.

Viewing television in the home has little apparent long-term effect on school achievement. It was hoped that Sesame Street and other programs would have a dramatic effect on learning. It appears, however, that reading improves a little, but that is about the extent of the impact of home viewing on school achievement (Hornik 1981). The use of instructional TV is hampered, in part, by various laws. To illustrate, the Veterans Administration's educational-benefit programs do pay for qualified "independent study," but televised courses do not qualify. To reach more veterans and other "nontraditional" students, many two-year colleges would like to increase their use of ITV, but until restrictive laws and regulations are modified, the frequency of offerings is unlikely to increase. Many colleges offer combined television and regular classroom instruction courses but do not count the television time toward full-time enroll-

OPEN UNIVERSITY OF GREAT BRITAIN

One of the most successful uses of ITV has been by the "Open University" in Great Britain. The students study mostly in their own homes or in regional study centers. More than 100 courses are offered through a system of correspondence materials, radio, and television programs offered through the BBC. There are over 70,000 students preparing to obtain college degrees in education, social science, arts, technology, science, and mathematics. Course materials are prepared by approximately 250 faculty members who are located at the University's Administrative Center at Milton Keynes, about 40 miles north of London.

A B.A. can be obtained in three years, although a student following this option would have to spend at least 20 hours each week on studies. At the current time, most students are taking five years to attain the B.A. degree. Each course is divided into blocks of 4 to 5 weeks, and then into units of a single week's work. Each week's unit requires at least 10 hours of work usually in this pattern: six hours of self-instruction, a half hour of TV, a half hour of radio, a half hour of self-assessment tests, about a half hour for subjective assignments to be graded by tutors, and an hour of objective assignments to be graded by a computer.

The courses are considered to be exceptionally good and the degrees are widely recognized. The dropout rate is much lower than in conventional British universities which have highly competitive entry tests.

The courses begin in January and continue for 32 weeks. This schedule allows the University to schedule one week of obligatory college attendance to college spaces in the summer. Over 32,000 individuals received their degrees in the first ten years (to 1979). The cost per student of providing an Open University foundation-level Humanities course is $130 per year if the total enrollment is 40,000. For comparison, the cost of a residential student in a university setting in Britain is $940 per year. For an Open University advanced-level physics course, the cost ranged between $350 and $500 compared to $1500 in a more traditional campus setting. Thus, the cost of educating each Open University student is one-fourth to one-third that of education in a traditional system.

ment status. This reduces the attractiveness of the ITV courses. The major reasons college officials give for not using ITV are that their institutions would not provide financial support, faculty are not sympathetic, and there are not enough appropriate courses adequately taught by TV. Nevertheless, it is estimated that in the United States there are over twenty-five hundred televised courses offered by about four hundred institutions of higher education. The courses are thought to enroll about two hundred thousand students. The most popular form of ITV distribution is through closed-circuit systems. Other distribution systems include public-television stations, cable stations, and commercial stations. Some educational programs are also available on videotape.

Television broadcasts are line-of-sight transmissions and do not follow the curvature of the earth as do AM radio broadcasts. Sending and receiving antennas are therefore usually built quite high. More recently cable systems, videotape recorders, videodiscs, and satellites are being used to increase the television viewing or service area. Television signals can be transmitted by coaxial cable anywhere the cable is available. Satellites, because of their height, can be seen over a wider area than a ground-based antenna and thus, with special antennas and amplifiers, can be used to broadcast to entire regions or nations.

SUMMARY

Due to the technical characteristics of media equipment and their accompanying materials, all have their unique characteristics. It is impossible for a sheet of paper to reproduce the sound of "middle C," for example. These characteristics must be considered by the instructional technologist when selecting one or more media to assist in the resolution of instructional problems.

The most significant conclusion concerning the use of instructional media is that they work. Students *do* learn from media. They tend to learn as effectively from instructional media as from traditional teacher-based systems. The lack of significant difference in research studies is probably due to testing instruments that are too imprecise to detect differences, or to uncontrolled critical training or learner variables. More research is obviously needed on how to select and effectively incorporate media into instruction.

Questions for Consideration and Discussion

1. If you had your choice of selecting full-color photographs of flowers or pen and ink sketches to teach parts of the flower, which would you choose? Why?
2. What factors would you consider in selecting either slides or filmstrips for a series of instructional lessons?
3. What problems would you expect to encounter in providing microfiche to learners for their direct use?
4. What are some of the advantages and disadvantages of this text compared to other media?
5. Some feel computers will revolutionize education while others feel they are only a fad and will have little lasting impact. What do you think?
6. What do you consider to be the five most important factors to consider in selecting a medium or media?

Suggested Activities

1. In order to illustrate the desirability of utilizing visual stimuli in instruction, develop a short instructional outline on the topic: "How would you teach the operation of a solar heater to a nontechnical person?" It is very difficult to do this effectively

without visuals. Choose other topics and observe the problems involved in designing an instructional sequence without incorporating visuals.
2. Select one of the references below and do a report on it for the class. The presentation may be oral or mediated (for example, a slide-tape presentation).
3. How large should your visuals be? Write on an overhead transparency using a variety of print or writing sizes; then project the transparency and go to the rear of the
room to determine the minimum size you can use with students in a classroom of
the size you are in. The same thing could be done with television materials, slides,
or other visual media.

Suggested Readings

Arnove, R. F., ed. (1976). *Educational Television: A Policy Critique and Guide for
Developing Countries*. New York: Praeger.

Barbatsis, G. S. (Summer 1978). The Nature of Inquiry and Analysis of Theoretical
Progress in Instructional Theory from 1950–1970. *Review of Educational Research*,
399–414.

Brown, J., Lewis, R., and Harcleroad, F. (1983). *A-V Instruction: Technology, Media,
and Methods*. New York: McGraw-Hill.

Chu, G. C., and Schramm, W. (1967). *Learning from Television: What the Research
Says*. Stanford, CA: Institute for Communication Research.

Fisher, J. E., Coyle, A., and Steinmetz, R. (September 1977). How to Choose a Good
Book. *Audiovisual Instruction*, 14–16.

Hartley, J. (November 1974). Programmed Instruction 1954–1974: A Review. *Programmed Learning and Educational Technology*, 278–291.

Heinich, R., Molenda, M., and Russell, J. D. (1982). *Instructional Media*. New York:
John Wiley.

Kulik, C. C., Kulik, J. A., and Cohen, P. A. (1980a). Instructional Technology and
College Teaching. *Teaching of Psychology*, 7(4), 199–205.

———(1980b). Effectiveness of Computer-based College Teaching: A Meta-analysis of
Findings. *Review of Educational Research*, 525–544.

Kulik, J. A., Bangert, R., and Williams, G. (1983). Effects of Computer-based Teaching
on Secondary School Students. *Journal of Educational Psychology*, 75, 19–26.

Levie, W. H., and Dickie, K. E. (1973). The Analysis and Application of Media. In
R. M. W. Travers, ed. *Second Handbook of Research on Teaching*. Chicago: Rand
McNally.

Locatis, C. N., and Atkinson, F. D. (1984). *Media and Technology for Education and
Training*. Columbus, OH: Charles E. Merrill.

McLuhan, M., and Fiore, Q. (1967). *The Medium Is the Message: An Inventory of
Effects*. New York: Random House.

Orlansky, J., and String, J. (September 1978). *Cost Effectiveness of Computer-Based
Instruction in Military Training*. San Diego: Cubic Corp. *Defense Management
Journal*, 1981, 46–54.

Schramm, W. (1977). *Big Media, Little Media*. Beverly Hills, CA: Sage Publications.

Sinofsky, E. R. (1984). *Off-air Videotaping: Issues, Decisions, Implications*. New York:
R. R. Bowker.

Thorndike, E. L. (1912). *Education*. New York: Macmillan.

Travers, R. M. W. (1982). *Essentials of Learning*, 5th ed. New York: Macmillan.

Well, S. (1976). *Instructional Technology in Developing Countries*. New York: Praeger.

10

Audio and Telecommunications Media, Simulation and Games, Media Selection

The book is one of the first, and very possibly the most important, mass-produced product, and its impact demonstrates the falsity of the common notion that mass production per se brings about the massification of men.
David Riesman

Objectives

After completing this chapter you should be able to:

1. Select an appropriate instructional medium when given (1) a statement about the learners and (2) the objectives to be taught.
2. Discuss (orally or in writing) the major research evidence and trends regarding each type of instructional media-based system.
3. Discuss (orally or in writing) both the advantages and limitations of three instructional media-selection models presented in this chapter.
4. List both the characteristics and limitations of six motion visual or audio media which affect their selection as instructional media.
5. List three characteristics of instructional simulations or simulation games not shared by other media.

The characteristics of audio media, telecommunications, and simulations and games will be presented in this chapter. Due to developments in telephone-line-based telecommunications, telelecturing, telewriting, teletext, and videotext are also included. Several instructional media-selection models will also be presented. Note how they differ and consider what implications, if any, these differences may make in designing instruction.

Before an instructional designer decides to design or select instructional materials he or she should preview the existing materials to determine which, if any, will work best with a given student or group of students. While some instructional-development models suggest creating new materials for each new instructional program, this is often unrealistically expensive and generally undesirable.

AUDIO MEDIA

Today we immerse ourselves in sound. We've all become acoustic skin-divers. Music is no longer for listening to, but for merging with.
Edmund Carpenter

There are a limited number of audio media available for instruction. They include teachers, audio tape, records, radio, television, and telephone.

Teachers

Although it may seem odd to regard teachers as audio media, they are, in fact, an excellent audio source since the audio channel is their principal means of communication. Excellent teachers are often the key to an outstanding instructional system. They provide a variety of audio stimuli and can also react to student feedback better than any other known medium. With chalkboard or paper, they can also provide written stimuli.

Conventional instruction is characterized by direct human contact. The use of this communication channel can create a high degree of teacher–student interaction and usually results in all students progressing at about the same rate.

Following are nine types of teacher–learner interactions listed from simplest to the most difficult:

- Drills (flash cards, algorithms, numbers, facts, vocabulary words).
- Practice (present problem, student answers and reviews each procedure). If the student provides an incorrect answer, then the teacher can have the student repeat the task.
- Problem review (may be randomly assigned). Locate the answers in a textbook and give rational answers.
- Diagnosis and prescription. Rationally figure out what the students know and then prescribe the next learning activities to them.
- Tutorial interaction (lead students from a known to an unknown).
- Simulation and games (for example, Hangman, to teach spelling).
- Computation (mathematical manipulations).
- Logical problem solving (setting goals, guiding and motivating).
- Exploration ("unstructured" exploration of one's environment).

In addition to providing motivation, guidance, and feedback unmatched by other media, the teacher is potentially the ultimate in instructional flexibility and adaptability. We say teachers *can* perform all these acts, yet many do *not* or cannot. Placing a teacher, for example, in front of a large group of students radically curtails the opportunity to guide individual students and provide relevant feedback. Moreover, the lower student–teacher ratio found in most classrooms, when compared to some programmed or computer-based systems, makes conventional teacher-based instructional systems appear relatively expensive.

What does research say about teacher effectiveness? Heath and Nielson (1974) observed that, "given the well-documented, strong association between student achievement and variables such as socio-economic status and ethnic status, the effects of techniques of teaching on achievement . . . are likely to be inherently trivial." A Rand Corporation study by Averch (1972) stated, "The research on teaching approaches, teacher differences, class size, and the like shows no consistent effect on student achievement, as measured by standardized cognitive tests." On the other hand, an Educational Testing Service (1976) study seems to show that teachers do make a difference, especially when they are in individualized instruction situations.

Studies of teachers' activities indicate that a majority of classroom time is spent on routine, noninstructional activities such as taking attendance, disciplining, grading papers, and the like. Less than an hour a day is spent on individual or small-group teaching (an average of 2 minutes per child in a class of 25). Research has also found that restructuring the classroom to provide greater instructional time usually results in higher levels of student achievement. The goal of instructional design should be to have teachers perform those tasks for which they are uniquely suited, and use other media for less demanding tasks.

Media-aided instruction is a term given to a teacher-based instructional system in which films, tapes, slides, transparencies, and similar media are used to assist the teacher. It typically involves using commercially prepared materials possessing high technical quality that require little or no preparation time (in or out of class). These materials should be chosen for their strengths. Filmstrips, for example, may have an advantage over slides and overhead transparencies because their order is fixed and cannot be put in the wrong order by the user. On the other hand, slides, overhead transparencies, and printed still photographs may be selected because they can be edited and reordered to reflect curriculum or content changes. When a media-based instructional system reduces teacher load without replacing it with a specific meaningful activity, frustration is likely to occur. Attention must be paid to the changed role of the teacher in a highly mediated environment. Negative aspects of media-aided instruction are a potential distraction to both teacher and students of the room darkening and time required to obtain and set up equipment.

Many types of still-visual materials can be made by an artistically inclined teacher. However, considering the time and expense required to produce these materials, it would be more practical to employ graphic artists who have all the materials, skill, and time at their disposal. Unfortunately, many education administrators give little consideration to teachers' time (it has to be expended anyway), so paraprofessional support to free teachers from performing these tasks is often inadequate. Many educators thus continue preparing their own still visual materials, but education and training administrators must be shown that it is expensive and wasteful to have instructors spend their time producing rather than employing instructional materials.

Telelecturing/Telewriting/Teletext/Videotext

Information can be transmitted long distances to students by telephone lines, radio, or broadcast television.

Telephone lines permit, to some degree, visual stimuli. Telewriting and slow-motion visuals are possible through the use of conventional voice-grade telephone lines, and if coaxial cable is available, full-motion television images may be distributed via wire.

Telelecturing is a relatively inexpensive method for providing audio stimuli to students who are bedridden, too far from school, handicapped, or otherwise unable to attend school. It is also an excellent way to have experts share their experience without having to travel to the students. When this system is used with a class, a loudspeaker system is rented to the school by the telephone company.

Telewriting permits transmission of simple visuals over the telephone, and is often done in conjunction with an oral presentation on another telephone line. The telewriting device is sometimes called an electric blackboard because the telewriter receiving unit usually incorporates an overhead projection unit to enlarge the visual images for group viewing.

Teletext uses a broadcast television system to send information to receivers. The viewer can determine when something is seen, but cannot ask clarifying

---

TELEPHONE INSTRUCTION

Kirkwood Community College in Cedar Rapids, Iowa, equipped some classrooms with telephone transmitting and receiving equipment (microphones and speakers). Six similarly equipped classrooms are scattered in smaller towns and a state reformatory throughout the seven counties served by the college. Students are encouraged to attend classes near their homes. The college delivered about 34,000 contact hours of instruction in 1979–80 with about 28.5 students per class. Both credit and noncredit courses are being offered to nurses and others. The college has begun to broadcast two-way color television instruction to these sites.

questions. Thus, this is a one-way (no feedback) medium. Teletext information systems permit a home or school television viewer to select news headlines, sports scores, recipes, current stock market reports, as well as many other types of information. Office workers, researchers, and even homemakers now have access to a wider variety of information relevant to their needs than the average classroom student. Teletext systems will further challenge the educator to design learning environments that can successfully compete for students' attention.

A teletext system may be designed which provides user-requested information on the bottom of the television picture while a movie or other television program is shown on the top of the screen. The British developed a system called CERFAX in 1974 using BBC broadcasting facilities and brought about two hundred pages of constantly updated information to viewers via their television sets. The commercial network in England, not to be outdone, developed a similar system called ORACLE. The French then developed a system called ANTIOPE. This technology could be invaluable in political science classes or a variety of courses dealing with current information.

Another technology, videotext, involves sending information from a central computer using conventional telephone lines. The access to information is virtually unlimited and the user can select what information to see and control the timing of the display on a local computer terminal. The BBC began by developing a system for transmitting captions to help deaf individuals understand television broadcasts, and later included a much broader range of data transmission. Their work was further expanded by the French and the Canadians, and finally in 1982 Time Inc., Times Mirror, and others began trial service in the United States via coaxial cable, satellite, and telephone systems.

Radio

Radio instruction has not been used extensively in the United States in the past few years. Of the over seven thousand AM and FM stations authorized, only about 10 percent are educational stations and almost all are FM. Many other nations, however, have made very effective use of radio instruction. Mexico, Nicaragua, Venezuela, Iran, Australia, and other countries have utilized it for many purposes over vast distances to provide quality instruction to a large number of users.

One exciting use of radio instruction is found in Australia where it is a reasonable solution to the problem of transporting information to learners spread over an extremely large, but sparsely populated geographic area. The school day typically begins at 5:30 every morning with lessons relayed through a transmitter. Pupils use small transceivers supplied by the Department of Education to enable them to participate in the discussions. They are also furnished filmstrips and projectors, audiotape cassettes, educational games, library books, work materials such as crayons and paints, and a school magazine. The Department of Education also provides a tape recorder for the cassettes if needed. Students eventually enter residential secondary schools in large towns and have been found to be articulate, well read, and able to relate naturally to adults. Government officials feel the results of using radio have proved it to be well worth this effort.

Mexico, too, uses radio extensively in its Radioprimaria program. In a large research project in the state of San Luis Potosi, fourth-, fifth-, and sixth-grade instruction was provided by radio, and tests were then given in mathematics and Spanish. An evaluation concluded that the radio students were superior in Spanish and learned about the same in mathematics as nonradio students. In another study in Mexico, the Tarahumara Indians, living in a remote region in northwest Mexico, experienced high drop-out rates in the radio schools. However, for students remaining in the radio-program school through the fourth grade, achievement test scores were comparable to those of students in urban Mexico receiving more traditional instruction. One of the major benefits of Mexico's Radioprimaria is presented in a United Nations study that concluded the cost of the program to be about five cents per student-hour as opposed to ten cents for television instruction and forty-five cents for traditional teacher-based systems.

Radio-based instruction has a number of advantages:

- It is an effective instructional medium when supplemented by appropriate printed materials.
- It overcomes physical distribution problems, such as lack of roads and mail.
- It has low electrical energy requirements.
- Radio messages can be rebroadcast for flexibility at little extra cost.
- For many types of instruction, audio is the primary stimulus and the visual channel is not required.
- Students can listen to lessons at home, on a tractor, in a car, or in a formal learning environment.

Some disadvantages to using radio as the primary instructional medium include:

- Radio has low emotional or affective appeal compared to television or teacher-based instructional systems. This often results in a large number of drop-outs.
- Unless a two-way radio or telephone is used, there is no immediate feedback to the radio teacher so the rate of presentation may be adjusted to learner abilities.
- Feedback to students on their progress is difficult to provide.
- With radio there is much more potential for distraction since visual stimuli usually do not accompany it.

Tape Recorders and Record Players

Tape recorders and record players may be used in the classroom by a teacher who has a prerecorded tape or record. Both offer good-quality reproduction of a prerecorded message. In commercial situations, a tape recorder is usually used because of its slightly increased recording quality and capacity for editing or adding additional audio stimuli. Classroom teachers too, may edit tapes or produce their own tape recordings. Tapes can also be easily duplicated for individual use.

Tape recordings may be on reel-to-reel systems and played at 7½ inches per second, 3¾ inches per second, or 1⅞ inches per second. Professional recorders often run at 15 inches per second or faster. Usually the faster the tape goes by the recording and playback head, the better the quality and fidelity. It is also easier to edit a tape which has been recorded at a faster speed. It is advisable to develop the master recording on a high-speed, high-quality reel-to-reel system and then duplicate in onto other reel-to-reel tapes or cassettes.

Be certain to select the appropriate tape player for the prerecorded tape you wish to play. Not only must the speed be correct, but so must the track format. The various track formats for monaural and stereophonic audio are:

1.   Full-track monaural
2.   Half-track monaural
3.   Half-track stereophonic
4.   Quarter-track monaural
5.   Quarter-track stereophonic (the most widely used today)

High-quality tape recorders usually can record at frequency ranges somewhere between 30 and 22,000 cycles per second. However, most instructional requirements can be met by a frequency range from 50 to 12,000 C/S.

A synchronizer can be used with a tape recorder to advance a slide or filmstrip projector. It can either use an audible tone on the same track as the audio being listened to by the students, or placed on a second (stereo) track so it cannot be heard.

Cassettes are very popular today and inexpensive compared to reel-to-reel systems. Most cassette players operate at 1⅞ inches per second, so the fidelity of these systems suffers from this low speed. For most classroom applications, however, cassettes offer all the quality needed.

Language laboratories and dial-access audio systems are expensive to build and maintain. An alternative is to develop a system using inexpensive tape playback devices which, compared to expensive facilities, are easier and cheaper to maintain. If cassette players and cassette are checked out of a library or instructional materials center, the cost per use and the convenience to the user are often enhanced.

Record players are not used much in schools today because the tape recorder system is so flexible. Records are available at speeds of 33⅓, 45, or 78 revolutions per minute. Appropriate transcription or record playing equipment must be obtained and used if the teacher is to play the desired record.

Speech compressors are being used today to reduce the time necessary to

SPEECH COMPRESSORS AND TRAINING COSTS

The Jack Eckerd Corporation, a large southeastern firm with over 1,000 drugstores, uses speech compressors to save over 26,000 student hours. It uses the speech compressor to shorten its basic courses in orientation, basic sales, camera department sales, and drug department sales. The students in these courses usually adjusted their listening rate to one-and-a-half times the normal listening rate. Their range extended from a little faster than normal to about twice the normal speed.

John Swinney, Eckerd's instructional system designer, says that even with employees earning entry-level wages, speech compression would save nearly $125,000 in training time. In addition, the students in the self-instructional programs exhibit less fatigue when using the compressed materials.

listen to a spoken presentation. For some recordings, compression of up to 50 percent can be done without a loss of comprehension and retention. A compression of 15 percent is hardly discernible but will reduce an hour lecture by almost ten minutes. There is some research to indicate that speech compression improves attention and retention by reducing a learner's tendency to daydream.

Speech compression hardware technology is fairly well developed. Frequency attenuation can be done so that the "Mickey Mouse" high frequency sounds of speeded-up tapes are eliminated. Searching for pauses and reducing or eliminating them is another approach to compression. A third method is to randomly delete tiny segments of the recording which, because they are so brief, are not missed by the listener. Hardware for speech compression is now available for a few hundred dollars. Only one compressor is needed to make the master compressed-speech tape, from which duplicates are made to play on regular tape recorders. Some compressors even allow students to control the rate of compression to meet their own listening abilities.

SIMULATION AND GAMES

Play is pleasurable exploration in its simplest form, and simulations and educational games are formalized expansions of play. They provide for social, emotional, and cognitive growth to occur. Increasingly, educators are using simulations and games as teaching tools to increase student affect, promote decision-making skills, and refine psychomotor skills.

Simulations are abstractions of the real world. For example, an aircraft simulator allows the practice of dangerous maneuvers without physical danger to the operator or others. A simulation in a health science classroom of a computer-driven plastic body model allows students to note the effects of rare diseases or practice diagnosing common ones, without endangering real patients. Simulations also permit simplification by having learners focus on desired specific elements without the confusion of encountering the entire supersystem. One popular game gives players a chance to sample the realities of faculty career development without the problems of actual teaching, serving on committees, and the like. Simulations can also be employed to have students experience an exchange of values as they would in distant countries. The dynamics of political science could be illustrated by having students alternately role play, for example, an industrialist and an environmentalist, to observe their impact on the local political scene.

Simulations thus aid in the teaching of processes that would be difficult or impossible to teach by other methods, including the concepts of parallel processing, allocation of resources trade-offs which must be made in real life, conflict-resolution strategies, intuitive problem solving, social negotiating, communications skills, and acceptable social behaviors in conflict situations. Simulations and games are effective teaching methods because they are usually highly motivating. They are dramatic representations of reality or aspects thereof and are relatively risk-free abstractions that permit active exploration of cognitive and psychomotor problems.

Of the currently available commercial simulations, about a third are in the area of business, and another third in the social sciences and related disciplines. These commercially prepared games are generally available and easy to use. Toy and bookstores, as well as regular educational suppliers, have games covering a wide choice of subject areas for almost every age level, ranging in cost from a few dollars to hundreds of thousands of dollars. Simulators for flight training, nuclear power plant operation, and other complex skills may cost hundreds of thousands of dollars to prepare and hundreds of dollars per hour to operate. A games bibliography published by the Clearinghouse on Teacher Education contains at least sixteen hundred entries on low-cost games and simulations in seventy categories. There are also several publications of the "how to do it" variety for would-be simulation and game developers.

The advent of the microprocessor is making computer-based simulations more readily available at a relatively low cost. An educational revolution is currently taking place in this medium of instruction. We predict that many more teachers will have computer-based simulations relevant to their objectives and to students' needs in the near future.

A distinction is generally made between simulation games and other educational games. All games are characterized by competition, but simulation games incorporate elements of the real world while others do not. By introducing the competitive element of having winners and losers, greater learner interest is generated than would normally result. However, simulations and simulation games for educational purposes are time-consuming to design, field-test, and revise, which makes the process expensive.

Instructional simulations and simulation games have generally been found to be no more effective than traditional classroom instruction, although it seems intuitively logical that they would be more effective for certain types of objectives (interpersonal interactions, abstract concepts, dangerous situations). Some reasons for these findings are (1) they may have been developed improperly; (2) they are not used as an integral part of the instructional program; and (3) research has not yet provided enough information on how to increase their effectiveness. This, however, is only speculation based on the *assumed* potential of simulations and simulation games. Unfortunately, there is little useful information available which would help an instructional designer. More research, therefore, is needed on these teaching/learning tools.

MEDIA-SELECTION MODELS

Man-machine identity is achieved not by attributing human attributes to the machine, but by attributing mechanical limitations to man.
Mortimer Taube

Instructional strategy and media selection decisions are interrelated and should be done concurrently, after instructional objectives have been developed. The model used to select an instructional medium can be fairly simple or quite complex. Robert Mager, a successful commercial instructional designer, has said that paper is the medium of choice unless a good case can be made for using another. Paper materials are inexpensive to design and produce, simple to reproduce, easy to use, and understood by most students. This is an example of a simple model for media selection. Complexity, as in most decision-making procedures, should be avoided whenever possible. (A comparable military maxim is KISS—"Keep It Simple, Stupid.")

The instructional medium should present instructional stimuli in an efficient, easily understood manner. Complex media, which tend to be costly and time-consuming, often prove to be inefficient and unreliable. Use the least expensive instructional medium that will result in students' attaining the desired objectives within a reasonable amount of time. However, remember that using a low-cost medium that does not produce good results can be just as inefficient as using an expensive and complex one.

In many schools, fourteen or fifteen pieces of instructional materials are used each day for an average of ten to fifteen minutes each. Time and motion studies indicate that between one-third and one-half of all instructional time involves instructional materials. The design of these materials is important! First-graders enter school with a speaking vocabulary of several thousand words, yet many first-grade teachers use curriculum materials limiting the student to 180 new words during the year—only one new word a day. Some curriculum designers feel that sensory deprivation is occurring in these classrooms.

Choose a medium appropriate for the majority of objectives that can serve as the primary medium of instruction throughout the instructional program or unit of instruction. Additional media, such as an unusual animated visualization, may be selected for emphasis or motivation. Frequent media changes within a short period of time are often confusing, time-consuming, and expensive.

Several instructional media-selection models will be presented for your consideration. Each represents a different approach to media selection. Note how the models differ and consider what implications these differences may have for an instructional designer. Note also that Figure 10.1 does not present a formal fixed media-selection procedure.

A simple media-selection chart is often useful for listing the media choices for each objective. The chart permits both easy examination of the various media and determination of which will serve as the primary instructional medium.

In the relatively simple If-Then model (Figure 10–2), a maximum of five decisions must be made by an instructional designer in order to choose an instructional medium. This model was developed by one of the authors of this text for a military instructional development project. It is relatively easy to use and is based on the behavior and condition statements in an objective.

Another media selection model was developed by William Allen at the University of Southern California. In his model, the instructional designer must determine the general classification of an objective and then maximize the ability of the instructional media to accommodate that type of objective (see Figure 10.3).

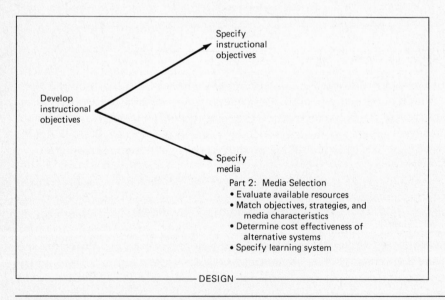

FIGURE 10.1   I.D. Model: Media Selection

MEDIUM OF INSTRUCTION

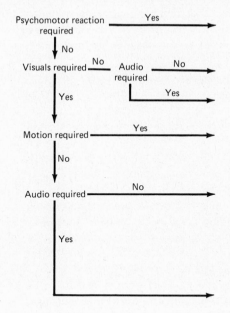

Psychomotor reaction required — Yes →

1. *Trainer*
2. *Simulation*
3. *Teacher* To analyze and feedback appropriateness of action

Visuals required — No — Audio required — No →

1. No instruction required

— Yes →

1. *Audio Tape* Print material optional, to provide reference
2. *Lecture* Print material optional

Motion required — Yes →

1. *VT*
2. *Film* Use for true color and greater definition; Usually more expensive than VT
3. *Models*

Audio required — No →

1. *Booklet/Handout*
2. *Programmed Booklet* Use if student is to learn a complex procedure and/or vocabulary
3. *Slide/Tape* Use tape for pacing or supplementary information; workbook optional
4. *Mediated Interactive Lecture* Use if few presentations are to be given or if student response analysis is required

Yes →

1. *Slide/Tape* Use if many presentations are to be given and/or if realistic audio is needed and if still visuals are needed. Workbook optional—provides reinforcement and data to refer to in the future
2. *Mediated Interactive Lecture* Use if few presentations are to be given or if student response analysis is required
3. *Booklet/Tape* Use if verbal description and/or visuals are to be given to the student and/or if individual pacing is required

FIGURE 10.2 If-Then Media-Selection Model

Allen's matrix is based on his review of hundreds of research studies. After discarding those not meeting rudimentary research criteria, he examined the effectiveness of the medium for the type of learning measured. From these results he created his matrix, which classifies media according to high, medium, or low achievement in that type of learning. Allen cautions that although the categories are his own and reflect his own opinion, they are nonetheless based on an extensive review of existing research. When using this model, the designer should attempt to avoid media rated low for that type of learning. If, however, the designer does select a low or medium format, he or she should be aware of its limitations and supplement it as tryout data indicates.

Reiser and Gagne (1982, 1983) reviewed several media-selection models and attempted to evaluate the learning effectiveness of the major features in those models. They also generated a selection model which identifies learner, setting, and task characteristics that should be given primary consideration in media selection.

Instructional Media Type	Learning Objectives					
	Learning Factual Information	Learning Visual Identifications	Learning Principles, Concepts, and Rules	Learning Procedures	Performing Skilled Perceptual-Motor Acts	Developing Desirable Attitudes, Opinions, and Motivations
Still pictures	Medium	HIGH	Medium	Medium	low	low
Motion pictures	Medium	HIGH	HIGH	HIGH	Medium	Medium
Television	Medium	Medium	HIGH	Medium	low	Medium
3-D objects	low	HIGH	low	low	low	low
Audio recordings	Medium	low	low	Medium	low	Medium
Programmed instruction	Medium	Medium	Medium	HIGH	low	Medium
Demonstration	low	Medium	low	HIGH	Medium	Medium
Printed textbooks	Medium	low	Medium	Medium	low	Medium
Oral presentation	Medium	low	Medium	Medium	low	Medium

Source: "Media Stimuli and Types of Learning." *Audiovisual Instruction*. Reprinted by permission of Association for Educational Communications and Technology. Copyright 1967.

FIGURE 10.3   Allen Media-Selection Model

Another approach to media selection involves applying criteria based on media characteristics. Gerlach and Ely (1980) presented five criteria that can be applied to the selection of instructional media after objectives have been identified and students' entering behaviors specified. They are (1) cognitive appropriateness (Can the medium transmit the stimuli required by the objective?); (2) level of sophistication (Is the medium understandable by the learner?); (3) cost (Can the expense be justified by the projected results?); (4) availability (Are hardware and software reasonably available?); and (5) technical quality (Are the audio and visual characteristics of the materials adequately produced?).

The form in Figure 10.4 graphically shows the relationship of objectives to each other and to the alternative media choices. The objectives listed in columns on the left side of the form are in the order in which they will be experienced by the learner. A check mark is then placed in the appropriate cell of the matrix. An instructional developer can thus easily see the suggested sequence of media usage. Using such a matrix is an excellent way of understanding and communicating media decisions, regardless of the media-selection model employed. It also helps avoid the problem of changing media too frequently.

Order media (1 high)	Psychomotor		Audio No Visual		Motion Visual			Visual No Audio				Audio and Visual		
Objective Number	Trainer/Simulation	Teacher	Audio Tape	Lecture	VT	Film	Models	Booklet/Handout	Programmed Booklet	Slide/Tape	Mediated Interactive Lecture	Slide/Tape	Mediated Interactive Lecture	Booklet/Tape

FIGURE 10.4   Media-Selection Report Form

MEDIA RESEARCH TRENDS AND SELECTION CRITERIA

Science is the refusal to believe on the basis of hope.

C. P. Snow

Another method of making media-selection decisions is to relate the general taxonomy position of each objective to student grouping requirements; that is, if the objectives are at the lower end of the cognitive taxonomy (for example, knowledge of specifics and comprehension), then certain types of teaching activities or media appear to be more appropriate for individualized instruction, whereas others are more appropriate for group instruction. Figure 10.5 presents three categories of learning: (1) lower-order cognitive, (2) psychomotor, and (3) affective and higher-order cognitive combined. For each category, instructional media are suggested for individual, small-group, and large-group instruction. Again, one of the main assets of this process is that it forces designers to carefully consider the range of available media before making a selection.

Objective Categories	Individual Instruction	Small Group	Large Group
Cognitive (lower order)	Textbooks Workbooks Audio tapes Programmed materials	Study groups Case studies	Lectures ITV Films
Psychomotor	Laboratory-directed practice	Simulation laboratory	Demonstrations
Affective and cognitive (higher order)	Research Fieldwork Application Internship	Discussion Simulation and gaming Human relations, feedback training	Field trips

FIGURE 10.5 Objective Taxonomy/Media-Selection Table

USING MEDIA AND INDIVIDUALIZED INSTRUCTION IN THE UNITED STATES ARMY

The U.S. Army has adopted a training philosophy requiring their Training and Doctrine Command (TRADOC) to export the expertise and training of the service schools via extension training packages to the units, where soldiers spend 90 percent of their time. Consequently, the job environment is where the soldier would undertake most of this training.

Due to the limited time soldiers can spend in service schools, TRADOC can only teach those areas demanding a large ratio of high-quality instructors to students or that require high-cost simulators and trainers. The remainder of the training is exported to the unit. Training packages based on critical job tasks are performance oriented and allow students to advance at their own pace. The mass-produced media that present the exported training must be cost-effective and be appropriate for the task and its intended users.

Integrated Technical Documentation and Training is aimed at decreasing institutionalized training, thereby reducing costs and increasing the effectiveness of equipment operation and maintenance. Presently, the media for the transfer of doctrinal, instructional, and technical material are predominately paper, Super 8mm film, or videotape. Experience indicates that as weapons systems become more complex, exportable training and technical manuals grow exponentially in complexity, quantity, and production cost. It is conceivable that videodiscs could reduce the problems and costs associated with the present media base.

Source: Abstracted from PIIN: DAAG39-78-R-9071, Page F.1, RFP, dated 26 Jan 1978.

The *economics* of alternative instructional systems also becomes a selection factor. In a specific situation in which all the systems are equally effective, the lowest-cost alternative would normally be selected. It should be pointed out that in many conventional instructional settings, media are an "add-on" cost over and above the teacher. Only when the total system is designed, and the teacher's role incorporated, can media use reduce cost. More will be said on this important topic in Chapter 12.

USING INSTRUCTIONAL MEDIA

The real danger is not that computers will begin to think like men, but that men will begin to think like computers.

Sydney J. Harris

Instructional materials often require some introduction by the teacher, and should be introduced in such a way that student attention can be directed to the most relevant parts of the materials. An introduction to media-based materials by a teacher can also include extrinsic motivation by way of content intended to increase student participation or attention. Announcing that a test will follow the presentation is one way of increasing attention. There is also some evidence that mildly increasing students' anxiety about the forthcoming presentation will result in increased attention. The instructor should check the equipment in advance to minimize its physical breakdown. There is also the problem of distribution of materials to student users and the storage of those materials.

It is often advisable to follow a media-based presentation with a summary and discussion. Some materials are designed to include all necessary introductory and summary information needed by the user, but many are not. Review exercises as well can provide additional reinforcement and examples specifically tailored to the situation. The teacher must evaluate both the instructional materials and the students to determine what will be required. In some instances, having students restudy materials (especially if they are short, high-information-density materials like many instructional films) will result in significantly increased learning. Again, the teacher must make decisions about the best way for students to use their time. To review, or not to review, *that* is the question.

All presentations used by students should be evaluated. Did the students learn what they were expected to learn? If the materials come from free sources, do they contain undesirable propaganda from the sponsor? Should the materials be used again in the future? What should the student do next? These and other questions concerning the evaluation of instructional materials will be discussed in further detail in the next chapter.

SUMMARY

Teaching today requires far too many people. It ought to be possible to do the job with far fewer. Teaching is where agriculture was around 1750, when it took some twenty men on the farm to feed one nonfarmer in the town. We have to make the teacher more productive, have to multiply his or her impact, have to increase greatly the harvest from his or her skill, knowledge, dedication, and effort.

Peter F. Drucker

Many of the media discussed in these chapters permit individualized instruction. The media provide channels of communication a single teacher could not begin to offer. One teacher faced with a group of students and no media usually has little choice but to provide grouped instruction. In a meta-analysis of fifty-one research studies Bangert, Kulik, and Kulik (1983) found that individualized instruction produced only a small effect on student achievement in secondary schools. An analysis of seventy-five college studies (Kulik, Kulik, and Cohen 1980), however, consistently showed that individualized instruction reduced variations in examination scores, raised student ratings of college courses, and reduced learning time. All the media discussed in this chapter may be chosen for individualized instruction for this older audience.

If an organization does not have the time, talent, or resources to produce a television program, it cannot select that medium for its courses. There are several sources of information on existing instructional materials to help determine whether a film or television program has been produced and is available. A list of these is included in Appendix B. Teachers may need to know when and how to produce their own instructional materials. However, this trade-off of time and costs to other professional activities is real and usually costly.

Often an instructional technologist's choice of available alternative media will be quite limited because of existing production facilities or administrative policy. In other cases, the costs of some media may be prohibitive when considering the limited number of users. For example, it is difficult to justify an expensive design and development effort for a seminar which will meet only once. After the media for the objectives in the lesson have been determined, it is usually advisable to list the objectives in their order of presentation, identifying the medium or media proposed for each. This is desirable so that the sequence of media use may be known. Then, if the media mix is too complex, simpler choices may be considered for substitution.

There are many media-selection models, each having unique strengths. But the major selection criterion for any program is: *Will it cause the student to learn the objectives?* If an instructional format or medium is not appropriate for the objectives, then it should not be considered. If there are alternative media that work equally well, the least expensive should be chosen.

Questions for Consideration and Discussion

1. Do you believe that there are always two or more alternative media for teaching a given set of objectives?
2. Should the least expensive medium that will work in conveying the desired stimuli to the learner always be used?
3. Under what circumstances would you decide to produce or use a motion-picture film rather than a television tape? How do these two media differ? To what degree do you believe that the instructional research involving film can be applied to television?
4. Would it be desirable to teach "television literacy" for the same reasons that written and spoken English are taught? Consider the following questions and activities as part of a visual or television literacy program:
    a. How does television make a food product or toy on a commercial look better than it really is?
    b. How does television influence your feeling about a character (consider laugh tracks, camera angles, use of light contrasts, special effects, music)?
    c. How does television make impossible things like Mork or the Hulk look real?
    d. What effect can an individual have on the television industry by writing to networks, stations, actors?
    e. What lasting impact do violent television programs, "Saturday morning" cartoons, "60 Minutes," or "Sesame Street" have on their viewers?

Suggested Activities

1. Identify the media you would select for the following circumstances and list your reasons.
    a. A ninth-grade English teacher would like to have the students hear an audio-instructional program of the "War of the Worlds." There is a competent A-V coordinator who can help locate materials.
    b. An adult-education instructor would like to teach the objective: "The students will be able to explain the components of a carburetor." The school has no facilities to produce elaborate instructional materials, but it can assist the teacher in preparing simple slides, transparencies, audio tapes, graphic materials, and the like. The room can be darkened with venetian blinds and there is an electrical outlet in the rear of the room.
2. What medium would you select to teach the media-selection models in this chapter? Why would it be desirable? What would the difficulties be in using the selected medium? Could you estimate the cost of using your proposed medium for this unit of instruction? Do you feel it is a reasonable cost?

Suggested Readings

Allen, W. H. (January 1967). Media Stimulus and Types of Learning. *Audiovisual Instruction*, 27–31.

Averch, H. S., et al. (1972). *How Effective Is Schooling?* Santa Monica, CA: Rand Corporation.

Bangert, R. L., Kulik, J. A., and Kulik, C. C. (1983). Individualized Systems of Instruction in Secondary Schools. *Review of Educational Research, 53*, 143–158.

Educational Testing Service. (1976). *Teachers Do Make a Difference.* Princeton, NJ.

Gerlach, V. S., and Ely, D. P. (1980). *Teaching and Media: A Systematic Approach.* Englewood Cliffs, NJ.: Prentice-Hall.

Hartley, J., Fraser, S., and Burnhill, P. (Summer 1974). A Selected Bibliography of Typographical Research Relevant to the Production of Instructional Materials. *Audio-Visual Communication Review,* 181–190.

Heath, R. W., and Nielson, M. A. (Fall 1974). The Research Basis for Performance-based Teacher Education. *Review of Educational Research, 44*, 463–484.

Hornik, R. (Summer 1981). Out-of-School Television and Schooling: Hypotheses and Methods. *Review of Educational Research, 51*(2), 193–214.

Jamison, D., Suppes, P., and Wells, S. (1974). The Effectiveness of Alternative Instructional Media: A Survey. *Review of Educational Research, 44*, 1–68.

Jamison, D. T., and McAnany, E. (1978). *Radio for Education and Development.* Beverly Hills, CA: Sage Publications.

Kulik, C., Kulik, J., and Cohen, P. (1980). Instructional Technology and College Teaching. *Teaching of Psychology, 7*(4), 199–205.

McAnany, E., Amison, D., and Spain, P., eds. (November 1975). Radio's Role in Informal Education: An Overview (paper prepared for *Radio's Educational Role in Development*). New York: World Bank.

Moldstad, J. A. (1974). Selective Review of Research Studies Showing Media Effectiveness: A Primer for Media Directors. *Audio Visual Communications Review,* 387–407.

Orlansky, J., and String, J. (August 1981). *Cost-Effectiveness of Maintenance Simulators for Military Training.* Arlington, VA: Institute for Defense Analysis. ED212252.

Reiser, R. A., and Gagne, R. M. (1982). Characteristics of Media Selection Models. *Review of Educational Research, 52*(4), 499–512.

———. (1983). *Selecting Media for Instruction.* Englewood Cliffs, NJ: Educational Technology Publications.

Schramm, W. (1977). *Big Media, Little Media.* Beverly Hills, CA: Sage.

Siegel, E. (1983). *The Future of Videotext.* White Plains, NY: Knowledge Industry Publications.

Stadsklev, R. (n.d.). *Handbook of Simulation Gaming in Social Education.* University, AL: Institute of Higher Education Research and Services, University of Alabama.

Taylor, J., and Walford, R. (1978). *Learning and the Simulation Game.* Beverly Hills, CA: Sage.

Wilkinson, G. L. (1980). *Media in Instruction: 60 Years of Research.* Washington, DC: Association for Educational Communications and Technology.

Well, S. (1976). *Instructional Technology in Developing Countries.* New York: Praeger.

PART THREE

Instructional Development

11

Instructional Materials: Location, Evaluation, Local Production, and Materials Management

A school should not be a preparation for life. A school should be life.
Elbert Hubbard

Objectives

After completing this chapter, you should be able to:

1. List the two primary components of information handling.
2. State four reasons why teachers should produce their own instructional materials and four reasons why they should not.
3. List six or more sources of instructional materials from memory.
4. List the items on an instructional materials evaluation form.
5. Identify, given a list of possible copyright violations, specific copyright violations.
6. Discuss problems of administrating the selection and evaluation of instructional materials.

After a learning problem has been identified and a solution designed, the instructional technologist determines whether appropriate instructional materials exist or new materials need to be created. The location and selection of current instructional materials is usually preferred to producing new ones, which is usually possible only with a large user population. However, large populations do permit the amortizing of costs over many users of the material. Hundreds or even thousands of potential users are often necessary to afford extensive instructional design. This amortization principle is basic to any technology. The more who use the instruction, the less costly it is per person. A single class of students may warrant four or five hours of preclass preparation by a teacher, but almost never several hundred hours.

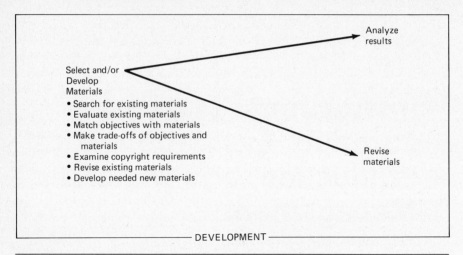

FIGURE 11.1   I.D. Model: Sources of Material Subsystem

In a school situation, the designer should check for available materials with the librarian, resource teachers, curriculum coordinator, and classroom teachers. If it is not possible to produce a new program to solve the instructional problem, it may then be necessary to use a labor-intensive lecture system to provide the necessary instruction. If there are no materials available that meet instructional-design requirements and a creative production is warranted from a cost standpoint, then production may occur. If the materials are to be duplicated and widely distributed or sold, copyright becomes a concern. While more will be said later concerning copyright, decisions on engaging in original production or using existing materials must take this factor into consideration.

SEARCHING FOR EXISTING MATERIALS

Education involves information handling. Educators, therefore, need to become information-handling specialists. The availability of information is increasing at a phenomenal rate. In many areas of study, the known information is doubling every ten years or less. Because teachers are the traditional channels of information for the students they must be concerned with information storage and retrieval. Instructional technologists, as problem solvers, also need access to information in order to identify and resolve problems.

Information storage and information retrieval are the two major components of information handling. The goal of information storage is to reduce space requirements in order to minimize cost. Storage costs are determined by the area required and the actual expenditure for this space. The storage system should also provide easy access to desired materials. Printed information originally published as books, pamphlets, periodicals, research reports, and the like can be more economically stored on paper, film, and magnetic tape.

The goal of information retrieval is to obtain desired information within minimum time at an acceptable cost. A textbook usually has two information-retrieval components: the table of contents and the index. The computerized information-handling system used by NASA illustrates an efficient storage and retrieval system for large volumes of information. It uses microfiche cards for storing information and a computer system to search for key words. Microfiche cards reduce the bulk of the material being stored, and make it available to users at relatively low costs. Even though a microfiche system requires camera equipment and technicians to operate the system, the space saved and the protection of the original more than offset the costs of this system. The computer rapidly searches a vast data bank to locate the documents most relevant to the user.

The Educational Resources Information Center (ERIC) is a similar information-handling system designed for educators. ERIC makes information available in either "hard copy" (paper) or microfiche form. ERIC-stored information is retrieved by either a manual or computer search. Both approaches to searching usually begin by identifying descriptors in the ERIC Thesaurus. The descriptors are then manually traced through Resources in Education (RIE), or entered for computer search. The ERIC collection contains both a citation index to periodical literature and ERIC documents stored on fiche and available in hard copy. Generally, searchers looking for sources of instructional material will find the ERIC documents more helpful than the literature citations. ERIC documents are identified by an ED prefix to the document number. Examples of ERIC documents are curriculum guides, course outlines, lists of sources, and descriptions of development projects.

The availability of instructional materials may be determined from sources that include:

- National Information Center for Educational Materials (NICEM)
- Publishers' and distributors' catalogs and brochures
- Media-center catalogs, such as film-rental libraries, IMCs, school libraries, community libraries
- *Epiegram* (a publication of Educational Products Information Exchange)
- Reviews of materials in professional journals
- Professionals such as instructional materials directors, resource specialists, and curriculum specialists
- Subject bibliographies for such categories as content area, medium, age level, free, inexpensive, and so on

Detailed lists of sources of instructional materials according to medium are found in Appendix A. These lists will be useful once you have made a decision concerning the desired medium. You will want to preview any of these materials before using them with students to ensure their quality and relevance to the targeted objectives. If the materials are not quite what you need, you may wish to ask permission of the copyright owner to purchase and modify the materials to meet your requirements. Some materials may be shown in part so that only their most relevant sections are presented to the learners.

The National Information Center for Educational Media (NICEM) publishes directories with the most complete listing of available nonprint materials in a wide variety of subject fields. The listings are updated frequently. Currently, information for over 300,000 main entries is available. Nonprint indexes include information about 16mm educational films, filmstrips, audiotapes, videotapes, records, 8mm motion cartridges, overhead transparencies, and slides. NICEM also has multimedia indexes for vocational and technical education, special education, psychology, and environmental studies. The NICEM data bank can be searched manually using the directories, or via computer data services. The NICEM data tapes are available through several database services.

The references mentioned thus far do not provide critical evaluations or comparisons of materials. Occasionally a reviewer will provide a critique of materials, but this occurs too infrequently for an instructional materials user to depend on reviews for current information. The Educational Products Information Exchange (EPIE) is a subscription service that evaluates selected instructional materials and equipment and publishes its findings in the *Epiegram*.

EVALUATING INSTRUCTIONAL MATERIALS

Selecting appropriate commercial instructional materials is desirable when developing instructional programs. As mentioned earlier, these materials must meet the needs of the lesson objectives. There may be times when an instructional designer will expand the lesson objectives to include those which are included in an outstanding set of instructional materials. Usually, however, the lesson's objective requirements will be the primary basis for selecting materials.

The following questions should be asked when evaluating instructional materials:

- Is the product well organized? A good set of instructional materials will clearly relate its facts to a few basic ideas in an organized manner.
- Do the materials prepare the learner for the presentation? Some designers feel that supplying the course objectives or advance organizers at the beginning of a lesson is useful in preparing the learner for the presentation.
- Do the materials keep the learners' attention? Color visuals, motion, music, surprise, novelty, drama, conflict, and other attributes may be used by the designer to attract the learner.
- Do the materials provide sufficient repetition through examples, illustrations, questions, and the like, to result in an understanding of the content? Is the

presentation well paced? Do the learners have time to think about and accept the presentation?

- Have the materials been presented in a technically competent manner? Audiotapes with distracting hissing sounds, visuals unintentionally out of focus, and music which drowns out the narrator are examples of technical problems that may inhibit a learner from benefiting from an instructional presentation.

One of the best ways to determine if the materials are usable for a particular student is to preview the materials. A materials evaluation form will suggest relevant questions to ask concerning the content and technical aspects of a set of materials. Such a form will also permit better comparison of materials if there are several from which to choose. A common materials evaluation form could probably be developed, but each medium has different characteristics which need to be examined. Films and television materials, for example, may use animated graphics, a characteristic unique to these media. Some media permit the use of audio stimuli, others do not. An example of an effective slide-tape materials evaluation form is presented in Figure 11.2. This form was chosen because it illustrates both audio- and visual-related questions. Keep in mind that evaluation of materials is difficult to do without actually testing the materials with students. Beware of free and inexpensive materials. Use them, but do so wisely. They are usually free for a reason, often because they are supported by commercial concerns with something to sell. The thousands of students who eat food, wear clothes, use soap, and buy records are seen as a captive audience by industrial producers and distributors. Thus, a film on nutrition may use all of one producer's products and discreetly plug its own "sugar-coated" products.

DECIDING WHEN TO PRODUCE MATERIALS

Producing instructional materials is both expensive and time-consuming. We suggest that when making the decision to produce instructional materials that will take over one hour, a market analysis should be performed to determine if the time and effort are warranted. Because of the cost associated with producing instructional material of high technical quality and proven effectiveness, it is almost always necessary to reproduce a large number of these materials to reduce the cost per use to a rational level. Reproduction will result in the design costs being amortized or shared by each set of materials so the overall cost per use declines as the number of copies increases.

For example, if a car manufacturer designed a model and then produced just one car, its cost would be in the hundreds of millions of dollars. But if the model were replicated over and over, design costs would be shared. This is a basic principle of both industrial and instructional technology. Just as cars can be produced in different colors and with many options, instructional materials may be designed to permit options, among which are responding to learners of differing abilities, learning styles, backgrounds, and interests.

Producer _____

Evaluator _____

Date _____

SLIDE TAPE EVALUATION FORM

A. Unit Topic:

B. Student Population:

C. Behavioral Objectives:

D. Slides: Technical

	Excellent	Average	Poor
Exposure	5	4 3 2	1
Color Balance	5	4 3 2	1
Focus	5	4 3 2	1
Framing	5	4 3 2	1
Legibility	5	4 3 2	1
Composition	5	4 3 2	1
Viewing Time	5	4 3 2	1

Slides: Content

Continuity	5	4 3 2	1
Originality	5	4 3 2	1
Use of Humor or Drama	5	4 3 2	1

E. Tape: Technical

Fidelity	5	4 3 2	1
Balance	5	4 3 2	1
Mix	5	4 3 2	1

Tape: Content

Support visuals	5	4 3 2	1
Originality	5	4 3 2	1
Vocabulary	5	4 3 2	1

F. Were the media appropriate for the objectives?

G. What I liked about this program is

H. What I did not like about this program is

FIGURE 11.2 Slide–Tape Evaluation Form

Teachers often make their own instructional materials at high cost to themselves and to their districts. Both parties may not realize that those who develop their own instructional material reduce the time available to develop lesson plans, talk with students, grade papers, or perform other tasks. Educational administrators often feel that a teacher's time is of little value—that is, the time a teacher devotes to making materials is "free" time—since the district has already paid for it. This, however, is not the case! There are always alternative uses of time. The key question should be, "What are the lost opportunity costs of engaging in this activity?" Using teachers as artists and producers of materials is frequently a misuse of time and talent. Most production should be done by skilled and specialized individuals who have the training and ability to rapidly produce inexpensive instructional materials. Moreover, many teachers are not artists or do not have voices that record well, and few instructors have the technical skill to develop their own photographs or other visuals.

Often a team of individual specialists works together to produce instructional materials. A curriculum specialist, an evaluation specialist, a management specialist, an instructional development specialist, a content specialist, and perhaps others may be brought together to design, develop, and refine a set of instructional materials. This group of specialists can produce a far superior product than an individual teacher because of the shared effort and expertise.

Before deciding to proceed with developing new materials, you must determine whether there is enough time, personnel, and financial backing with which to produce the needed materials. Estimates for the development of materials range from fifty to a hundred fifty person-hours of development time to one hour of instruction. This range is usually true in the development of computer-assisted instruction materials, filmed materials, and taped materials using a systematic model that includes an assessment of the problem as well as an evaluation and revision of the materials until they meet the specified instructional objectives. It may take, however, as many as two thousand hours to develop one hour of instruction. The physical act of writing and photographing materials is trivial compared to the analysis and design. If the resources to produce materials are available, then objectives should be collected and personnel scheduled using a PERT chart or other management techniques.

Before beginning production, instructional objectives should again be reviewed to confirm their sequential order. The objectives may then be arranged into units of instruction (often described as modules of instruction) and, if necessary, into full courses of instruction.

If the project is sizable, or if a technical writer is to be used, it may be advisable for the designer to write lesson specifications before developing a storyboard. The lesson specifications contain an outline of each module, objectives, key points to be included, illustrative examples, sample test questions, illustrative graphics, and anything else which will assist the writer in completing the script. Designers who will also be the writers may wish to proceed directly to developing the storyboard. A storyboard is the bridge between the message and the audience. A sample storyboard form is shown in Figure 11.3. The scripting of materials requires the instructional designer to:

- Clarify difficult points through visual illustration.
- Simultaneously engage two senses that may attract and maintain the user's attention without the senses interfering with each other.
- Determine the best approach to convey the message quickly and clearly.
- Isolate and focus student attention on the main points required by the objectives.

A scriptwriter must think visually. Sound and the written word are often not as reliable as a mere visual presentation for developing student retention. Visuals may be allowed to carry the message by using narration to clarify and reinforce the message. You should be certain that the graphics, written material, and audio support each other. Making complex material easy to understand is the goal of good instruction, so reduce difficult material into simpler segments. The duration of visual exposure will depend on the complexity or detail of the image, the learners' familiarity with the subject, and the affective reaction desired. Generally, a long shot will be shown longer than a close-up because there

Lesson No. _____   Page No. ____

STORYBOARD

Title _____

Scene No. _____

(Graphic art
or
narrative
description)

(Verbal/written
script)

Scene No. ____

(Second visual)

(Script)

FIGURE 11.3   Storyboard Format

is more to see. A still visual should generally not be shown for more than forty seconds. Usually, the faster images change, the more exciting the presentation.

Many additional design guides should generally be followed. Know your audience. Do not repeat what they already know. Use a vocabulary the students understand. Do not present more than they can grasp. Keep their attention by changing the format or the activity. (Most presentations, even good ones, begin to lose their effectiveness after thirty minutes.) Talk to your audience and be as concrete as possible. Do not repeat too much, but do review the major points at the end of each presentation.

Effective visuals can be designed using simple images. The narrative should clarify and amplify what is in the visual. Charts, outlines, and other graphic presentations should be used whenever possible to promote long-term retention, and color can be utilized for emphasis, coding, or realism. Above all, design readable graphics! Emphasis can be added or subtracted by the choice of shots. A close-up says to a viewer, "This is important!" A medium shot suggests that this information is more general and less specific than that presented in a close-up. A long shot is usually used to provide background information: an orientation.

Narration should be simple and concise. Deadwood such as "In this slide we will see . . . " should be avoided, as well as jargon and cliches. Background music should be used with caution, so that it does not interfere with the narration in an audio presentation.

Much of the formative evaluation can and should be done on the presentation by having students from the target population read a storyboard. Revision of a storyboard is much less costly than that of a finished product. Moreover, research shows that students will learn as much from reading the storyboard as from the completed product.

If the storyboard requires many visuals, use a quick-draw artist to facilitate its development. This will permit the subject-matter experts reviewing the storyboards to see actual rough visuals and will also allow students who use the materials for formative evaluation purposes to better understand the presentation. Final artwork will then be redone to conform to higher quality standards.

The next steps involve producing the materials, completing the formative evaluation, performing a summative evaluation of the entire package, and adopting the materials. A more complete discussion of the process involved in producing materials is beyond the scope of this book, but Appendix E provides some additional general guidelines.

COPYRIGHT

Copyrighting of print materials began in England with the Statute of Anne in 1710 to protect publishers from the unscrupulous who pirated their materials. The first national copyright law in the United States was passed in 1790 and revised in 1831 (to include musical compositions), 1870, and 1909. Additional laws were passed in 1976 because of a dramatic increase in the ability to duplicate articles, books, and radio and television programs. The 1976 copyright law is an attempt to balance the rights of the copyright holder with the information needs of a democratic public; that is, to determine the "fair use" of published materials.

The following guidelines are minimum standards for fair use of copyrighted materials for educational purposes under the copyright law of 1976. This information on copyright law will change due to court interpretations and is presented here to serve only as a guide to acceptable copying practice. Instructional technologists should continue to monitor court decisions and legislative action to determine currently acceptable practices.

First of all, copyright infringement is a crime. It is a crime against the producer and distributor who will not be paid for their ideas and products. It attacks creativity and the willingness of an individual writer or artist to risk publishing original ideas. The laws regarding print copyright are found in the Congressional Record as House Report 94–1476 (1976).

The following guidelines are abstracted from the American Publishers Association:

A single copy of the following may be made by or for a teacher for his or her scholarly research or instructional purposes:

1. Chapter from a book
2. Article from a periodical or newspaper
3. Short story, short essay, or short poem, whether or not from a collective work
4. Chart, graph, diagram, drawing, cartoon, or picture from a book, periodical, or newspaper

Multiple copies, not to exceed more than one copy per pupil in a course, may be made by or for the teacher giving that course, providing that:

1. The copying meets the tests of brevity and spontaneity as defined below.
2. The copying meets the cumulative effect test as defined below
3. Each copy includes a notice of copyright.

Some of the key definitions in the "fair use" doctrine include:

Brevity: 1. *Poetry:* a complete poem if less than 250 words and if printed on not more than two pages or, from a longer poem, an excerpt of not more than two hundred fifty words. 2. *Prose:* (a) either a complete article, story, or essay of less than twenty-five hundred words, or (b) an excerpt from any prose work of not more than one thousand words or 10 percent of the work, whichever is less. 3. *Illustration:* one chart, graph, diagram, drawing, cartoon, or picture per book or periodical issue. 4. *Special works:* certain works in poetry, prose, or in "poetic prose," which combine language with illustrations and are intended sometimes for children and at other times for a more general audience, and that are less than twenty-five hundred words in their entirety. Such special works may *not* be reproduced in their entirety; however, an excerpt comprising not more than two of the published pages of such special work and containing not more than 10 percent of the words found in the text thereof may be reproduced.

Spontaneity: The copying is at the request of an individual teacher, and the inspiration and decision to use the work and the moment of its use for maximum teaching effectiveness are so close in time that it would be unreasonable to expect a timely reply to a request for permission.

Cumulative: The copying of the material is for only one teacher for one course in the school. No more than one short poem, article, story, or essay or more than two excerpts may be copied from the same author; nor more than three used from the same collective work or periodical volume during one class term. There should not be more than nine instances of such multiple copying for one course during one class term.

Notwithstanding the above, the following are prohibited:

1. Copying is not to be used to create or replace or substitute for anthologies, compilations, or collective works. Such replacement or substitution may occur if copies of various works or excerpts therefrom are accumulated or reproduced and used separately.
2. No copying is allowed of or from works intended to be "consumable" in the course of study or teaching. These include workbooks, exercises, standardized tests, and test booklets and answer sheets, and the like. Copying cannot substitute for the purchase of books, publisher's reprints, or periodicals; be directed by higher authority; or be repeated with respect to the same items by the same teacher from term to term.
3. No charge shall be made to the student beyond the actual cost of the photocopying.

In 1983 a group of book publishers settled out of court a lawsuit charging New York University and several of its professors with copyright infringement. The university and the scholars were charged with using photocopies of protected works for an anthology-like text, without seeking the publishers' permission. In return for the publishers' dropping the suit, the university agreed to control unauthorized photocopying of copyrighted works by faculty members. A representative of the Association of American Publishers cautioned other institutions that it would continue to closely monitor the photocopying done at colleges across the nation. Teachers and trainers at all levels should be aware of the potential consequences of violating copyright laws.

School teachers and university professors can easily make video- and audiotapes from television and radio broadcasts. They regularly use off-air copying equipment in order to record broadcast programs for their classes. Guidelines for copying of off-air broadcasts which are within the fair-use doctrine include:

- Off-air recordings may be made only at the request of and used by individual teachers, and may not be regularly recorded in anticipation of requests. No broadcast program may be recorded off-air more than once at the request of the same teacher, regardless of the number of times the program may be broadcast.
- A limited number of copies may be reproduced from each off-air recording to meet the legitimate needs of teachers under these guidelines.
- Do not transfer, distribute, or use the copy outside of the school where it was produced.
- Taping for research purposes is a legitimate reason for copying materials off-air.
- A videotape copy of an off-air broadcast may be retained for a limited amount of time—not to exceed forty-five consecutive calendar days after date of recording. You can show it to a class once within the first ten days; remaining time is for evaluation purposes.
- All copies of off-air recordings must include the copyright notice on the broadcast program as recorded.
- Educational institutions are expected to establish appropriate control procedures to maintain the integrity of these guidelines.

An instructional resources coordinator may not make an audiocassette of a record for more efficient storage or retrieval purposes unless, under certain circumstances, a replacement is unavailable at fair prices (Section 108). The coordinator may not make copies of records or audiotapes in order that the original be preserved as a master. This practice clearly deprives the producers of additional sales. On the other hand, a student preparing an audio project for a course may use copyrighted music as background music. Individuals in their homes may also tape musical works for their own personal use. Teachers, though, may not make copies of musical works for distribution to students.

Writers or developers of software for computers are becoming increasingly concerned with obtaining legal protection for their programs. The Federal Computer Software Copyright Act of 1980 protects images but it does not prevent someone from studying the logic and writing their own parallel program. Trade secrets are established by having an attorney draw up a software license agreement with a provision that specifies what the secret is, who may have access to it, and for how long. Trade-secret protection protects ideas, designs, and concepts, as well as the software image. Another form of protection for the computer programmer may be obtained from patenting his or her idea. In one decision, the court declared that the more a program is embodied in the hardware, or the more significant the post-algorithm activity, the more possible it becomes to patent the program.

The above are only guidelines and are not provided as legal advice. See the list of references at the end of the chapter for additional sources of information on copyright guidelines. Instructional technologists should also be aware that their role and liability concerning copyright are not completely clear. The language used in the above description consistently uses the term "teacher." It is not clear whether instructional technologists will be defined as teachers or not. Also, the issue of spontaneity will no doubt result in several test cases in court. Can a designer claim spontaneity when the models clearly and specifically state that planning, testing, and reviewing are integral to the process? Obviously, designers associated with large or highly visible projects should seek copyright clearance, as well as keep an eye on future developments in the field of copyright.

SUMMARY

It is not always possible to locate commercial materials that will completely satisfy the objectives of a lesson. When this occurs, trade-offs must often be made. Can the available materials be used in part, or modified and combined with other materials to attain the desired ends? Will this modification result in undesirable consequences such as the violation of copyright? Will it be acceptable to modify the instructional objectives to incorporate the existing materials?

A central concern of any instructional evaluator or designer is whether or not the materials attain the stated objectives. If they do not, the materials should not be adopted and used. All materials should be used only insofar as they are directly related to one or more of the instructional objectives.

Using other people's ideas without crediting and rewarding them is unethical and often illegal. Those who develop or create should be rewarded for their efforts. We presented several guidelines for the use of copyrighted materials in this chapter. Ignoring them could be hazardous to your professional health.

Questions for Consideration and Discussion

1. The research on the effectiveness of instruction via storyboards suggests they teach almost as well as the finished instructional materials. If this is correct, why would instructional developers elect to proceed with this relatively expensive production phase of instructional development?
2. How does copyright affect the ability of instructional technologists to modify existing materials?

Suggested Activities

1. Develop a list of sources of free or inexpensive materials which might be useful to you in the future.
2. Evaluate two different types of instructional materials and discuss your judgments with your fellow students and your instructor.

Suggested Readings

Abt, C. C. (1970). *Serious Games.* New York: Viking.

Allen, S. (1981). *A Manager's Guide to Audiovisuals.* Hightstown, NJ: CRM/McGraw-Hill.

Allen, W. H. (Summer 1975). Intellectual Abilities and Instructional Media Design. *Audio-Visual Communication Review,* 139–170.

American Library Association. (1977). *The New Copyright Law: Questions Teachers and Librarians Ask.* Washington, DC: National Education Association.

Association for Educational Communications and Technology. (1977). *Copyright and Educational Media: A Guide to Fair Use and Permissions Procedures.* Washington, DC: The Association.

Brown, J. W., and Norberg, K. D. (1965). *Administering Educational Media.* New York: McGraw-Hill.

Chisholm, M. E., and Ely, D. P. (1976). *Media Personnel in Education: A Competency Approach.* Englewood Cliffs, NJ: Prentice-Hall.

Copyright Office. (1977/1978). *General Guide to the Copyright Act of 1976.* Washington, DC: Library of Congress.

Cruickshank, D. R., and Telfor, R. A. n.d. *Simulations and Games: An ERIC Bibliography.* Washington, DC: ERIC Clearinghouse on Teacher Education.

Greguras, F. M. (June 1981). Software Security: A New Look at Patentability. *Mini-Micro Systems,* 161–164.

Horn, R. E., ed. (1978). *The Guide to Simulations/Games,* 3rd ed. Cranford, NJ: Didactic Systems.

Johnston, D. (1981). *Copyright Handbook.* New York: R. R. Bowker.

Sinofsky, E. R. (January 1984). Issues: Copyright in a Nutshell. *Instructional Innovator,* 84(1), 44–47.

———. (1984). *Off-air Videotaping: Issues, Decisions, Implications.* New York: R. R. Bowker.

Sirkin, A. F. (September 1979). A Guide to Video Resources. *Journal of Library Automation,* 233–241.

Troost, F. W. (December 1979). Copyright Today: Current Areas of Controversy. *Audiovisual Instruction,* 24(9), 52–53.

U.S. Congress. House. *Copyright Law Revision,* House Report 94–1476 to accompany H.R. 13136–8, 94th Cong., 2nd sess., 1976.

12

Choosing a Teaching/
Learning System:
Economic Considerations

Replication is the key which unlocks the economics of technology.
K. Gustafson

Objectives

After completing this chapter, you should be able to:

1. List three reasons why instructional technology students need to be aware of the cost of different instructional systems.
2. Define and contrast cost-effectiveness and efficiency.
3. Discuss the relationship between goal or objective attainment and effectiveness.
4. Define the following terms: accountability, performance contracting, management by objective.

Can anyone afford to use instructional technology? Should they afford these procedures or materials? These are difficult questions about which to generalize. Most of the answers to date have resulted from the research on cost-effectiveness (producing the desired results with minimum costs) in education. From these studies we derive the central question: "How can one maximize learning and minimize cost and time requirements for student learning?" Concern for cost-effectiveness appears throughout the field of instructional technology. The instructional technologist develops programs or systems that will minimize development and implementation time, as well as evaluation costs. And, as we have said, if there are alternative teaching strategies or media, the least costly is often the best choice.

Instructional technology-based teaching and learning systems provide alternatives to teacher-based teaching systems. It has long been known that some teachers are more effective than others for particular students. Student learning (output) is greater, whereas the requirements of the system (input) are the same or less. More specifically, some teacher systems:

- Help students better appreciate or like the course content and the act of learning. *(Output)*
- Help students to better attain the objectives. *(Output)*
- Require less time to achieve the learner objectives. *(Input)*
- Require less money to help students attain their objectives. *(Input)*

Thus, some teacher-based systems are more cost-effective than others in the sense that the outputs of the system are higher and the inputs are the same or lower.

If a low-salaried teacher is effective in keeping the objectives growth high and the requirements of the system low, then a school-board member can be fairly certain that the teacher is cost-effective. Unfortunately for this illustration, first-year teachers are seldom outstanding in this respect.

Educators generally do not seem to make very efficient use of their instructional dollars; we are not cost-effective. A Rand Corporation study entitled *How Effective Is Schooling?* concluded that "there is virtually no examination of the cost implications of research results. This makes it very difficult to translate research results into policy-relevant statements." (p. ix) The study also says that increasingly, expenditures on traditional educational practices are not likely to improve educational outcomes substantially. A third major policy implication suggests that "there seem to be opportunities for significant reduction or redirection of educational expenditures without deterioration in educational outcomes." (p. 155) Money alone does not seem to buy quality education. Comparisons of teacher salaries and the total cost per pupil do not result in an output that is consistent with the increased expenditure level.

As Figure 12.1 shows, educational costs (input) have no direct relation to output as measured by SAT achievement scores. The average verbal score nationally on the SAT was 478 in 1963, but it declined steadily thereafter and hit bottom in 1980 at 424. It remained at 424 in 1981 and rebounded slightly to 426

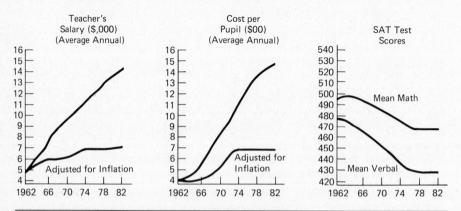

FIGURE 12.1   Does Money Buy Quality Education?

in 1982. The average math score nationally fell from 502 in 1963 to 466 in 1980 and moved up to 467 in 1982. Only 9 percent of the students taking the SAT scored over 500 on both portions of the test.

The single largest budget item in an elementary, secondary, or higher education budget is for teaching personnel. It may be as high as 45 percent of the total annual operating budget or 75 to 80 percent if capital outlay is not included in these figures. As classes are reduced in size, the personnel cost is dramatically increased. However, at present, there is little evidence that this cost increase will improve output. According to research, there is no consistent relationship between class size and student achievement.

One of the reasons school teachers do not have as much impact on learning as might be expected is suggested by time/motion studies. Teachers, on average, appear to spend approximately 30 percent of their time in activities that are related to academic instruction or learning. Typically, less than an hour a day is spent in individual or small-group teaching, averaging about two minutes per

"Please feel free to call on me if any of you think you need individual attention."
(Gotham)

DECENTRALIZED EMPLOYEE TRAINING AT
METROPOLITAN PROPERTY AND LIABILITY

Metropolitan Property and Liability, a division of Metropolitan Life, expects to dramatically increase its policyholders in the next few years. This growth will demand many more trained (and updated) employees. They say, "You simply have to find an easier and cheaper way [to provide training] or you buy stock in airlines [to bring the employees in for centralized training]." Vice President of Claims Salvatore De Salvo feels that once-a-year centralized office sessions may be manageable, but he adds, "Constant changes in state laws coupled with our own policy changes require frequent updating of personnel—at least quarterly. And assuring a consistent body of knowledge in a field requires close control on training. We're always on the lookout for ways to convey such information cheaply and concisely." De Salvo continued, "We have found we can now produce an entire film for what it used to cost to fly one student in from California for centralized training."

---

student in a class of twenty-five. Routine activities such as clerical work, housekeeping, and behavior control often consume about 40 percent of the school day. About 10 percent of the day is devoted to nonteaching tasks such as making announcements, participating in ceremonies, and the like. The remaining 20 percent of the day is devoted to class planning, student evaluation, administration, and out-of-class activities.

In the Rand study mentioned earlier, when the effect of teacher activities on learning was studied, it was concluded, "The research on teaching approaches, teacher differences, class size, and the like shows no consistent effect on student achievement, as measured by standardized cognitive tests." Jamison, Suppes, and Wells (1974) summarized the impact of teacher behavior, stating, "given the well-documented, strong association between student achievement and variables such as socioeconomic status and ethnic status, the effects of techniques of teaching on achievement . . . are likely to be inherently trivial." (p. 481)

In a summary of thirty-five studies considering class size, Bridge, Judd, and Moock (1979) found five in which increases in class size had a positive effect, five in which increases had a negative effect, and fifteen in which increases had no effect. Nonetheless, traditional teacher-based systems do at least partially work. Some students learn very well and most progress, at least to some degree. The use of alternative instructional systems, however, is effective with other students and thereby may increase the average amount of learning per unit of time. The key to developing instructional systems that really work is systematic design. Making cosmetic changes in classrooms and instructional strategies is not likely to produce significantly different outcomes. Only major reexamination of the entire instructional process holds out much hope for substantial increases in output.

MANAGEMENT BY OBJECTIVE (MBO)

A manager, making the assumption that employees are trustworthy and open-minded, may wish to ask them to participate in setting their own objectives. Employees and management will then agree to a periodic review to see if the objectives are being met. The employees are usually rewarded for their efforts depending on how well their objectives are attained.

Many businesses in the United States use MBO to some degree. A number of motivational benefits often result from the use of this technique. The process of sharing in objective setting often results in a sense of acceptance, belonging, and importance. The use of MBO techniques can also arouse an urge to achieve as the employee meets self-selected objectives. This two-way objective setting can be a powerful force for increasing job satisfaction.

The educational counterpart of MBO is contract learning. Under this arrangement, student and teacher decide on a set of objectives (and perhaps the strategies for achieving them). An evaluation procedure is identified and progress checkpoints established at predetermined intervals. It then becomes the student's responsibility to achieve the terms of the contract. Evidence suggests that contract learning works well with highly motivated, independent learners but is less successful with poorly organized students who lack self-discipline. Some teachers also have great difficulty with this strategy. Like all instructional formats, contract learning is no panacea. It must be carefully planned and implemented so students and teachers will benefit from its use.

ECONOMIC DECISION GUIDELINES

When there are two or more instructional strategies which result in the desired level of student learning, the least costly method should be selected.

F. Knirk

To relate learning outputs with their required cost and time inputs, it is advisable to visualize the relationship of inputs to outputs in terms of efficiency. Efficiency is maximized by high objective attainment, minimum cost, and minimum student time requirements. This relationship is summarized by the following equation:

$$\text{Efficiency} = \frac{\text{Objective Attainment}}{\text{Cost} \times \text{Time}}$$

It is important to recognize the value of cognitive, psychomotor, and affective objectives when considering this equation. School personnel and parents want their students to like the learning process and the content as well as develop cognitive and psychomotor skills. Behavioral measures of affective objectives may be reflected by attendance trends, tardiness, number of books checked out of the library, and so on. Unfortunately, affective objectives are seldom included in the determination of cost-effective instruction. If the desired level of objective attainment is not obtained from a teaching system, eliminate it from any further cost-effective analysis. A system that does not meet the requirements of the task is neither efficient nor cost-effective.

A number of models for making instructional decisions involving qualitative as well as economic decisions have been developed and used. For example, Wagner (1982) evaluated several existing innovative systems, such as the Open University in Great Britain and the Telesecundaria radio project in Mexico, and then proposed an economics-based decision-making model for media selection.

A great deal of research effort in education is devoted to studying individual differences. Most studies compare individuals using achievement and intelligence test scores. These tests compare the performance of students of common age on norm-referenced instruments, which compare students with each other. *Norm-referenced* grading assumes students will be distributed across a range (often the normal curve) and will thus evaluate some as "high" and others as "low." In contrast, *criterion-referenced* grading compares each learner to pre-established external criteria. There is no assumption of distribution; all can earn an A or an F or anything in between. In contract learning, students can agree to achieve some specified amount of performance to obtain a C, an additional amount for a B, and so on.

In any event, the output of the system—the attainment of the desired objectives—must be realized before time or cost requirements become relevant.

Systematically developed instructional systems can also be compared to conventional instruction in terms of effectiveness and efficiency. Only in the last two decades have instructional technology-based systems undergone the extensive evaluation and revision cycle required to ensure that they would work.

TIME-EFFICIENT INSTRUCTION AT THE POLICE ACADEMY USING CRITERION REFERENCED INSTRUCTION

Using a Criterion Referenced Instruction model to design its instructional program, the Metropolitan Washington, D.C., Police Academy has redesigned its curriculum. Following demonstrations on videotape and "lectures" on paper, students are required to practice using the content of the presentation. Instructors are available at all times to provide assistance as required.

Because of the use of the CRI instructional model to design the program, the academy has been able to attract a broader range of trainees. The entry level of the trainee is assessed and instruction begins at that point. As a result of the new program, the former sixteen-week training program has been reduced to an average of twelve weeks. Graduation time ranges from eight to sixteen weeks.

After being fully developed, instructional technology-based systems often require minimal additional lesson preparation by a teacher. The materials themselves provide the structure, examples, reinforcement, and often part of the motivation required for learning a specific subject. They also provide the basis for teaching systems that allow students to maximize learning in a shorter period of time than traditional teacher-based methods. Although initially more costly to develop than traditional instruction, technology-based systems help to amortize development costs for large numbers of students.

In the early 1970s the California legislature attempted to mandate a Program Planning Budgeting System (PPBS) for public education. A few California school systems still use the basic PPBS approach, which relates specific expenditures to specific instructional programs in order to determine the relative effectiveness of their instructional programs. For the most part, however, it has failed to solve the instructional management problems of school funding for the majority of school districts in the state. Until schools come to grips with the issue of defining goals and then deriving meaningful and measurable objectives, there will be little progress in determining efficiency.

ACCOUNTABILITY

Who is responsible when a student does not learn? The student? The teacher? The school board? In 1975, parents in San Francisco sued the school board because their son graduated from high school without knowing how to read. Teachers are sued for their students' lack of learning and students are regularly failed by teachers as though they were accountable for their own learning success. Are the students, the teachers, or the school boards accountable for the degree of learning that occurs in school? The concept of accountability implies that the person performing a task should be accountable for the results of his or her performance; that is, teachers are responsible for the student's learning as evidenced by change in achievement. In turn, it is reasonable to assume that school boards are accountable for the assessment of teachers' skills.

Many factors promoted the movement in education to assess educational results. The Elementary and Secondary Education Act of 1965 provided for the funding of systematic evaluations of programs in terms of outcomes and cost-effectiveness. In the early 1970s several states passed legislation requiring school boards to report to the legislature on the expenditure of their funds using PPBS. During this same period, school boards were writing performance contracts with private businesses which stipulated that no payment for the instruction would be made unless students attained certain given objectives.

In the late 1970s, many states began to develop minimum-competency programs following the New York State Regents Examination model. These programs established a minimum set of criteria to be met by students before a regular high-school diploma would be awarded. Indeed, one of the purposes of these programs was, to develop a sense of accountability on the part of both students and teachers.

Recent public opinion polls indicate that upwards of 85 percent of Americans feel teachers should be required to pass a state exam in their subject areas and be continually retested. Even more dramatic is the increasing appearance of legislated minimum-competency tests for students. It is possible that legislation will someday require evaluation of teachers, and possibly even instructional materials. But accountability is unsettling to those teachers, teacher unions, and school board members who have to supervise the accountability system. Accountability is not synonymous with performance contracting, PPBS, or Management by Objectives, but all of these management concepts are related to the construct of accountability. Accountability will "work" only when all parties can agree on goals and objectives and develop an ongoing system of assessment and revision. The role of instructional technology in such a system should be obvious.

The use of educational vouchers may also result in instructional accountability. Parents whose children participate in a voucher program often show an interest in exerting influence on school decision making. They may elect to put their children in schools that reflect the best situation for their children. The factor that has shown the most influence on school choice is the school's location. During the first year of most voucher systems the vast majority of the children attend the school nearest their home, but the influence of location decreases after the first year, whereas the contents of the curriculum, a child's satisfaction with a program, and a child's test scores gain more importance.

Before any accountability system is recommended for wide adoption, the problems of measuring learning must be considered. Without adequate measurement techniques, the assessment of an individual teacher or program in terms of student learning cannot be performed. Learning must be measured in terms of identifiable, measurable objectives. Any assessment format can be used if it provides valid, reliable, and measurable results. Assessment formats include nonstandardized tests, norm-referenced and criterion-referenced tests, inventories, and questionnaires. To what degree should teachers be held accountable for the growth or deficiencies of their students? This question relates to a number of variables, a few of which are:

- Class size. An interesting question: Would some teachers elect to have larger classes if they were paid on the cumulative success of each student?
- The accuracy of the students' cumulative records that provide their entering or starting point data (it is from this point that the teacher could take credit for "growth").
- The availability of instructional materials. Would a teacher elect to have one more student in class for an additional $800 of instructional materials? Since this is about the amount for personnel cost for an individual student, this trade-off would result in no extra cost to the school district.
- Access to the students' parents.

- The use of reliable measures for assessing student growth.
- A differential for teachers in undesirable school situations where students' values of school and schooling are less.

Although no teacher or instructional program will be successful with all students, it is possible that these variables would average out in a system where a teacher was held accountable for student achievement.

PERFORMANCE CONTRACTING

Performance contracting is a managerial concept that guarantees students' learning or the instructing agency does not receive compensation. Performance contracting was used in the early 1970s, but soon went out of vogue. It is within the context of accountability that renewed interest in performance contracting may occur in the 1980s. In performance contracting, the school district makes a contract with a teacher, a teachers' group, or a commercial firm to deliver instruction. Frequently the contracts are aimed toward deficient learners in subject areas where measurable objectives can be defined and mutually agreed upon by the administrators and the contracting agency. To date, the majority of the contracts have been written for mathematics and reading objectives at the elementary level.

The economics of performance contracting are as follows: if the average cost for educating a child for one year is $1600 in a given district, then about $1300 or 75 to 85 percent goes for direct instructional costs. Most of this is teacher cost. Assuming there are six periods, subjects, or hours in a school day, the cost for each is $267. Thus, the cost of teaching mathematics to a fifth-grade student might be assumed to be $267. The performance contractor would guarantee that this fifth-grade student and others in the grade would raise their math ability "one grade level" or the contractor would forego the $267 for teaching each student mathematics. (The usual guarantee is a 1.0 grade level gain in one academic year for the subjects covered in the performance contract.) In reality, the performance contractors will often agree to teach for less than in this illustration. In many cases a contract will state that if the student learns significantly more than the "one grade level," then a bonus will be paid. Often, the contractors will insist on obtaining their own teachers or paraprofessional aides who are familiar with the system of materials they plan to use. It is not unusual that, in order to afford the materials, the contractor will have a larger than normal teacher–pupil ratio.

One of the best-known and most troubled performance contracts was awarded by the Texarkana school board in the fall of 1969. Dorsett Educational Systems guaranteed a one grade-level increase for $80 per pupil. In May 1970, it was noted that some of the test items used to determine the effectiveness of the program had been included in the instructional materials. It appeared that

PERFORMANCE CONTRACTING IN CHERRY CREEK

The Cherry Creek School District in Denver, Colorado, signed a performance contract in the 1970–71 school year with two schools. The Dorsett
Educational Systems of Norman, Oklahoma, was contracted to improve students' reading abilities. Dorsett was to be paid $60 per pupil for those who
gained one year of growth as measured on a standardized reading test
after eighty hours of instruction. The results were inconclusive, and at the
end of the year the faculty in one school voted to discontinue the program.
The second school used the program for another year.

A second contract was written with a team of the district's own teachers
who called themselves the "I- Team." They agreed to work with fifty high-
school pupils identified as probable dropouts. The team agreed to work for
a bonus if the students' scores on tests and their attitudes improved. The
bonuses were paid to the team for the first two years. It was felt that the
incentive pay to teachers had merit, but when the superintendent left, the
programs were discontinued.

Dorsett had been "teaching to the test." The outside evaluation service felt that
the procedure made the promising test results invalid. The results, however,
indicated that the students achieved approximately a 1.5 grade-level gain in
reading and just slightly less in mathematics in approximately eighty hours of
instruction. It is unfortunate that problems clouded the effort and made further
research undesirable in this case.

Another major performance contract that received much attention occurred
at the Banneker School in Gary, Indiana. A contractor entered into an agreement guaranteeing to raise the achievement level of all elementary students in
all subjects. For $640,000 the eight hundred students in the K–6 school were to
be brought up to grade level. This contract was constantly faced with teacher
strikes and teacher resistance and ultimately decommissioned by the state. The
decommissioning occurred after teacher organizations, concerned about the
modified teacher–pupil ratios, successfully lobbied the legislature for its elimi-
nation.

There are, nevertheless, many other performance contracts that have gone
smoothly but never got the publicity of the two contracts mentioned above. In
one study, for example, gains ranged from 0.4 to 1.7 grade levels in nine
months. Studies of resource allocation indicate quite different patterns between schools and performance contractors. About 75 percent of the total cost
of a traditional instructional system is spent on teachers' salaries and only 1 to 2
percent on instructional materials. In contrast, performance contractors spent
about 60 to 65 percent on teachers and 15 to 20 percent on instructional materials. Studies indicate that in about one-third of the cases a school's adoption of a
contractor's instructional program would reduce operating costs. Nevertheless,
negative pressures from various groups have sharply curtailed the number of

PERFORMANCE-BASED TEACHER EDUCATION

A performance-based teacher education program developed at Ohio State University's National Center for Research in Vocational Education is exciting! It is exciting enough that McDonald's Hamburgers, United Airlines, U.S. Steel, the Department of Defense, 300 colleges and universities, 175 other postsecondary educational institutions, and over 250 businesses, industries, and other organizations are using it.

The curriculum requires students to demonstrate specific teaching competencies in actual classroom situations. It is a self-paced individualized program consisting of 100 modules in ten categories: program planning, development, and evaluation; instructional planning; instructional execution; instructional evaluation; instructional management; guidance; school–community relations; student vocational organization; professional role and development; and coordination of cooperative education. The students are evaluated by how well they perform in the classroom, not how well they do on paper-and-pencil tests.

The curriculum is a result of an eleven-year development effort funded by the U.S. Office of Education and the National Institute of Education. The field testing was conducted in eighteen institutions of higher education.

Each of the modules includes three elements: information about the competency or competencies to be acquired; practice activities; and a final evaluation of the student demonstrating the competencies in a classroom situation. Performance objectives, based on the competencies, are stated at the beginning of each module. At the end of most sections is a "self-check" in the form of an essay test.

Immediate feedback is used along with continual student practice via simulations and case studies. Field assessments are encouraged and used whenever possible immediately following the formal instruction. Instructors lead group discussions and act as resource persons.

performance contracts. The National Education Association, for example, has long opposed these accountability procedures. NEA Resolution 771 suggests that performance contracts are detrimental to public education.

ECONOMICS OF INSTRUCTIONAL SYSTEMS

Why in the world are salaries higher for administrators when the basic mission is teaching?

Former Governor of California Jerry Brown

Instructional costs for any given or projected program can be estimated depending on the:

- Availability of equipment and materials and their amortized per-hour costs.
- Availability of trained personnel and their per-hour costs.
- Overhead items such as facilities.
- Creative skill and experience of the producer and the design team.
- Amount of formative and summative evaluation needed.
- Extent of revision needed to ensure the lesson objectives are attained by learners.

Care should be taken to include equivalent cost components in all comparisons of teacher-based and media-based systems. Not only must the cost for the school plant, teacher aide, counselor, and others be included in determining the total cost of a teacher-based system, the requirements and cost for these components must also be determined for the alternative systems. These specific costs can be estimated for any given situation, so the approximate cost of using alternative instructional systems can be obtained in the design or planning stage by the instructional technologist. The more experience a designer has in a specific situation, the more precise these approximations can become.

Program costs in specific situations can be estimated or determined by first identifying personnel costs. Teacher cost can be determined in per-student-per-hour units as shown in this example:

1. Determine the annual salary for the year; for example, $18,000.
2. Determine the number of hours the teacher will spend in class-related activities; for example: 180 school days per year multiplied by six contact hours per day equals 1080 hours for each school year.
3. Determine the average number of students assigned to the teacher while working in the system being projected; for example, 30 students per hour.
4. Determine the cost per student per hour. Using this example, 18,000 divided by 1080 divided by 30 equals 60 cents per student per hour.

By following this procedure, one can determine the cost per hour for each of the personnel involved in implementing the projected system.

Next, determine the cost of the other components of the instructional system. The cost of a textbook can be determined by projecting its lifespan. Typically, school districts expect to use a textbook for five years before replacing it. If students purchase their own books, however, the designer would not include them. The procedure for determining the cost of the textbook would be to take the purchase price of the book, $15 for example, and divide it by the number of hours the text will be used each year. If the books are assigned to each student, the book may get one hour of use a day for 180 school days (or 180 hours of use). If the books are left in a classroom and used by several groups of students, this figure will be increased appropriately. The cost of the textbook per student per hour in this illustration would be $15 divided by 180 divided by five (years), or just over a penny per student per hour.

To determine the per-pupil cost of renting a film for an hour as part of the instructional system, the procedure would be to determine the rental cost of the film, for example, $12. Next, determine the number of students who will view the film during the rental period—for example, five classes of 30 students each, or 150 students. By dividing $12 by 150, we determine the cost of the film to be .08 cents per student per hour.

The estimated costs of the other media can be similarly determined. Another illustration would be a programmed text. Assume that a year-long programmed text had been determined to work well and was well liked by both teachers and students. Now the question becomes whether or not the school district should spend $35 per unit for the programmed text for that subject area. Again, assume a five-year use. Also assume that on average, four groups of students will have access to the programmed texts per day. The cost figures might be projected to look like this: $35 divided by 180 (school days) divided by 4 (students using each book a year) divided by 5 (years projected to be used) equals less than one cent per student per hour.

Courses developed for instructional television can cost less than $100,000 or as much as a million dollars for a series of thirty half-hour programs. These costs are minimal when compared with those incurred for commercial television in the United States. Major broadcasting networks usually send their film crews to a location and shoot about twenty times more film than they will ultimately use. The cost of an hour-long documentary news program with salaries and overhead often exceeds $250,000. An hour-long drama program costs about twice as much. The Children's Television Workshop, on the other hand, spent about $40,000 per hour for a typical *Sesame Street* program. The British Open University usually spends $20,000 to develop a one-hour course for college-level students.

For high-cost media, the key economic question is: How many students will experience the program over its economic life? Also, distribution costs and equipment and facilities requirements must be included. If it is an "add-on" to the already-incurred costs of the teacher without increasing learning, cost-efficiency suffers. It is also worth restating the above discussion assumes the program achieves desired learning objectives. A soap opera may be cheap, but not necessarily efficient!

Another item, fixed cost, must be either estimated or left out of calculations for all alternative systems. Fixed cost includes space and administrative costs, maintenance, transportation, and similar expenses. Most school districts have these figures available. They may be as high as 25 percent of the total educational cost. Some instructional systems require greater administrative support than others. Individualized instructional systems, for example, often require more record-keeping support than conventional systems. Some require specialized equipment and facilities such as learning carrels, rather than conventional classroom space. The difference in the cost of these spaces needs to be determined. In some cases the fixed cost may be expected to remain approximately the same for alternative systems and may be eliminated from the calculations.

In the following illustrations we will assume the fixed cost to be 15 cents per student per hour.

The big question is, however, how much will the total comparative cost be for alternative instructional systems? First let us estimate the cost of a teacher-based instructional system having the following components:

1. Teacher cost = .60
2. Fixed costs = .15
3. Textbook = <.01
4. Total cost of a teacher-based instructional system = .76 per student per hour

If anything (a film for example) is added to this basic system, the cost per user-hour will be increased. Costs will further increase as additional items are added to the basic cost structure.

Does this mean that the use of all instructional hardware and software will result in more costly instructional systems? Not necessarily! Not if the component parts of each system are designed to reflect the needs of that system. In the programmed text example, we determined that the cost for a highly developed and workable text was about one cent per student per hour. However, if the programmed text is effective and requires little teacher intervention, what do the teachers do while students are working with the text? They are able to work with the occasional student who has a problem (content or personal), ensure that the content is understood, and so on. But these activities often do not require constant attention. Many programmed instruction labs could have one teacher supervising from forty to eighty students depending on behavior problems, the quality of the materials, administrative policy, and the like. If we assume that a teacher is supervising 60 students in a laboratory, the teacher cost is about half of that in the conventional classroom containing 30 students. The cost for this alternative programmed instruction-based system would be determined thus:

1. Teacher cost = .30
2. Fixed costs = .15
3. Programmed text = .01
4. Total cost of a programmed instruction-based instructional system = .46 per student per hour

Note that the single most expensive component of both instructional programs is the teacher. If the teacher–pupil ratio can be modified, instructional costs can in turn be dramatically altered. Even the addition of a single student to a classroom could release approximately $800 for purchase of instructional materials or other expenditures.

Instructional efficiency (objective attainment per unit of cost) can be enhanced by:

1. Increasing the teacher–pupil ratio.
2. Reducing learner time (if student time is given an economic value).
3. Reducing instructor time.
4. Increasing the degree of objective attainment (if exceeding the required degree level of the objective is desirable).

The relative cost of traditional instructor-led and self-instructional systems can also be figured out for industrial training.

COST COMPARISON IN INSTRUCTOR-LED VS. SELF-INSTRUCTIONAL SYSTEM

The effect of development cost and of a reduction in training time (classroom and study time) on total training cost can be readily seen in this example. Assume a 20-hour classroom course to be taken by 200 middle managers with an average salary of $25,000 a year (instructors and course developers earn the same).

Factors	Instructor Led	Self-Instruction
No. of students	200	200
Course length	20 hours	20 hours
Student contact time	4000 hours	4000 hours
Development time	20 hours	1000 hours (1)
Student study time	4000 (2) hours	0
Instructor prep time	200 hours (3)	20 hours
Total times	8,240 hours	5,040 hours
Cost at $12.50/hour for students and staff (4)	$103,000 (5)	$63,000

Notes:

1. Assuming 50 development hours for each instructional hour; 20-hour course × 50 = 1000 hours.
2. Assuming the students spend one hour doing homework for each hour in the Instructor-Led class and that all of the homework was done in the Self-Instruction sessions.
3. Assume the instructor has 20 students in a class; thus there are 10 classes × 20 hours/class = 200 hours preparing for classes and administrating them. Assume the Self-Instruction requires some preparation time.
4. $25,000/year with a 50-week year, 40 hours/week = $12.50/hour.
5. 8240 hours × $12.50/hour = $103,000; 5040 × $12.50/hour = $63,000 for the Self-Instruction-taught students.

Industrial organizations will usually calculate the costs of personnel time spent in instruction. Because the employees are being paid to attend class, it is necessary to add their salaries and benefits to the other instructional costs in order to obtain the actual total cost of instruction. The longer an instructional program, the more expensive it is. Experience indicates that the more time and effort devoted to the design and development of a course of instruction, the higher the probability of a time-efficient instructional program. Increasingly, training programs are investing in these "up front" development costs to reap the benefits of more efficient training. As employees' salaries, as well as travel and per diem costs, rapidly rise, we can expect to see even greater interest in a systematic development of training.

PROPOSAL WRITING

Due to the relatively large investment that must initially be made to purchase or develop instructional technology, it is often necessary to secure funds from federal, state or local agencies, or from philanthropic organizations, such as the Carnegie Foundation and the Ford Foundation. After determining funding sources, the initial procedure involves writing a proposal for the agency that describes the planned activity and the specific funding needs. The proposal must be clear, motivating, detailed, and comprehensive. Information must be presented in a logical and exciting manner. Part of the success of the instructional technologist depends on how well proposals are developed.

Instructional designers in business and industry usually do not prepare proposals for outside funding, but often must be prepared to "sell their case" inside the organization. Internal proposals usually contain fewer "academic trappings" such as extensive footnoting and eloquent rationale. Rather, they focus on the problem, the proposed solution, pay-off to the company, and project cost. Generally, a short, crisp proposal that quickly gets to the point will receive greater attention than a voluminous detailed narrative. Economic analysis of the type described in this chapter may be particularly helpful in selling the idea. A single-page executive summary may also be desirable if the proposal is to be reviewed higher in the bureaucratic hierarchy. Usually, the higher the position of the reviewer, the less operational detail desired. As in any organization, check the local customs and norms.

A fully developed proposal for outside funding may have the following components:

Cover letter—Remind funding officials of previous contacts you have made with them, outline your project in one or two sentences.

Title page—List project title, your name, address, and telephone number, project duration, date, funds requested.

Abstract—Write one to two pages summarizing your request, including objectives, need, methods, evaluation design, dissemination procedure, the proposal's relationship to the funding organization's policies or interests, and benefits of the project to the funding organization.

Procedure—How you are going to conduct the project. If it is a statistical study, describe the population, your design, what statistics you will use, what level of significance you will use, and what measures or instruments you will use.

Introduction—Describe who you are and explain what you do; outline your goals; describe the accomplishments of your organization and staff to date; describe your competency and local support; show the relationship between this project and your organizational goals.

Problem and/or need statement—Document the problem with facts and expert opinions; show how your project is unique and how this project fits into the organization's long-range goals; show that you cannot financially support this project internally; identify other potential or existing donors; provide a concise outline of the plan to solve the identified problem.

Objectives—What specifically do you want to do? By what date? Are the objectives cost-effective? Are the objectives measurable? Describe the methods you will use to accomplish each objective. Identify who will be responsible for implementing each objective.

Evaluation—Describe your measurable criteria for success and how you will collect and process the data; identify the evaluator or evaluation agency; outline the reporting procedures.

Dissemination—Describe how you will share the information you have generated with others who could use the conclusions or materials you have developed.

Budget—Identify the personnel or the categories and specify the costs for each; show fringe benefits; show consultant or contracted service costs; show space, equipment, travel, telephone, and other costs, as well as the total cost.

Appendix—Include endorsement letters, vitas or resumes of key personnel, and certifications.

To prepare yourself for proposal writing, outline your ideas and plans. If the potential funding agency specifies a certain format, follow it and nothing else. Do *not* change it simply to fit your personal preference. Remember, the agency will be reviewing many proposals and comparing them category by category. If yours doesn't fit it will almost certainly be discarded. Also, follow submission procedures precisely. If they call for five copies, don't send six. It may foul up their sorting procedures and make them think you cannot follow directions. If only a general format is specified by the prospective funder, you have considerably more latitude, but you should still study its guidelines carefully. As a first step, develop at least one paragraph on each of the proposal components. Once you have summarized your ideas, you may then assign members of your group (if you are working with a group) to write the various sections. After the initial writing has been done, review the proposal with other knowledgeable and interested individuals before putting it into final form for submission to the funding agency. Needless to say, both internal and external proposals should be double-checked for accuracy and readability. Many good ideas don't receive funding due to their sloppy appearance.

SUMMARY

Instructional technologists must be keenly aware of the economics of their profession. Traditionally, instructional improvement has been an "add-on" cost over and above current expenditures. However, as education and training costs have rapidly increased, alternative arrangements are beginning to be employed. By totally redesigning the system and incorporating the teacher (the most expensive component) as a planned part, total cost can remain equal or perhaps be reduced.

Cost-efficiency is determined by dividing the outputs of instruction by its costs or inputs. Outputs typically include cognitive, psychomotor, and affective changes in behavior. Inputs include personnel, facilities, equipment, materials, and learner time. Cost-efficiency analysis rests on the assumption that both inputs and outputs can be measured with some degree of validity and reliability.

The general social movement toward increased professional accountability is being felt in education and training. Increasingly, we are being asked to specify what we are attempting to do and how well we are accomplishing those goals. These forces, coupled with the economic reality that educational costs cannot forever continue to rise faster than inflation, suggest a much greater interest in instructional technology in the future.

Questions for Consideration and Discussion

1. Which of the following do you believe would help avoid teacher malpractice law suits? Discuss your reasons.
   a. Student-oriented behavioral objectives should be made available to a parent or to the school administrators for all classes for which you are responsible.
   b. The materials and assignments should always be consistent with the objectives.
   c. Student grades should always be assigned based on actual performance and not on effort or other standards.
   d. Learning materials should be distributed to students only if they are adapted to their abilities and needs.
   e. Punishment should always be consistent with parental wishes, district policy, and state law.
   f. Physical punishment should only be inflicted on a student of your own sex and then only with another teacher present.
   g. You should always avoid leaving your class without adequate supervision for visits to the teachers' lounge or to the office.

    h. You should always protect the personal rights of your pupils and avoid punishment of a student in front of other students.

    The answers to all of these questions on malpractice seem to be true.

2. Class size, according to the following research reports, has little or no effect on performance in the classroom. Do these reports coincide with your knowledge and beliefs?

    a. Bridge, R., Judd, C., and Moock, P. (1979). *The Determinants of Educational Outcomes*. Cambridge, MA: Ballinger.

    b. Hedges, L. V., and Stock, W. (Spring 1983). The Effects of Class Size: An Examination of Rival Hypotheses. *American Educational Research Journal, 20*(1), 63–86.

    c. Kean, M., Summers, A., Raivetz, M., and Farber, I. (1979). *What Works in Reading?* Philadelphia: Office of Research and Evaluation, School District of Philadelphia.

    d. Marsh, H. W., Overall, J. U., and Kesler, S. P. (Winter 1979). Class Size, Students' Evaluations, and Instructional Effectiveness. *American Educational Research Journal*, vol. 16, no. 1, 57–70.

    e. Shapson, Stan M., et al. (Summer 1980). An Experimental Study of Class Size. *American Educational Research Journal*, 141–152.

    f. Van Matre, N., et al. (February 1981). *Computer-Managed Instruction in the Navy: II. A Comparison of Two Student/Instructor Ratios in CMI Learning Centers*. San Diego: Navy Personnel Research and Development Center.

    g. Want to Prove Class Size Is Unimportant? Harris Will Help. (March 1978). *Phi Delta Kappan*, 463.

    h. For an alternative view, see: Smith, M., and Glass, G. (Winter 1980). Meta-analysis of Research on Class Size and Its Relationship to Attitudes and Instruction. *American Educational Research Journal*, 419–433. For a rebuttal to this article, see: Educational Research Service. (December 1980). Class Size Research: A Critique of Recent Meta-analyses. *Phi Delta Kappan*, 239–241; or Hedges and Stock (1983).

Suggested Activities

1. Determine the cost of this course. How could it be made more cost-efficient?
2. Analyze the effect of your IT classroom on student learning. How could it be redesigned or remodeled to promote learning?

Suggested Readings

Brown, B. W., and Saks, D. H. (1981). The Microeconomics of Schooling. *Review of Research in Education*. Washington, DC: American Educational Research Association, 217–254.

Doughty, P. L. (n.d.). *Guidelines for Cost-Effectiveness Analysis for Navy Training and Education*. San Diego, CA: Navy Personnel Research and Development Center.

Dyer, H. (1973). *How to Achieve Accountability in the Public Schools*. Bloomington, IN: Phi Delta Kappa Educational Foundation.

ERIC Clearinghouse on Educational Management. (December 1978). *The Best of ERIC: Educational Vouchers*. Eugene, OR: University of Oregon.

Humble, J. W. (1973). *How to Manage by Objectives*. New York: American Management Association.

Jamison, D. T., Klees, S. J., and Wells, S. J. (1978). *The Costs of Educational Media: Guidelines for Planning and Evaluation*. Beverly Hills, CA: Sage Publications.

Jamison, D., Suppes, P., and Wells, S. (Winter 1974). The Effectiveness of Alternative Instructional Media. *Review of Educational Research, 44*(1), 1–68.

Machlup, F. (1962). *The Production and Distribution of Knowledge in the United States*. Princeton, NJ: Princeton University Press.

National Education Association. (September 1975). *Briefing Memo: Should Teachers Say No to MBO?* Washington, DC.

Orlansky, J., and String, J. (1978). *Cost Effectiveness of Computer Based Instruction in Military Training*. San Diego: Cubic Corp.

Ornstein, A. C. (1973). *Accountability for Teachers and School Administrators*. Belmont, CA: Fearon.

Rand Corporation. (1972). *How Effective Is Schooling?* Santa Monica, CA.

Roberson, E. W., ed. (1971). *Educational Accountability Through Evaluation*. Englewood Cliffs, NJ: Educational Technology Publications.

Strickland, R., Phillips, J. F., and Phillips, W. R. (1976). *Avoiding Teacher Malpractice: A Practical Legal Handbook for the Teaching Professional*. NY: Hawthorn Books.

Swope, W. M. (November 1979). *Incremental Costing Model for Use with the CNET Per Capita Course Costing Data Ba ·: System I*. TAEG Report no. 77.

Umans, S. (1973). *How to Cut the Cost of Education*. New York: McGraw-Hill.

UNESCO. (1977). *The Economics of New Educational Media*. New York.

Wagner, L. (1982). *The Economics of Educational Media*. New York: St. Martin's Press.

13

Evaluation of Programs

Every sentence I utter must be understood not as an affirmation, but as a question.

Niels Bohr

Objectives

After completing this chapter, you should be able to:

1. List three purposes of evaluation in education.
2. Define norm-referenced and criterion-referenced measures and identify their differences.
3. Define process and product evaluation and show how they differ.
4. Define formative and summative evaluation and identify their differences.
5. Discuss major aspects of at least three different evaluation models.
6. Discuss five major data-collection methods used for collecting information in an evaluation.
7. Discuss the primary research trends in instructional technology.

Evaluation is a form of quality control. It looks at questions like: Was the right problem resolved? Were the objectives taught to the degree specified, under the designed conditions? Do the same results occur repeatedly? Ralph Tyler perceives evaluation as "the process of determining to what extent the educational objectives are actually being realized." Evaluation, then, involves the measurement of how effectively the learners are meeting the objectives as a result of instruction.

When a child fails to learn, it is not necessarily the teacher's fault. On the other hand, if a student doesn't learn, we often take the position that the teacher or instructional system isn't doing its job. Just as giving implies receiving, teaching implies learning. Evaluation, however, must be performed to determine if learning did occur, and, if it did not, why. The learner, the teacher, and the instructional design or methodology must all be looked at and evaluated as a whole.

Formative evaluation looks at the process of learning and teaching while the instructional design is being developed and the materials produced. The primary purpose of formative evaluation is to improve the process or instructional methods and their resultant products. *Summative* evaluation is performed near the conclusion of the teaching/learning process to draw inferences or conclusions about the effectiveness of the instruction. Some say formative evaluation is to improve, whereas summative evaluation is to prove.

Both types of evaluations examine the learner, the teacher, and the instructional design, and while both attempt to determine what the student actually learned, their focus is different. The data sources are also unique for each form of evaluation. Formative evaluation might ask about the learner's study habits, class attendance, learning preparation, and participation in class activities. In contrast, summative evaluation might ask: How much did the student learn concerning each objective? Formative evaluation of teachers addresses their implementation of educational methods, personality, use of media, and the thoroughness of class preparation. The intent of this evaluation is to provide feedback for improving classroom performance. Summative evaluation focuses on how well the students learned what the teacher taught. The instructional design is formatively examined for the appropriateness of the educational method, level of objectives, grading system, use of feedback to the student, media selection, and so on. Summative questions regarding the instructional design address its costs, logistics requirements, ease of maintenance, and level of acceptance by parents, administrators, teachers, and students.

Formative and summative evaluation are really two sides of the same coin. During the early stages of a development project, most evaluation questions revolve around making improvements to the system. As the project progresses, emphasis shifts toward documenting its effects. In some cases, the same data may serve both formative and summative goals (as with an item analysis of a post-test). In others, unique procedures must be employed particularly to obtain data for making revisions. It is one thing to know revisions are needed—it is another to know *what* specific revisions to make.

The evaluation design should be planned at the same time as the instructional design and, if possible, should be done by a different person or agency than the one responsible for developing the materials. This helps ensure that the evaluation is objective and believable. The evaluation design should include:

- The evaluation question(s).
- The evaluation criteria.
- The evidence used in the evaluation (the types of questions or test instruments).
- The role subjective judgment is to play in the evaluation (who is going to make which subjective judgments about the effectiveness of the program).
- A plan for implementing the evaluation design.

The analysis of instructional strategies and materials is an ongoing activity. It must continue from the time of development until it has been determined that the entire instructional system is workable, which may require several evaluation and revision cycles. As can be seen in the "development" subsystem block below, the analysis or evaluation occurs in the same time frame as the revision activities.

Evaluation involves the collection and use of information to make decisions about an instructional program. Evaluation is performed to:

- Make decisions about individual learners. What are the learners' needs? How should instruction be planned or designed? How should student groupings be determined? How and when should the students be informed of their progress?
- Make decisions about course improvement. Decide what materials and methods are the most promising, and where and how to revise the materials.
- Make administrative decisions to determine how effective the school program is and how well individual students or teachers function in specific situations.

There are two general yardsticks against which to measure student performance. Norm-referenced measures compare a group's or an individual's performance with the results of a previously tested group, or for individuals it may be their own group. Measurements can rank learners according to achievement and are thus often used to assign grades and IQ scores. These measures tend to result in competition among individual students. Criterion-referenced measures, on the other hand, compare a student's performance with objective criteria. These measures test individual mastery to a criterion as stated in an objective, and tend to foster competition within the individual rather than between individuals. Criterion-referenced testing is generally preferred by instructional technologists since individual performance is compared to the behavior con-

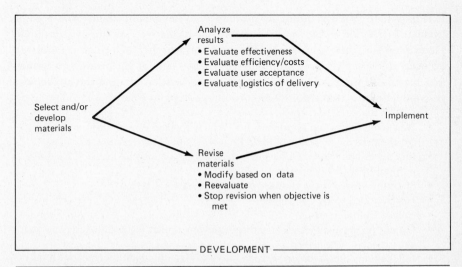

FIGURE 13.1   I.D. Model: Analyze and Revise Subsystems

tained in the objectives. Under these conditions it is possible for all students to perform at an acceptable level. In contrast, when norm-referenced testing is conducted, learners are often compared and their performance is plotted on a curve. This practice guarantees some learners will be evaluated as successful and others unsuccessful. In reality, all might have done very poorly compared to what was stated in the objectives, but some will be declared competent. Of course, the reverse is also true. If all learners have learned almost all the behaviors, minor differences might become major determinants of who passes or who fails. Also, since what constitutes "passing" can float up or down, revision of the instruction to improve it has less meaning.

Evaluation may focus on the instructional process or on the product of the instruction. *Process* evaluation examines the means or methodology used to reach the objectives. Determining whether programmed materials displayed on videotapes are more readable than equivalent materials in text form is a process evaluation. The evaluation is performed while learning is occurring and examines the process itself. *Product* evaluation looks at the results of a program after its implementation; for example, determining the effectiveness of a specific film.

Process evaluation tends to focus on formative questions about what does and doesn't need revision. However, summative process questions about time, cost, and acceptance can also be examined. Product evaluation tends to focus on summative questions, but can also examine the content for accuracy or obsolescence, which are formative questions.

THE EVALUATION PROCESS

It is important when planning an evaluation to be specific about what is to be evaluated. Decide if the evaluation will be formative, summative, or both. Determine how the evaluation will be used and whether criterion- or norm-referenced measures should be employed. The process of performing an evaluation may differ according to the theoretical perception guiding the evaluation. In conducting an evaluation there are many steps to follow:

- Plan needed program improvements. Who will plan? When? How often? What are the priorities? How will plans be carried out? Make recommendations.
- Identify the audience. Determine which decisions must be made. What is the purpose of the evaluation?
- State the objectives of the instruction in behavioral terms.
- Develop measuring instruments.
- Collect the information.
- Display progress information and comparisons so that the decision makers will have reliable information.
- Judge the evidence for success and need. Who will judge? When? How often? What decisions will be made? How will they be made? Delayed evaluations often provide useful data about retention.

When an evaluation plan is designed, decisions should be made involving the desirability of program objectives. Objective studies, it is argued, are free from subjective inputs. They adhere to the scientific method of investigation to eliminate bias and permit generalization. Objective data are more useful in medicine (where things tend to be seen as black or white), but subjective data are often more useful in the behavioral sciences. Both play important roles in designing and implementing instructional systems.

Subjective studies are often useful precisely because they do not eliminate potentially relevant parameters that might complicate a "tight" research design. High reliability and validity in a study are desirable, but too much is often lost in achieving these values. Many research studies are too far removed from the interactions of the real world. The design of evaluation studies should be based on both personal professional knowledge and formal design if practical curriculum decisions are going to be made. Firmly grounded objective studies can perhaps then be performed once a solid grasp on the variables has been obtained. Eventually, fine points or comparisons can be made with research designs rather than with evaluation designs.

RESEARCH METHODOLOGY IN INSTRUCTIONAL TECHNOLOGY

Research and evaluation assessments in education ensure that effective and efficient educational systems are designed, developed, and implemented. The focus of research and evaluation in instructional technology should be to determine the relative effectiveness and efficiency of specific instructional designs and materials.

Now we will examine research and evaluation tools, their contribution to education, and their uses by instructional technologists, designers, producers, evaluators, and change agents.

Good ongoing research is necessary because it provides a foundation for instructional technology. In addition, research:

- Reveals reality.
- Exposes program effects.
- Exposes costs.
- Helps order priorities.
- Suggests the design of proposed programs.

Research and evaluation efforts are being questioned today in many academic communities. Appropriate research designs using "statistics" or projection techniques to determine statistical differences are sometimes thought to be irrelevant because the studies are too controlled, or out of touch with reality. During the 1970s, Congress curtailed federal research funds in education because of concern regarding the utility of many of these studies. Independent reviews of educational studies by John Goodlad and others conclude that few of the research studies employed appropriate experimental design. Studies of irrelevant, insignificant factors or parameters also occur far too often. Data based on techniques useful for studying rat mazes or electron movement seem to have little relevance in the more complex domain of human learning. Learning based on trivial questions in "laboratory" situations may also have little relevance to a classroom teacher or an instructional technologist.

Many of the questions useful to instructional technologists cannot be answered by physical science methods of research. The instructional technologist needs to look at the interrelationship of multiple variables and complex problems, such as: What are the most relevant composition objectives for a second-grade student?

The questions that can be answered by traditional research designs are often of a lower order and less relevant. After analyzing numerous research studies over an extended period of time, Gage (1978) was convinced that correlational studies are inevitably weak in identifying causal effects. He stated, "Only an ethically impossible experiment would end the doubt in terms of the logic of scientific method." (p. 235) We cannot know whether direct, structured, formal research-based methods really promote higher achievement than, for example, progressive, open, and informal methods. Gage believes our only acceptable alternative is a combination of logic, insight, raw experiences, common sense, and the writings of persuasive prose stylists.

Barbatsis (1978) suggests that ITV research has not led to theoretical progress in answering the question, How can television be used to teach? One is left to conclude, says Barbatsis, that "the major factor contributing to the domination of research which has produced so little progress in the field of instructional television has been the bias of the academic community to inquiry dedicated to scientific validation." (p. 412) The same conclusions can be drawn from the lack of impact of research on other media and processes used in instructional technology.

Easy yet now irrelevant questions are still being asked by researchers. For example: Is televised teaching as effective as the traditional lecture method? The fact that after two decades the same question is still being asked indicates the difficulty of attacking the questions beyond this level.

The futility of past research is seen in the summarizations of research on instructional technology. Instructional technology studies have not provided enough information to eliminate the uncertainties involved in making choices. Another weakness in the media research is pointed out by Wilkinson (1980) in his summary of research involving media. He states, "Many of the studies in the files were set up to demonstrate prior convictions rather than to examine carefully drawn hypotheses. The results of several decades of research nevertheless . . . can be summed up as 'no significant difference.'"

EVALUATION MODELS

Figure 13.2 presents some comparative information on several evaluation models, all of which will be discussed to examine their usefulness.

Systems Analysis Model: In this approach to evaluation, there are usually few quantitative output measures other than test scores. The focus is on relating differences in programs to a variation in test scores. The data is often survey data and is processed by correlational analysis. This approach has served many of the projects funded by the Department of Health, Education and Welfare since 1965.

Behavioral Objectives Model: Once the program objectives are spelled out in terms of specific student performance, the behaviors can be measured by norm-referenced or criterion-referenced tests. Ralph Tyler used this model as far back as 1942 to measure student progress.

Decision-Making Model: The nature of the decisions to be made structures the evaluation. This model uses questionnaires and interview surveys extensively because it is more sensitive than others to user input and feedback. The results are usually intended for administrators concerned with the efficiency of a program and assumes that the objectives are appropriate. This may be a good model for affective objectives.

Goal-Free Model: This model reduces the effects of bias in evaluation. The evaluator is not informed of the intent of the evaluation, and thus must search for all possible outcomes.

Art Criticism Model: This model evolved from the art and literary criticism tradition. An experienced and trained educational critic judges the important aspects of a given program. This model is not often used in IT-related evaluations.

School Accreditation Model: Collection of data is primarily accomplished by local personnel before an on-site evaluation by outside professionals. This type of staff self-study may have little relevance to a classroom teacher or an instructional technologist.

Adversary Model: Legal or quasilegal procedures to present the pros and cons of a program are specified by this model. A "jury" then makes the evaluation decision. This model has little application in the instructional development process.

Transaction or Countenance Model: This approach concentrates on the instructional processes themselves and reports ways in which different people view the curriculum. Case studies and other informal methods are generally used. This approach may stir up value conflicts and ignore causes, but it does paint a broad picture of the curriculum and pinpoints conflicting expectations of a program.

Model	Proponents	Major audiences	Assumes consensus on	Methodology	Outcome	Typical questions
Systems analysis	Rivlin	Economists, managers	Goals; known cause and effect; quantified variables	PPBS; linear programming; planned variation; cost-benefit analysis	Efficiency	Are the expected effects achieved? Can the effects be achieved more economically? What are the most *efficient* programs?
Behavioral objectives	Tyler, Popham	Managers, psychologists	Prespecified objectives; quantified outcome variables	Behavioral objectives; achievement tests	Productivity; accountability	Are the students achieving the objectives? Is the teacher producing?
Decision making	Stufflebeam, Alkin	Decision makers, esp. administrators	General goals; criteria	Surveys, questionnaires, interviews; natural variation	Effectiveness; quality control	Is the program effective? What parts are effective?
Goal-free	Scriven	Consumers	Consequences; criteria	Bias control; logical analysis; modus operandi	Consumer choice; social utility	What are *all* the effects?
Art criticism	Eisner, Kelly	Connoisseurs, consumers	Critics; standards	Critical review	Improved standards	Would a critic approve this program?
Accreditation	North Central Association	Teachers, public	Criteria; panel; procedures	Review by panel; self-study	Professional acceptance	How would professionals rate this program?
Adversary	Owens, Levine, Wolf	Jury	Procedures and judges	Quasilegal procedures	Resolution	What are the arguments for and against the program?
Transaction	Stake, Smith, MacDonald, Parlett-Hamilton	Client, practitioners	Negotiations; activities	Case studies, interviews, observations	Understanding; diversity	What does the program look like to different people?

Source: Earnest R. House, "Assumptions Underlying Evaluation Models." *Educational Researcher* (March 1978), pp. 4–12. Copyright 1978 by American Educational Research Association, Washington, D.C.

FIGURE 13.2 Taxonomy of Major Evaluation Models

DATA COLLECTION

Collecting information for an evaluation can be accomplished in many ways.

Achievement tests can be administered to large groups at low cost. These tests measure student knowledge over a wide spectrum of subject areas.

Aptitude or IQ tests are somewhat useful measures of potential.

Paper-and-pencil self-reporting measures ask individuals to express their attitudes, beliefs, perceptions, and feelings.

Questionnaires are self-administered surveys consisting of sets of questions. They are inexpensive to construct, but the type of information they provide is often limited, biased, and incomplete.

Rating scales can be used for evaluation of individuals, events, or products. Student attitude, for example, can be rated on a scale of one to five. These scales are easy to develop and provide objective data which may, however, be biased due to differences in definitions.

Ranking scales arrange a set of items into a hierarchy according to a value or preference. A teacher may be asked to rank students or textbooks. Because ranking is forced, raters may make some distinctions despite their not really noting any differences.

Semantic differentials may be used to measure attitudes and affect according to the indirect meanings of words. The format of a semantic differential question might be:

Instructional Technology is:

Good	____ ____ ____ ____ ____	Bad
Powerful	____ ____ ____ ____ ____	Weak
Desirable	____ ____ ____ ____ ____	Undesirable
Effective	____ ____ ____ ____ ____	Ineffective

In this illustration, the semantic differential reveals the attitude of an individual toward instructional technology, which was being assessed for its goodness, power, desirability, and effectiveness.

The *Q-Sort* permits individuals to rate items or statements by prioritizing them. Teachers could be asked to rate ten textbooks from "very good" to "very bad" in such a manner that at least two texts are assigned to each category. In essence, it is a forced-choice classification exercise.

Diary techniques require individuals to keep hourly, daily, or weekly accounts of specific activities, attitudes, thoughts, or events.

The *critical incident technique* requires the recording only of particularly important information. Emphasis is placed on recording or reporting those incidents or situations that seem to make a big difference in system performance. If an event occurs frequently, but does not have major impact on other events, it is not a critical event, whereas uncommon events that have major consequences are. Diary and critical incident techniques are difficult to interpret and score.

Observations can be used to determine what instructional materials are being used. Eyewitness observations, self-completed checklists, rating scales, field notes, and summary reports are all examples of observation instruments. Standard observations require careful planning to ensure accurate information. Many individuals, however, do not behave normally while being observed. It is also difficult to train accurate observers. Time-sampling observations provide repeated observations of a given situation. While this technique overcomes some of the limitations of the standard observation techniques, it does not permit the program as a whole to be observed.

An *interview* may be performed by talking to an individual or group. Interviews can be either unstructured and spontaneous, or highly structured. A face-to-face interview permits the probing of sensitive issues like attitudes or values. This process, however, can be time-consuming and expensive and requires extensive training of the interviewer. Telephone interviews, although less sensitive to attitude and value information than face-to-face interviews, are much less time-consuming and expensive.

Performance tests require individuals to complete a task. Evaluation may focus on the performance itself, the end-product of the performance, or both. Rating scales may be used to evaluate the performance. They are often time-consuming, expensive, and difficult to develop, but if related carefully to objectives they will provide excellent data.

Record reviews use score data such as tests and grades, from which inferences about achievement or attitude can be made. This method can be used to assess individual achievement.

In summary, an evaluation technique closely matching the objective should be selected and used. Usually, the decision is easy to make. To determine the consistency of objectives and a corresponding test, the condition statement should be examined to determine whether the evaluation or test can be given under those specified conditions. The degree statement should also be examined to determine the scoring standard. And of course, the behavior statement should be examined to determine specifically what behavior the student is to exhibit.

A review of the use of verbs in behavioral objectives suggested in Chapter 6 will permit you to relate the verbs directly to one of the testing formats discussed earlier in this chapter. If the behavior involves recall or recognition, then the most appropriate test formats are those that require this of the student. Matching, multiple-choice, and true-false questions are examples of recognition tests. Recall objectives require short-answer, fill-in-the-blank, or list-type responses.

Measuring a concept, procedure, rule, or principle objective usually requires a short answer, fill-in-the-blank, listing, or a performance test item. A procedure objective typically requires a short answer, fill-in-the-blank, narrative description, or a performance test. Problem-solving performance is often based on projects, case studies, or performance simulations.

EVALUATION PROJECTS

Some of the first coherent observations on the quality of education came from the National Assessment of Educational Progress (NAEP) in 1970. This government-sponsored project measured student achievement in art, careers, citizenship, literature, mathematics, science, social studies, music, reading, and writing. The facts provided by the NAEP helped curriculum developers, textbook writers, and other educators to better assess their students and consequently design better instruction for them. Another federally-funded source of educational statistics is the National Center for Educational Statistics (NCES). These large evaluation efforts provide data that tend to be both valid and reliable and should be studied by all professional educators including technologists.

Coleman, Hoffer, and Kilgore (1982) published data from the "High School and Beyond" study by National Opinion Research Center involving information on fifty-eight thousand sophomores and seniors. This data has been reviewed by many additional researchers. In their post-hoc analysis, Walberg and Shanahan (1983) found that private schools, even the most elite, did not produce superior cognitive achievement once fixed characteristics of their students and their backgrounds were statistically controlled. They concluded that quantity of instruction is the only educationally alterable variable that emerges as a strong correlate of performance. Their results are based on year-long courses taken in English, mathematics, French, German, Spanish, history, and science. This time-on-task conclusion is important because it stresses that our instructional designs should not focus primarily on reducing time to the attainment of given objectives. Rather, it should result in more time spent on learning activities.

The College Entrance Examination Board also regularly evaluates student aptitude. Its Scholastic Aptitude Tests (SAT) provide data annually which suggest that over the last few years the nation's youth have been performing less well on verbal and mathematics measures than in earlier years.

Research Trends in Instructional Technology

As much as possible, research involving the various aspects of IT have been included within the appropriate chapters. However, it now seems appropriate to provide a listing of major research reviews. Some of the best research summary statements have been prepared by Anderson (1967), Gagne and Rohwer (1969), Glaser and Resnick (1972), Levie and Dickie (1973), McKeachie (1974),

Jamison, Suppes, and Wells (1974), Glaser (1976), Salomon and Clark (1977), Wittrock and Lumsdaine (1977), Kulik, Kulik, and Cohen (1980), Wilkinson (1980), Resnick (1981), and Glaser (1982).

The research reviews generally suggest that for any given set of objectives there are usually several media that can be used with equivalent cognitive and affective results. Research involved in determining the best medium of instruction was unproductive and is no longer of interest to most researchers. The only area consistently reporting "significant difference" media-comparison studies involves "programmed" materials, which usually show reduction in learning time, but not necessarily greater achievement. Kulik, Kulik, and Cohen (1980) summarized eight CAI studies showing time reductions (often approaching 33 percent) over other instructional media. Jamison, Suppes, and Wells (1974) reported this trend with programmed materials about ten years ago. Many military training research reports also suggest that CAI can reduce learning time between 30 and 50 percent. Instructional radio, film, and television appear to require about the same time as more conventional techniques while achieving the same results. We therefore conclude that these media are real alternatives to each other and teacher-based instruction.

In an eight-month study involving eighty-five sixth-grade math students randomly assigned to either traditional instruction or an instructional-systems approach Hannafin (1983) found that the systems approach increased retention. The students in the systems-developed classes obtained higher scores in adding fractions and in a few other tested areas. He also found that Anglos earned higher scores than Hispanics. Hannafin, however, did not find a significant difference in the students' test scores involving whole-number math problems. He concluded that the systems approach to designing programs may be most effective for learners when the criterion task is not heavily influenced by the acquisition of prerequisite skills. Additional research is needed to determine when and where these systematic procedures should be used.

There is little consistent research related to which instructional methods or strategies are best for which subjects/objectives and which students. Instructional materials designed to adapt to an individual's abilities, special aptitudes, entering competencies, and en route performance are now being researched. It is unclear whether the results will be positive. A number of educational researchers are also continuing to examine the interaction between learner aptitudes and treatment variables. However, the intuitive appeal of this concept has yet to be proven through research.

In summary, a review of the above trends suggests that the ATI research, although logical and reasonable, has failed to provide a useful position from which to observe and understand the instructional/teaching process. It is also apparent that something about the self-paced, programmed materials does make a difference to learning. The frequency and intensity with which students cognitively process instructional input should be further studied. Constructed responses may facilitate achievement with new content, but the advantage disappears when familiar material or content is being taught because it requires less time to be mastered. Their superiority may be due to the fact that students spend more time with the instructional material when they have to construct answers. Generally, the more time the students spend on a task, the more they will learn. Tobias (1982) summarizes it well: "Any teaching method, instructional organization, media, or instructional technology that stimulates students to actively attempt to comprehend the material, organize what is learned with what has been learned previously, and relate it to their prior experience will facilitate student learning." (p. 6)

A promising line for further research in IT involves a cognitive research paradigm involving a "training approach." This approach begins with a detailed analysis of the task and the cognitive processes it demands. This leads to the design of a training sequence to instruct new learners to do the task. The analysis must be sufficiently detailed so the instructional materials can be constructed to simulate task acquisition. The training approach begins with a microanalysis of the content's structure to be learned and of the learning processes required by it. Several military training models have been developed that reflect this analysis and design paradigm.

SUMMARY

The evaluation of both individual materials and complete instructional programs is the key to the success of any instructional technology activity. The assessment that occurs during the development of a program is called formative evaluation, which is usually done with individuals or small groups of students taken from the intended user population. It ensures that the vocabulary, pacing, examples, reinforcement, and other variables are appropriate. Summative evaluation is performed with groups after a program's development to ensure that the entire program works and that the objectives are met. As a result of evaluation, several revision cycles are likely to occur. These cycles will continue until the behaviors, criterion levels, and degree statements in the objectives are attained.

Because most instructional technology assessments are based on objectives rather than norms, criterion-referenced measures are most common. Both process and product evaluation are common in IT activities. Not only do we want to know if our programs and materials work, we also want to be able to generalize from these specific activities into the future. Process evaluation is therefore important to the development of a solid instructional technology. Without it we would quickly revert to an audio-visual or resource-provider level of problem solving. To learn from specifics and develop theories or models that will allow us to generalize into the future are two of the more complex yet challenging rewards of the IT profession.

There are several evaluation models that are useful at varying times, depending on the problem and its parameters. Because of its usefulness, the skill of evaluation must be mastered by all IT professionals.

Questions for Consideration and Discussion

1. Read each question and determine whether it is formative or summative:
    a. Did the students learn anything from the film *Roots?*
    b. How can I make the film *Roots* more interesting to the students?
    c. Which visuals can be eliminated or improved?
    d. Can the students learn as well from the film on an individual basis as on a group-viewing basis?
2. Read each question and determine whether it is process- or product-related:
    a. Can the students learn as well from the film on an individual basis as on a group-viewing basis?
    b. Do the students who are viewing *Roots* attain the desired objectives?
    c. Does the new projector work as well as the old film projector?
3. What research question would you like to see studied? Answers: Question 1: a. summative b. formative c. formative d. summative. Question 2: a. process b. product c. product.

Suggested Activities

1. Have each member of the group bring to class perplexing problems dealing with the assessment of an ongoing program. The details may cover as many relevant parameters as desired. Three or four paragraphs should be sufficient. In groups of five or six, select one problem from the group for discussion. The group can determine what type of evaluation is needed and how to collect and organize the data so it can be used to revise the program. This is not a "front-end analysis" of the problem to select alternative solutions. The focus is oriented toward improving the existing program.
2. Use the above problems, but determine for each whether it requires norm-referenced or criterion-referenced measures; formative or summative evaluation; process or product evaluation; and which evaluation model would be of help in resolving the assessment problem.
3. Determine for the above problems how the data-collection instruments should be developed. What kinds of questions need to be asked? What data-collection methods or techniques should be used? If time permits, write sample questions for the problems examined in numbers 1 and 2 above.

Suggested Readings

Anderson, R. C. (1967). Educational Psychology. *Annual Review of Psychology,* 129–164.

Barbatsis, G. S. (Summer 1978). The Nature of Inquiry and Analysis of Theoretical

Programs in Instructional Television from 1950–1970. *Review of Educational Research, 48*(3), 411–412.

Bastian, R., et al. (June 1983). Formative Evaluation in Industry. *Performance and Instruction, 22*(5), 20–22.

Bloom, B. S., Astings, J. T., and Mandans, G. F. (1971). *Handbook on Formative and Summative Evaluation of Student Behavior.* New York: McGraw-Hill.

Briggs, L. J., et al. (1967). Limitations of Current Media Research. *Instructional Media: A Procedure for the Design of Multi-Media Instruction.* Pittsburgh: American Institutes for Research, 137–142.

Coleman, J. S., Hoffer, T., and Kilgore, S. (1982). *High School Achievement: Public, Catholic, and Private Schools Compared.* New York: Basic Books.

Glaser, R. (1976). Components of a Psychology of Instruction: Toward a Science of Design. *Review of Educational Research, 46,* 1–24.

Glaser, R., and Resnick, L. B. (1976). Instructional Psychology. *Annual Review of Psychology, 46,* 1–24.

Golas, K. C. (June 1983). Formative Evaluation Effectiveness and Cost. *Performance and Instruction, 22*(5), 17–19.

Hambleton, R. K., Algina, J., and Coulson, D. B. (Winter 1978). Criterion-Referenced Testing and Measurement: A Review of Technical Issues and Developments. *Review of Educational Research, 48*(1), 1–47.

Hannafin, M. J. (Summer 1983). Fruits and Fallacies of Instructional Systems: Effects of an Instructional Systems Approach on the Concept Attainment of Anglo and Hispanic Students. *American Educational Research Journal, 20*(2), 237–249.

House, E. R. (March 1978). Assumptions Underlying Evaluation Models. *Educational Researcher,* 4–12.

Jamison, D., Suppes, P., and Wells, S. (Winter 1974). The Effectiveness of Alternative Instructional Media: A Survey. *Review of Educational Research, 44*(1), 1–68.

Kerlinger, F. N. (1979). *Behavioral Research: A Conceptual Approach.* New York: Holt, Rinehart and Winston.

———. (September 1977). The Influence of Research on Education Practice. *Educational Researcher,* 5–12.

Kulik, J. A., Kulik, C. C., and Cohen, P. A. (Winter 1980). Effectiveness of Computer-based College Teaching: A Meta-analysis of Findings. *Review of Educational Research, 50*(4), 525–544.

Levie, W. H., and Dickie, K. E. (1973). The Analysis and Application of Media. *Second Handbook of Research on Teaching,* R. M. W. Travers, ed. Chicago: Rand McNally & Co., pp. 858–882.

McKeachie, W. J. (1974). Instructional Psychology. *Annual Review of Psychology,* 61–193.

Montague, W. E., et al. (June 1983). Instructional Quality Inventory. *Performance and Instruction, 22*(5), 11–14.

Nevo, D. (Spring 1983). The Conceptualization of Educational Evaluation: An Analytical Review of the Literature. *Review of Educational Research, 53*(1), 117–128.

Resnick, L. B. (1981). Instructional Psychology. *Annual Review of Psychology,* 659–704.

Rivlin, A. M. (1971). *Systematic Thinking for Social Action.* Washington, DC: The Brookings Institution.

Roid, G., and Haladyna, T. (Summer 1980). The Emergence of an Item-Writing Technology. *Review of Educational Research,* 293–314.

Salomon, G., and Clark, R. (Winter 1977). Reexamining the Methodology of Research on Media and Technology in Education. *Review of Educational Research, 47*(1), 99–120.

Scriven, M. (1972). Objectivity and Subjectivity in Educational Research. *Philosophical Redirection of Educational Research*, H. B. Dunkel et al., eds. Chicago: National Society for the Study of Education.

———. (1980). *Evaluation Thesaurus*, 2nd ed. Inverness, CA: Edgepress.

Shaver, J. P. (January 1979). The Productivity of Educational Research and the Applied-Basic Research Distinction. *Educational Researcher, 8*(1), 39.

Stake, R. E. (1967). The Countenance of Educational Evaluation. *Teachers College Record, 68*, 523–540.

Stufflebeam, D. L. (1969). Evaluation as Enlightenment for Decision Making. *Improving Educational Assessment and An Inventory of Measures of Affective Behavior*, W. H. Beatty, ed. Washington, DC: Association for Supervision and Curriculum Development, NEA, 41–73.

Stufflebeam, D. L., and Webster, W. J. (1980). An Analysis of Alternative Approaches to Evaluation. *Educational Evaluation and Policy Analysis, 2*(3), 5–20.

Tobias, S. (1976). Review of the Response Mode Issues. *Review of Educational Research, 43*, 193–204.

———. (April 1982). When Do Instructional Methods Make a Difference? *Educational Researcher, 11*(4), 4–9.

Tyler, R. W. (March 1942). General Statements on Evaluation. *Journal of Educational Research*, 492–501.

Walberg, H. J., and Shanahan, T. (August/September 1983). High School Effects on Individual Students. *Educational Researcher, 12*(7), 4–9.

Wilkinson, G. L. (1980). *Media in Instruction: 60 Years of Research*. Washington, DC: Association for Educational Communications and Technology.

Wittrock, M. C., and Lumsdaine, A. A. (1977). Instructional Psychology. *Annual Review of Psychology*, 417–459.

Wolf, R. M. (1979). *Evaluation in Education: Foundations of Competency Assessment and Program Review*. New York: Praeger.

14

Diffusion of Innovation and the Future of Instructional Technology

He who fears the unknown may one day flee from his own backside.
Sinbad

Objectives

After completing this chapter, you should be able to:

1. List three ways diffusion of innovation studies or techniques can be used by instructional technologists.
2. List the primary characteristics of an innovation and the environment in which it is to be adopted and predict the rate of adoption of that innovation.
3. List two future forecasting technologies and discuss when they might be used by an instructional technologist.
4. List and discuss the significance of five emerging instructional technologies.

Analysis of an instructional development project often includes an assessment of future requirements that may assist the instructional technologist in making wiser decisions.

The instructional technologist must, therefore, be concerned with forecasting the future. There is little need for materials or products or systems that will not be used! If projections of requirements indicate that the proposed product will be viable in the future, there is a much stronger rationale for conducting the project.

Similarly, unless the product is likely to be adopted by intended users after it is developed, there is no reason to produce it. The diffusion of new or innovative programs must be considered from the time they are first conceived. The potential adopters are much more apt to adopt and use a program if they feel they were involved in its creation.

Unless the new innovative solutions to the instructional problems are actually adopted by the client, all the analysis, design, and production effort is wasted. Variables to consider that will enhance the probability of the innovation being adopted and used are: characteristics of the problem situation, the nature of the personnel who will work with the innovation, attitudes of the administration or policy makers, and the methods used to involve personnel in the adopting organization.

DIFFUSION OF INNOVATION

There are two kinds of fools: Those who say, "This is new and therefore better" and those who say, "This is old and therefore good."
William Ralph Inge

To be an effective change agent, an instructional technologist should be able to:

- Identify and work effectively in situations where there is an instructional problem.
- Identify the characteristics of an organization that make it a likely candidate to adopt an innovation.
- Understand the characteristics of an innovation that make it more adoptable.
- Recognize the impact of individual and organizational attitudes on the adoption of an innovation.
- Recognize the stages normally occurring in individuals and organizations as they progress from awareness to the adoption of an innovative process or materials.

Individuals or groups usually proceed through the following steps in deciding whether to adopt new materials or processes:

- *Awareness*—becomes aware that new material or process exists.
- *Interest*—develops a curiosity about how the new material or process works and what its benefits may be. Begins to seek information.
- *Appraisal*—considers the advantages and disadvantages of the innovation. This may also include a trial use of the innovation.
- *Adoption*—decides to make continued use of the innovation. It is now integrated into the person's decision and behavior patterns.

An instructional technologist helping potential users through these four phases should avoid rushing them through too quickly. Adopters must have sufficient time in the early steps to understand the implications of the innovation.

A model for relating the factors that affect the adoption of an innovation in education is shown in Figure 14.1. This model assumes that in education, individuals rather than organizations make the decision to use a new procedure or

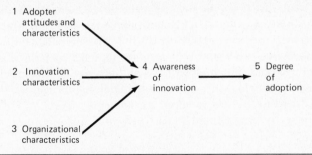

FIGURE 14.1   Diffusion of Innovation Model

set of materials. The individual may be a classroom teacher, principal, or someone else, but in many educational settings the individual instructor is the one who ultimately decides what goes on in the classroom. In military training, the model would include a centralized intervention component to reflect a command decision to use a new set of training materials. But even in the military, individual instructors can strongly resist innovations they do not support.

Some individuals are more flexible and willing to change than others. Potential adopters can be classified according to their willingness to try new ideas. By ascertaining aspects of clients' personalities, it may be possible to predict if they will use new materials or procedures. As a change agent, one should be able to identify the more promising members of the adopting unit. The primary types of adopters are the:

- *Innovator*—curious and eager to try new ideas, a risk taker; usually not integrated into the social structure of the school or organization.
- *Early adopter*—respected, knowledgeable leader within the social system; a discreet user of innovative ideas and products.
- *Early majority*—follower rather than leader; deliberate in coming to a decision.
- *Late majority*—skeptical and cautious about adopting a new idea; responds to peer pressure; typically has less education than the early majority.
- *Resister*—wrapped up in traditional values, oriented toward the past and has a local (provincial) outlook as opposed to a national or world orientation.

Although this classification scheme has been found to have some validity, it should be used with caution. These are generalized traits that may not be valid for a specific innovation in a specific setting. The innovator may be a resister under some conditions and vice versa. Also, do not assume innovators or early adopters are "better" people. Instructional technologists tend to share many values with these types, but all members of the organization are important and make significant contributions. In fact, "super-innovators" can be very disruptive of systematic development efforts because of their impatience to try every new idea. Often, after a system has been carefully developed, tested, and implemented, they will be the first to suggest abandoning it in order to try something else! Generally, innovators do not make the best clients for the technologist. Other things being equal, early and middle adopters are a better choice.

Individuals who respond with rich imagery and empathy tend to be persuadable. Intelligence and sensitivity are apt to make an individual more accepting of new ideas. Individuals with low self-esteem (or who lack social poise or are shy and passive) may be easily swayed. Dull, highly aggressive, or hostile personalities tend to be slow to adopt an innovative idea.

Characteristics typically found in early adopters include:

- Receives higher professional ratings and will accept greater risks.
- Seeks advice and information from more persons outside of the local area.
- Has an active imagination.
- Is sensitive to others and to their problems.
- Is sought less often for advice by local educators.
- Has shorter tenure in current position and is upwardly mobile.
- Exhibits greater accuracy in judgment of the rate of previous adoptions.
- Is known well by few peers, but is socially active.
- Is young, at least in his or her outlook on life.
- Tends to travel extensively.
- Has more contacts with the media.
- Is less fatalistic, less negative.
- Can cope better with abstractions.

Keep in mind that you will never find all these characteristics in one individual, but the more the above characteristics match the individual, the higher the probability that the innovation will be adopted.

When assessing the climate for potential change, the technologist should also examine the *innovation's characteristics*. The probability of adoption of an innovation increases in proportion to the number of the following characteristics it displays.

1. The innovation has obvious advantages over the existing process, materials, or equipment.
2. It is compatible with the existing system.
3. Significant research and/or case studies are available concerning its use in other similar situations.
4. A rational sequence for its adoption and application is apparent.
5. It relates to an identified need.
6. Projections are for a long duration of the program.
7. It requires a minimum of new skills by the adopter.
8. It can be tried out on a limited basis before the decision is made whether or not to adopt it.

It appears that the relative impact of an innovation is very important to its rate of adoption. In their summary of studies of innovations Nelson and Sieber (1976) concluded that popular low-quality innovations that have relatively little impact on the overall system are likely to be adopted. In contrast, high-quality innovations that are low-cost and that will have a lot of impact on existing practices, like continuous progress programs and independent study programs, are usually not implemented. They concluded, "it appears that practitioners have been constrained to adopt expensive low-impact practices by virtue of the organizational problems posed by high-impact practices."

A third aspect of the diffusion model that can be used to predict the potential for adoption of an innovation involves the adopting organization's characteristics. Positive factors include:

- High status and high credibility of the perceived adopter leader (who may or may not be the acknowledged organization leader).
- Placement of the adopter near the top of the administrative ladder.
- Leader newly appointed from outside the adopting unit, who is not necessarily personally well known by the rest of the organization, and who still has the halo of an expert.
- Relatively highly educated individuals in the organization.
- High interaction among the administrators and the staff in the adopting unit.
- Individuals in the group are perceived as being highly professional.
- Communication channels exist in the organization so that interested individuals can easily obtain relevant information.
- The innovation can be made available in a participative rather than authoritative manner.

Research studies involving the diffusion of innovations are complex and multivariant, often lacking a sound theoretical base. However, models such as the one proposed earlier can be useful in examining and understanding the relationships of the factors affecting change. In reality, much of what was discussed above concerning change was first and best studied in the 1920s and 1930s by agriculture extension agents who were urging farmers to use contour plowing, fertilizers, and hybrid seed. For example, the results of using the new seeds could be seen in a few months. This made it relatively easy to evaluate how change could be affected. Unfortunately, in education this kind of obvious change is seldom visible after only a few months.

Once an innovation has been adopted, the following factors are positively correlated with its continuance:

- The longevity of the project director.
- Open management climate.
- The new procedure or materials work as well as projected.

Having considered characteristics of clients, innovations, and organizational settings, we now turn to the characteristics of change agents.

Effective change-agent activities are positively correlated with:

- Being client- and need-centered rather than material- or innovation-centered.
- Being somewhat more educated than the client.

- The degree to which the change agent seeks, empathizes with, and gets the support of leaders in the adopting organization.
- Being open to information from various sources.
- The extent to which clients believe the change agent is knowledgeable and competent.
- How hard the change agent works at communicating information about the innovation.

In many cases, the instructional technologist, as change agent, must work to achieve these facilitating characteristics. They are not automatically part of one's repertoire as a result of formal training as a technologist. This process can be enhanced by using public relations techniques. The instructional technologist has a number of roles to fill regarding facilitation of diffusion and adoption of an innovation:

- *Change agent*—determines strategies that will result in the adoption of the process or product the team is working on.
- *Researcher*—researches the characteristics that can alter effectiveness.
- *Idea person*—inventor of a better product that has high relative advantage over the existing "mousetraps."
- *Public relations contact person*—interacts to persuade clients to adopt and use an innovation because it is good for the community.
- *Instructional designer*—designs appealing and effective materials that sell.

There are many strategies available to the change agent for informing, advising, and assisting clients contemplating adoption of an innovation. Some have been shown to be more powerful than others, but each should be selected based on client needs and on their placement in the adoption phases. Distribution of print material is, for example, an inexpensive vehicle for making people aware of an innovation. However, it has almost no ability to convince them to try it. Personal assistance is very powerful, but also very expensive and should be employed only when clients are ripe for action. A list of diffusion strategies is presented below with some indication given of their relative power and application:

- *Talking to people*—a good, all-purpose technique. Face-to-face interactions are expensive but generally effective if engaged in by a good communicator.
- *Pilot testing*—can arouse interest but is often time-consuming.
- *Site visits*—an all-purpose activity. Visits permit people to acquire additional information and mentally test an idea.
- *Print material*—useful for creating awareness.
- *Group presentations*—can be used to enhance awareness.
- *Demonstrations*—can persuade people to move from mere interest to the trial stage.
- *Materials workshops*—some of the most potent activities to stimulate interest and trial among teachers. They should focus on producing materials for specific classes.

THE DVORAK KEYBOARD AND CHANGE

Even changes that are clearly for the "better" may be difficult to implement. An example is that of a new typewriter keyboard developed by August Dvorak in 1932. A keyboard called the standard keyboard, or "Qwerty" keyboard, had been developed a year earlier for the Sholes typewriter in a manner that would prevent the keys from jamming. The Sholes keyboard was designed to make many commonly used letter sequences awkward to reach and slow to execute so the operator would be forced to slow down. As the technology developed to permit faster typing, the keyboard did not evolve. Dvorak, a researcher at the University of Washington, received two Carnegie grants to analyze the problems and the teaching of typing. In conducting his research on keyboards, he found that even random keyboard arrangement was superior to the Qwerty board. As a result of analyzing the problem, he engineered (not "antiengineered" as with the Qwerty) an effective improved board called the DSK or ASK (American Simplified Keyboard). The home row included all vowels and the most frequently used consonants. Most of the typing could be done on the home row, and finger movement was reduced by more than 90 percent. Typing productivity could be increased by over 50 percent.

Although the ASK board first appeared early in 1939, few have been sold. As we can see in this example, although an innovation may clearly be an improvement, it does not necessarily follow that the innovation will be adopted and used.

The fear of technology, sometimes called "technophobia," is common to many people, just as many fear a change of any kind. This fear inhibits the adoption of innovations in education. Arabic numerals are obviously superior to Roman numerals for business and everyday living, but when they were introduced in Europe by Leonardo Fibonacci in 1202 they were rejected and resisted for several centuries before they were widely adopted. In the United States today, the metric system of measurement with its logical system based on units of ten is obviously superior to the mishmash of twelve inches to a foot, three feet to a yard, sixteen ounces to a pound, and so on. Although every other "hi-tech" nation has adopted this system, the United States has not, but we suspect they will within this century. The opposition to changing the typewriter keyboard from the Qwerty system, which was developed to keep the mechanical keys with their long wire levers from getting stuck, has not been changed for a keyboard system that makes more balanced use of the two hands and uses the home keys for the most frequently used letters. A third area where we are resisting change involves the adoption of a worldwide calendar with months of equal length. Yet another area in which we resist change involves the refusal of many English-language speakers to consider a system of rationalized spelling. Is it not reasonable to expect users of pencil and paper (or the modern typewriter) to resist using computers?

Why this resistance to change in our culture? It seems we fear the process of reeducation and/or embarrassment. As the decision makers, adults have invested years of learning how to convert ounces into pounds, remembering the number of days in each month, and so on. To change these comfortable, commonly understood processes would result in people's having to begin all over again, to become ignorant again, perhaps even run the risk of failing to learn.

Another fear is that a particular technology will cost an individual his employment. Another reason that some say they resist using computers and other technology is they fear the technological change will harm the environment. Almost every invention from fire (if it can be called an invention) to the use of nuclear energy can either be used for good or evil, but discussion of the trade-offs is beyond the scope of this book.

A final fear to be discussed here involves the fear that our humanity will be replaced—that the computer will become "more intelligent" than a human being. Built of protein and nucleic acid, after millions of years of random, hit-and-miss biological evolution, it does not seem scary to believe that our brain can rationally build a computer of electronic switches and electric current to serve our purposes. It is true that computers can solve highly complex math problems with far greater speed than humans with much less error, but they are still tools we have developed to serve our ends. In the future, computers may identify their own problems to solve and obtain the necessary information to solve those problems, but as long as we design them they will be our tools.

FUTURE FORECASTING TECHNOLOGIES

Education which is not modern shares the fate of all organic things which are kept too long.

Alfred North Whitehead

An instructional technologist should be aware of techniques for predicting the future. For example, it is necessary to have some idea of future curriculum needs before advocating the expenditure of manpower and funds for developing and creating instructional materials for a specific curriculum. There is no scientifically based forecasting procedure, but some techniques have proved to be of value in approximating future events and needs. There are three general categories of forecasting techniques. One type involves *qualitative* methods, which include the Delphi method and market research techniques. A second category consists of time-series analysis and projection methods, which include trend projection, the moving-average technique, and exponential smoothing. The third category of forecasting techniques involves *causal* methods, which include the use of regression models, leading indicators, and econometric models. A few of these techniques will be discussed in further detail.

Delphi Technique

The Delphi technique is used to reach consensus on a specific subject and to predict a future occurrence. The Delphi was developed by Norman Dalkey and Olaf Helmer at the Rand Corporation in the early 1950s. The rationale for the technique is based on the belief that several knowledgeable persons are more likely to attain a better solution to a problem than one or two. The Delphi technique incorporates three procedures to identify potential future events and reach consensus on those believed most likely to occur.

1. Anonymous responses are required to ensure that neither personalities nor political stresses will affect the evaluation of information. Initial anonymous information is gathered by a formal questionnaire. This questionnaire may be mailed or the individuals may interact from physically isolated areas using a computer program or telephone to reduce the time required between "rounds." A round consists of obtaining information, summarizing it, and returning this summary to the participants. They can take weeks if the information is gathered by questionnaires mailed to the participants.

2. Feedback is provided to the participants so they can review the obtained information. Several rounds or iterations may occur, enabling respondents to the Delphi to sharpen their projections. Since no one knows what any other individual has previously stated, it is easy for participants to change their minds and responses based on information or feedback given to them from the previous round. If the response differs from the consensus, panel members are asked to either support their original estimates or to change them.

3. A statistical group response is used to provide information or feedback to the participants. This type of response reduces group pressure. The aggregate of the group opinion on the final round is the output or product of the Delphi.

The process begins with the construction of a data-gathering instrument, or questionnaire, which is then sent to a selected group of experts who rank the importance of the items on the questionnaire and return it to be processed. The questionnaire may have up to fifty items that relate to the issue under consideration, and each of the participants will select the fifteen or twenty that he or she considers essential.

Respondents are selected because they are considered experts in the field being studied. They must have:

- Basic knowledge of the problem area.
- High degree of objectivity and rationality.
- Good performance record in the area being studied.
- Commitment to the project and the time to participate to the conclusion of the Delphi.

The nature and composition of the panel will depend on the nature of the problem. If the group is homogeneous, a panel of ten to fifteen members is sufficient. As the degree of homogeneity decreases, a larger number of members will be necessary. If the goal is consensus among the members of an organization, all should participate.

For the second round, the fifteen or twenty most highly rated concerns, variables, or issues are identified from the first-round responses and a new questionnaire is developed using this information. It will ask for additional information and determine a procedure for identifying the importance of each item. This procedure may be stated thus: "Select the 10 items which you believe are of the greatest importance."

This step may occur several times, with a summary of information provided after each round. The list may be condensed each time. Respondents may be asked to establish a time priority for each event. As the respondents reach consensus, a usual occurrence, the Delphi is considered finished. A final report summarizes the goals, processes, and final results of the study. The Delphi method is a medium-cost method (often around $2,000) that requires at least two months to complete unless the participants are involved in a real time-computer series of rounds. The estimated accuracy of the method is fair to good.

Research has shown that face-to-face interaction results in predictions much less accurate than the Delphi process. It is useful in identifying the purposes and relationships between future quantitative occurrences, but has not been shown to be especially reliable in long-range forecasting. It can, however, be very helpful to groups who must reach consensus on what the future will be. For example, a group of educators can, by using Delphi, reach agreement on what a curriculum will contain. In so doing, however, they are not predicting the future, they are creating it.

Scenario Construction

Scenario construction is another method of forecasting the future. The purpose of a scenario is to provide decision makers with a realistic picture of those aspects of the future that seem important for their decision making. Because there are usually several developing trends that could affect the future, several scenarios are developed to reflect these different directions. The study of these various scenarios encourages flexible and adaptive planning by suggesting alternative contexts for decision making.

Most educational scenarios are in narrative form, although they may be developed in quantitative form as mathematical models. Each scenario is based on a theory or set of explicit assumptions specified by one or more experts in the field. Various scenarios relating to the same issue can be evaluated and decisions made from assumptions evolving from the analysis. It is also possible to examine the relationship of one part of the scenario system to its other parts, since a change in any part affects the entire system.

The range of uncertainty of future possibilities may also be examined through scenario construction. For example, alternative scenarios may be rated effective and ineffective. They can also be judged as suitable or unsuitable. If a scenario describes a high degree of human interaction as being socially desirable, it may judge the use of videotape systems unsuitable in that future. Investment in video equipment would, therefore, not be supported, nor would the personnel that recommend it.

Trend Extrapolation

Trend extrapolation techniques point to the future using history as the baseline for the projection. When examining current changes and forces, we find several trends that may influence the use of IT in the future. In 1975, Congress passed the Education for All Handicapped Children Act, P.L. 94-142, which requires that many handicapped students be placed into "normal" classrooms. Extrapolation predicts that this "mainstreaming" will result in a greater range of ability in a classroom, and consequently the same high degree of IT utilization that has been found in "special education" classrooms.

Trend extrapolation predicts fewer students in the nation's schools. This may have an adverse impact on the use of media and materials. With an excess of teachers, there may be pressure from teachers' unions and others to employ teachers rather than spend scarce dollars on materials.

Trend projections result in good to very good predictions on a short to intermediate-range basis, but are weak at identifying specific turning points. At least five years of data is usually required before this technique can be used. One advantage is that frequently a day or less will be sufficient time to develop an application and to make a forecast using a mathematical equation and a trend-line procedure.

DEVELOPING FUTURE TECHNOLOGIES

> *. . . like the transportation system of 100 years ago, the present delivery system of education is no more capable of the desired level of productivity than was the horse.*
>
> *John D'Angelo*

No discussion of the future would be complete without considering the emerging ideas, knowledge, and techniques that will almost certainly have a profound impact on education and training. Most of these forces lie outside traditional disciplines associated with education, but their impact will be of no less consequence because of this. The next twenty-five years will see major changes in the way people learn and are taught. Some of the ideas we present may discomfort or alarm you, but they cannot be dismissed or ignored. Either we will control them, or they will control us—ignorance will be no defense! We will first examine emerging knowledge in the behavioral sciences, and then turn our attention to what the physical sciences have to offer.

Brainwave Analysis

Recently developed techniques for analyzing how the brain responds to stimuli hold promise for improved ability to predict mental illness, learning disabilities, and decision-making capability. *Evoked potentials* can be measured as an outgrowth of advances in electroencephalograph (EEG) and computer analysis techniques.

An EEG device is used to assess the brain's response to electrical activity on its surface. A computer extracts the response-evoked potentials from the background noise. About three hundred milliseconds after the onset of an unpredictable response, a large positive wave appears, thus earning the name P300. This wave seems to represent a decision-making activity indigenous to the cortex. It is used by neuroscientists to measure such complex variables as decision-making ability. Perhaps in the future this could be monitored so that when a learner's attention begins to wander, a switch could be triggered and the student's attention brought back to the instruction. A relatively simple EEG device activated by alpha brainwaves could perform the monitoring.

Four basic levels of awareness have been identified. The beta level occurs when the individual is in full consciousness. The alpha level is an altered state of awareness, and is commonly identified as the transition state between full consciousness and sleep, and during meditation or under hypnosis. The theta level is experienced in the early stages of sleep, in deep meditation, or under deep hypnosis. The delta level typifies deep sleep. Everyone, thus, experiences an altered state of awareness at the alpha level at least twice daily, when going to sleep and when waking up. Some individuals can use this state of awareness to recall forgotten names, but most of us have not yet learned to use it to its full potential. The alpha state can also be used for deliberate relaxation. Instances of precognition, telepathy, and other little-understood forms of communication during this time have been reported. It is possible that a technology of learning and performance using the unique abilities of an individual in these altered states may be developed in the future.

Meditation may also have an impact on learning as individuals change their state of awareness from the thinking beta level to a more relaxed alpha level. Recall is greatly enhanced when students have lower anxiety levels. The ability to control anxiety is also of considerable use to teachers of hyperactive students. Meditation, when combined with biofeedback techniques, can help individuals become aware of the functioning of their bodies, and may help those with behavior problems to identify and control their problems. Use of these techniques may enable hyperactive children to become aware of conditions that lead to unacceptable behavior, and thus to greater control over their bodies.

One promising use of the altered states of awareness is known as suggestive-accelerative learning and teaching, or suggestology. Lozanov (1978) found that by inducing a state of altered awareness and obtaining relaxation prior to instruction (and by using music and drama during a lesson), adults could learn foreign languages in short periods of time with a high retention rate. Suggestology also studies the ways individuals respond to cues, or suggestions, in the learning environment. In this process, the instructor learns to change these suggestions in order to help students internalize a new approach to their own learning. These experiments have been repeated and are reported in some of the references found at the conclusion of this chapter.

If a person is aware that he or she should take some action in the near future, the frontal area of the brain tends to develop a steadily increasing negative electrical potential. The contingent negative variation (CNV) is influenced by psychological factors such as motivation, interest, and the ability to focus attention. This CNV pattern may have application by instructional technologists who are concerned with gaining learner attention.

Brain-monitoring research offers a more direct method for determining an individual's reaction to aural and visual messages. The EEG has been used to monitor beta level waves of subjects viewing various advertisements. (EEGs measuring beta waves that indicate brain alertness are most commonly monitored.) This technique can measure whether an individual's response to an ad is chiefly rational/verbal (left-hemisphere activity) or emotional/visual (right-hemisphere activity). Goeman (1979) at General Electric found this measure useful in analyzing commercials that have not done as well as expected. He showed commercials to several individuals and found that the right hemisphere was more active while viewing ineffective ads. This greater right-hemisphere activity suggests that viewers were responding strongly to the visual stimulus while ignoring the verbal stimulus. The sales message is usually carried verbally.

There is data to suggest that the left hemisphere of the brain does linear processing, such as interpreting a book, and also controls the functioning of the right side of the body in most people. Thus, it may be possible to design print materials with the text on the right side of the paper and the visuals on the left side. This format may be most effective for textual materials. Obviously, more research needs to be done on this topic to determine its potential contribution to a predictive instructional technology.

The processes of the two hemispheres of the brain seem to have these characteristics:

Left Hemisphere	Right Hemisphere
verbal	nonverbal, visuo-spatial
sequential, temporal, digital	simultaneous, spatial, analogic
logical, analytic	gestalt, synthetic
rational	intuitive
western thought	eastern thought

Attempts by anthropologists to characterize the thought processes of various cultures suggest that this dichotomy is consistent throughout all known cultures. Some individuals do make different use of the two hemispheres. Artists, in general, make greater use of the right hemisphere than do lawyers or accountants. It seems logical to assume that schools in the United States place strong emphasis on left-hemisphere development, thereby neglecting nonverbal, intuitive development.

Growth Groups

Can encounter groups, sensitivity training, human potential marathons, T-groups, or other growth-oriented group-based training sessions be used by educators as instructional technologies? Some researchers feel that a useful instructional technology that will predictably affect learning may be developing based on these techniques. Berman and Zimpfer (1980) summarized a large number of studies concerning growth-group techniques. They noted that at least one study from each of the topics reviewed documented meaningful and enduring changes resulting from a growth-group intervention. It appears group membership can result in lasting changes toward self-actualization following marathon-group participation. Growth-group intervention, human relations training, and microcounseling appear to have the potential for producing positive enduring outcomes. In many cases, however, the studies failed to confirm lasting effects of these techniques. But individual behavioral goals identified prior to group participation sometimes seem to be achievable and are maintained over time.

Subliminal Communication

In an effort to improve the chances of increasing sales, advertising agencies have used heart-rate measurements, pupil dilation, and galvanic skin responses of test subjects to determine a buyer's focus of attention. It has been suggested that consumer behavior in terms of response to advertising can be altered by subliminal communication. In department stores where shoplifting was a problem, shopper-behavior control was being studied using audio phrases such as, "I am honest and I will not steal." The messages were so low in volume that they were not readily perceived by shoppers, but were still audible when mixed with taped background music. One chain store reported a 37 percent reduction in theft after using these subliminal messages. Behavior modification in the schools using subliminal techniques may be a possible yet questionable practice. Moral issues related to changing behavior without conscious knowledge must first be resolved.

Athletes meditate to increase their psychomotor abilities. Some top Soviet athletes are trained to attain a state of deep relaxation before a game. In preparation for the contest they visualize the event, their functioning at top perfor-

"Hey Fred, will you hurry and swallow your math lesson so we can go eat?"
(Bartenstein)

mance, and their winning. Just like stories of the 110-pound grandmother lifting a car to save a grandchild, the Soviets are attempting to use this psychological-physiological-connecting technique to improve their abilities. It appears that this ability can be developed by training, and may someday become a useful instructional technology in the United States.

The use of chemicals to enhance perception and increase retention may be possible in the near future. Health-science investigators at Creighton University have identified a compound that apparently improves memory processes:

3-(2-benzylmethyl amino ethyl) benzoic acid methyl ester hydrochloride, or PRL-8-53, appears to improve ability to remember lists of nonsense syllables, reproduce sets of geometric figures, and supply missing letters in incomplete words.

Long-term memory is laid down in the brain, apparently in the form of a chemical code. In order to effect a synthesis of the informational molecules for long-term memory, it may be necessary to effect a transition from the short-term memory code. This process appears to depend on the mediation of another chemical system using noradrenaline as a chemical messenger. PRL-8-53 has been shown to enhance recall over a considerable dose range, which decreases the probability of accidental overdosing. Another drug, Piracetam (2-pyrroldine acetamide), has been studied by Dr. Stuart Dimond and E. Y. M. Brouwers at University College in Cardiff, Wales. Sixteen psychology students were given a battery of tests, including one for verbal memory that had them memorize six lists of nine two-syllable words. Based on the test results, the students were divided into eight matched pairs. One member of each pair took three 400-mg Piracetam capsules every day for two weeks. The other students took placebos. After one week, and again after two weeks, the students took the memory tests. After the second week the students taking Piracetam improved markedly. This drug has also been used on animals, chronic alcoholics, and individuals suffering from senile dementia with some degree of success.

The National Institute of Mental Health has identified a chemical that seems to improve memory and learning. The substance is vasopressin, a hormone secreted by the pituitary gland. A synthetic relative of this hormone called DDAVP was tested on animals and then in humans. The drug was administered by a nasal spray for several weeks. College students scored 20 percent higher on retention tests related to categories such as fruits and cities by listing the words according to their category. It is suspected that the chemicals may affect motivation and pleasure—important aspects of learning. If proven safe, the drug may be useful in the treatment of forgetfulness common to elderly people (and professors?). It might also be used by those preparing for exams.

Children exceptionally gifted in mathematics are twice as likely to be left-handed, six times as likely to have allergies, and five times as likely to be nearsighted as the population at large, according to Camilla Benbow at Johns Hopkins University. It seems that these characteristics may result from an abundance of testosterone, a male hormone. If such a link is found, it could help account for boys, as a group, doing significantly better than girls on tests of mathematical reasoning. It is possible that this chemical may, in the future, be more closely monitored in the fetal and later stages of childhood.

Brainwave analysis, biofeedback techniques, drugs, self-hypnosis, and meditation techniques are not yet in general use, but may develop into safe, predictable, and useful instructional techniques. Split-brain research may also become a tool to improve instructional design and presentation practices. Instructional technologists should continue to monitor developments in these areas.

LEARNING ENVIRONMENT

The location and form of schools seem important to learner achievement. Indeed, form should follow function! The better the design of the learning environment, the greater the chances that learning will occur. The selection of visual, acoustical, and thermal factors in an environment do affect individuals in the school. They should be considered when designing schools and planning solutions for instructional problems.

The physical environment of a school can affect student learning, affect, and physiology. Specific environmental variables that can influence the student are temperature and humidity; noise, light and color; seating position; openness; density; privacy; and the presence or absence of windows.

Consideration and control of temperature, relative humidity, air movement, and air quality are essential to providing a comfortable learning environment. While the human organism is highly adaptive, student attention can be distracted by an "uncomfortable" physical environment. A student may think about the disturbing quality of the physical environment rather than the instructional presentation. It is not possible to make absolute statements at this time relating cognitive, affective, and psychomotor learning to temperature, lighting, or other environmental conditions. Simulation facilities that control many of these stimuli are expensive to construct and program. NASA has done so, but their focus has been directed on outer-space rather than educational environments.

We do know that individual metabolic rates differ and influence perception of "ideal" classroom temperature. Men prefer a lower temperature than women. Elementary and secondary students prefer a cooler environment than adults. Since teachers control the thermostats in the classrooms, younger students often tend to be uncomfortably warm. Air temperatures of 68 to 70 degrees Fahrenheit (20 degrees Celsius) at 30 inches (76 cm) from the floor for elementary students engaged in sedentary activities (such as reading or writing) is considered optimal. In the summer, temperatures as high as 80 degrees are permissible in a classroom without excessive loss of concentration or learning ability. Temperatures of 68 to 74 degrees Fahrenheit (20 to 23 degrees Celsius) 30 inches from the floor for older students seem both healthful and comfortable during the heating season if the humidity is kept between 30 and 60 percent. A maximum of 85 degrees Fahrenheit is desirable for adults performing sedentary tasks; 65 degrees for very active tasks.

The acoustical environment should not cause injury, interfere with voice or any other communications, cause fatigue, or in any other way degrade the ability to learn. Noise levels seem to influence heart rate, blood pressure, and blood cholesterol levels. Short-term noise levels of 135 decibels may cause physiological effects such as nausea, fatigue, and a loss of muscular coordination. Generally, noise in excess of 70 decibels (the din of ordinary expressway traffic) will cause, according to the Environmental Protection Agency, tempo-

"Our architect has come up with an interesting concept in building design that might create an atmosphere in which students could achieve excellence."
(Ford Button)

rary stress reactions including increase in heart rate, blood pressure, and blood cholesterol levels. Lower-intensity background noise may simply be annoying or result in distraction from desired learning tasks. They are not, however, the distractors educators once thought them to be. The highest level of background noise in a classroom should be 45 decibels (30 dB is a better goal). These guidelines are also appropriate for conference rooms, libraries, and offices.

Instructional technologists may recommend the use of background noise to mask undesirable noises that are usually sudden rather than continuous. In a classroom, they are in the same frequency range as the teacher's voice and relatively loud, such as the amplified soundtrack from a motion picture. One of the best ways to control noise is through the use of carpeting. The cost of carpeting is very favorable when compared to tile or other flooring materials. Noise generated outside the school may be controlled by using shrubs or earth embankments near the outside wall of the school. The school itself may have few or no windows to further reduce the annoyance of fire sirens or students on the playground. Draperies also control sound by absorbing instead of reflecting it, as do hard plaster walls or chalkboards. They can also provide desirable color, form, and texture in the learning environment.

Measurable increases in learning have been found by simply changing light levels, contrast ratios, the color of the learning environment, or the light source. A brightness ratio of 4 to 1 should not be exceeded. The amount of light on the page of a book, for example, should be no more than four times brighter to the viewer than the light reflected from the surrounding desk area and the flooring. It is for this reason that the dark desk surfaces of the past have been replaced by lighter surfaces today.

Recommended light levels vary depending on the detail required in performing a task. Reading generally requires at least 540 LUX (50 foot-candles), but 755 LUX (70 foot-candles) is recommended. Bench work requires at least 540 LUX, but 1000 LUX (150 foot-candles) is recommended. A hallway requires a minimum of 215 LUX (20 foot-candles).

Color can be selected to affect learning behaviors. Bright, light, warm colors tend to spur outward activity and action while cooler, softer colors tend to foster withdrawal. Research indicates that ideas and actions emerge from red backgrounds. However, green is desirable for meditation and the fulfillment of tasks. In other words, the ideas and actions created in a "red" environment need "green" for development and execution. Perhaps it would be desirable to design two different learning environments for students.

Since students are often nervous and anxious when taking tests, perhaps a cool-colored room is best for an examination room. Avoid red, as this color would further upset those already biting their nails. Research has found that children tested in rooms perceived as beautiful (light blue, yellow, yellow-green, or orange) scored up to twelve points higher on IQ tests. Those in "ugly" rooms (white, black, or brown) scored as much as fourteen points lower than the norm. A learner's attention span seems to be affected by color preference. If you can determine a child's color preference and use it in his or her school surroundings (in desk covers, chairs, study materials printed on paper in the preferred colors), you might be able to lengthen the child's attention span.

Here are a few suggestions about using colors in learning spaces:

- To increase visibility of signs and displays, the following eleven combinations are offered: yellow on black, white on blue, black on orange, black on yellow, orange on black, black on white, white on red, red on yellow, green on white, orange on white, and red on green.
- Determine a learner's favorite colors and use them in the learning environment to increase interest and attention span.

- In crowded rooms (small reading rooms and offices) use lighter tones to create a feeling of spaciousness.
- Use green in areas where the student is to accomplish a task, and brighter colors like reds when the student is generating ideas and needs to become more involved.
- In examination rooms, use cool colors to reduce test anxiety and avoid bright colors like red (unless the students are not anxious about the tests).
- In primary grades, use tints of red, blue, and yellow. In secondary classrooms or laboratories (requiring close visual and mental tasks) use tints of blue-green, green, gray, or beige. In dining areas or auditoriums use peach, pink, or turquoise to relax the students. In gyms and play areas use cool or neutral tones to reduce distractions and attention on increased body heat. In health-service areas, recommend the use of green or neutral colors, but avoid yellow-green colors.

Seating position also seems to affect learning. Students seated near windows or in the rear of a classroom are generally less successful in school than students in the front and center of the class area. As the density increases in a classroom, there will tend to be dissatisfaction, nervousness, less social interaction, and increased aggression.

Despite the differences in personal preference for classrooms with or without windows, research data supports neither the claim that windowless classrooms will allow increased concentration, and thus higher achievement, nor the fear that the absence of windows will have harmful psychological or physical effects. Instructional technologists, however, may wish to consider the ability to control temperature, light level, and vandalism in windowless spaces. This positive control over the learning environment may be offset, however, by energy-related concerns. In many parts of the country, the most cost-efficient way to cool buildings in the summer is to open the windows at night and let the outside air cool them. The use of natural light may, at times, reduce electrical lighting requirements.

Human-factors engineering, to allow for better learner-machine interface, becomes increasingly important as more hardware is used in instruction. If students are to use microfilm viewers, filmstrip viewers, typewriters, or computer terminals it is desirable to design the furniture to permit easy, relaxed use of the equipment and reduce eye fatigue. The study of ergonomics (how to minimize human energy to accomplish tasks) has resulted in specifications for seat height, table height, keyboard or operator controls, and screen or viewing zones such as those suggested in the following table. Note that all of the dimensions depend on the user's size.

The Department of Defense recommends that computer screens or CRTs have a viewing distance of sixteen inches, but be designed to permit the observer to view the screen from as close as desired. The ambient illuminance should not contribute more than 25 percent of screen brightness. Reflected glare can be minimized by proper placement of the screen relative to the light

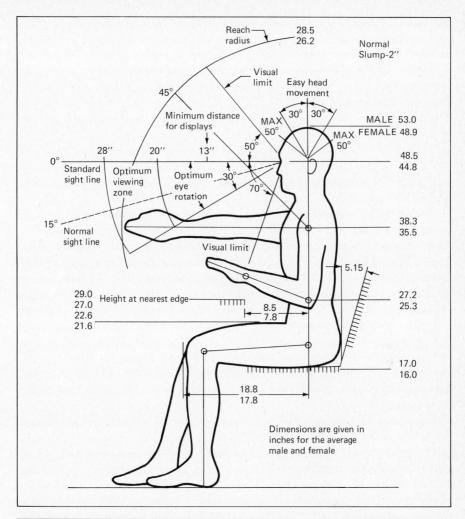

FIGURE 14.2 An Ergonometric Study by Hammond Manufacturing

source and installing a hood or shield to reduce glare. Surfaces adjacent to the scope shall have a dull matte finish and have reflectances such that the resultant luminances will be consistent with the above criteria. The duration a student should be permitted to sit in front of a CRT screen while being exposed to radiation has not yet been ascertained.

The Information Revolution

Workers in the physical sciences are predicting a cornucopia of ideas and devices that will affect future education and training. Among the most obvious are those in the fields of computers, satellites, and lasers. Students in the near future will be using computers in a variety of ways. Some institutions are currently assisting their entire student bodies in acquiring personal computers. Carnegie-Mellon and Clarkson, for example, now require that every student have a computer to process information for communication, word processing, and data handling.

Stanford University has already equipped its chief administrators with computer terminals so they can send "electronic messages" to each other. These messages are typed in by the sender and transmitted "immediately" to receivers who would normally check their "mail" between telephone calls and other activities. Communication effectiveness is increased and response time dramatically reduced.

One of the specialized computers that will be used by almost all professional educators and trainers will be the word processor. Word processors connected to printers and typesetters are emerging as a new writing and printing technology. Offices of the future will use computers to facilitate mailings, draft and edit proposals, and prepare letters and other written forms of communication, in addition to performing a multitude of other tasks. The computer system will also store "copies" of the correspondence, thus eliminating the need for file cabinets. Instead of going to the office to write scripts, letters, and so on, terminals may be located in many homes as well as most offices. Students may even have access to this data bank from their own homes (or offices). Word processing will greatly increase the efficiency of preparing drafts of instructional materials for tryout. Revisions can then be easily made and further tryouts conducted.

Because of the time saved from not having to retype a rough, or intermediate draft, more efficient communication can occur. Typing in recognizable abbreviations to the computer can speed up input even for less-proficient typists. Built-in dictionaries can also prompt or correct incorrectly spelled words. Computer packages are also becoming available that will analyze the grammar and readability of text. These hold much promise for improving both the teaching of grammar and production of quality writing. Authoring languages for producing computer-based instructional material will also become easier to use. All these developments will reduce the required knowledge of computer programming but will increase the required knowledge of effective instructional design.

The annual industry growth rate for microcomputers is about 30 percent and is expected to increase to 50 percent in the late 1980s. More than three million microsystems were in use in 1985, and it is expected that ten million will be operating by 1990. Sixteen- and 32-bit microprocessor-based computers with high-resolution color displays, voice and/or music frequency generators, and more interactive/user-friendly software programs will be widely available. Much of the software will be self-documenting and more programs will use compatible operating systems.

The cost of good-quality computers is certain to decrease over the next few years, but the cost of software is expected to increase substantially. However, the price escalation of software may slow as competition increases and as the younger generation, growing up with computers, finds it relatively easy to develop programs. The most significant problem for educators to overcome will be an old one—how to design good instructional programs.

An ongoing problem facing instructional technologists involves the interface between learner and machine. How does a typical three-year-old or functionally illiterate adult or handicapped individual input data to a computer? Speech-activated input and output holds great promise for these people. Speech synthesis—the production of speech by machines—has advanced rapidly in the past twenty years. Devices permitting speech synthesis may be purchased at most personal computer stores for a few hundred dollars. But the problem of a complete interaction using speech lies in speech recognition. Devices costing $2000 can now recognize only a small set of single-word commands from only one or a few speakers, and then only after a period of training. Only a few commercial machines can recognize continuous speech, and they have vocabularies of fewer than a thousand words (the English language has more than three hundred thousand words). These complex devices currently cost over $60,000, far beyond the range of most educational/training budgets. However, prices are expected to fall and their power to increase rapidly in the next few years. In any case, speech recognition research is progressing, and in a few years we may be able to carry on a relatively significant conversation with a computer in conversational English.

Additional Developing Hardware Technologies

There are several other equipment inventions that may dramatically change instruction in the future. The use of lasers in a videodisc system provides long-wearing, long-playing, inexpensive still visuals, motion visuals, and stereo audio all on the same disc. When these videodisc systems are coupled with microprocessors, they will be able to analyze student responses and direct the student to the required instruction by branching to any information on the disc. Semiconductor chips may now contain a million functions in a square-centimeter chip. This hardware technology will allow the digitalization of broadcast or recorded signals so that noise and interference are almost eliminated. Tape recordings will lose very little quality as they are replicated. Digital recording is currently restricted by the costs—about $100,000 for a simple stereo recorder and digital editor, but it is felt that digitalized audio will become rapidly accepted as prices fall, and its superior quality accepted as the norm.

The sending of signals from one point to another may be dramatically increased with optoelectronics using optical fibers. The use of glass instead of copper or aluminum wire should reduce the per-mile costs of transmission, and provide immunity from interference by electrical or electromagnetic fields. Satellite communications will also be increasingly used for education in regions of the world with a common language. Through the use of separate audio channels, multiple languages may be provided for television visuals. The current development of high-resolution television systems (perhaps 1000 lines compared with today's standard of 525 lines) and high-speed computer-based information systems will tax the capability of coaxial cables resulting in a further increase in demand for satellite television distribution. Direct broadcast satellite systems (DBS-TV) may answer this need with 12-GHz channels, allowing homes and schools to receive the transmissions on two-foot dish antennas.

Instructional television will be improved by the development of high-resolution television systems that will enhance the quality of picture, especially on large screens like those obtained by television projectors. The use of digital signals will eliminate much electromagnetic interference and reduce loss of definition when the signal is copied. Systems are being designed so that a television picture can clearly show an eight-by-eleven-inch typed page.

SUMMARY

There is nothing permanent except change.

Anonymous

There are many emerging instructional technologies discussed in this chapter. They include both behavioral knowledge and physical devices. While their individual impact can only be speculated upon, collectively they will almost certainly revolutionize education and training. In the behavioral science area, psychologists continually provide educators with new insights into perception and memory. Split-brain research, for example, suggests a variety of innovations for instructional material development.

In the physical science area, development of the microprocessor, integrated circuits, laser communications, interactive video systems, digitalization of information, and satellite communications will certainly change some aspects of the education process. An extremely wide variety of sources of information may soon be available for educational uses. But two underlying questions must always be asked. First, What does the learner need to know?, and second, What is the most effective or efficient learning environment? Failure to ask these questions will ultimately result in wide misuse of all these promising devices and ideas. The instructional technologist must keep a sharp eye on the learner first and the hardware second.

Questions for Consideration and Discussion

1.   What training/educational media are needed that do not now exist? Why? Is it true that software for the existing media is the number-one problem facing instructors today?

2. List additional processes or techniques which, when applied in learning situations, will affect individual behaviors in a predictable manner. Would these processes be considered instructional technologies that should be included in this text? Where are these processes weak and what are their strengths?

Suggested Activities

1. Design and conduct a forecast of the future of instructional technology using participants who are not members of the class. The class should design the instruments, analyze the data, provide feedback to the participants, and develop a final report.
2. Use the Delphi Technique in class to predict how much wheat was grown in Kansas in 1948, or any other verifiable historical statistic in an effort to validate the Delphi and to experience how it would be run.
3. Identify a problem area in which innovative solutions have been developed in society, but have not been adopted locally. Use the techniques discussed in this chapter to plan for its further adoption. Be sure that you feel the innovation is worthy of being adopted.

Suggested Readings

Ascher, W. (1978). *Forecasting*. Johns Hopkins University Press.

Berman, J., and Zimpfer, D. G. (Winter 1980). Growth Groups: Do the Outcomes Really Last? *Review of Educational Research, 49*, 505–524.

Caskey, O. L. (1980). Suggestive-Accelerative Learning and Teaching. *The Instructional Design Library, 36*. Englewood Cliffs, NJ: Educational Technology Publications.

Cornish, E. (1977). *The Study of the Future*. Washington, DC: The World Future Society.

Department of Defense. (May 1981). *Military Standard: Human Engineering Design Criteria for Military Systems, Equipment and Facilities*. MIL-STD-1472C, Washington, DC.

Dill, D., and Friedman, C. (Summer 1979). An Analysis of Frameworks for Research on Innovation and Change in Higher Education. *Review of Educational Research*, 431–435.

Dodge, B. F., and Clark, R. E. (April 1977). Research on the Delphi Technique. *Educational Technology*, 58–60.

Elphick, M. (March/April 1982). Unraveling the Mysteries of Speech Recognition. *High Technology, 22*, 71–78.

Fleming, M., and Levie, W. H. (1978). *Instructional Message Design: Principles from the Behavioral Sciences*. Englewood Cliffs, NJ: Educational Technology Publications.

Hansl, N. R., and Hansl, A. B. (December 1979). Learning and Memory Improvement through Chemistry: Dream or Reality in the Offing? *Phi Delta Kappan*, 264–265.

Hayes-Roth, B. (November 1980). *Projecting the Future for Situation Assessment and Planning: A Cognitive Analysis*, N-1600-AF. Santa Monica, CA: Rand Corporation.

Helmer, O. (1966). *Social Technology*. New York: Basic Books.

Horn, J. (February 1977). Learning: On the Horizon—a Pill to Remember. *Psychology Today,* 92.

Hurst, P. (December 1975). Educational Technology and Innovation in the Third World. *Educational Broadcasting International,* 160–165.

Kline, P. (February 1982). Suggestopedia. *Instructional Innovator,* 27(2), 20–21.

Knirk, F. G. (1979). *Designing Productive Learning Environments.* Englewood Cliffs, NJ: Educational Technology Publications.

Lewis, P. (March 1977). Noise in Primary Schools. *Journal of Architectural Research,* 34–37.

Lilly, J. C. (1972). *Programming and Metaprogramming in the Human Biocomputer.* New York: The Julian Press.

Lozanov, G. (1978). *Suggestology and the Outline of Suggestopedy.* New York: Gordon and Breach Science Publishers.

Margulies, N., et al. (1973). *Organizational Change: Techniques and Applications.* Glenview, IL: Scott, Foresman.

McCormick, E. J., and Sanders, M. S. (1982). *Human Factors in Engineering and Design,* 5th ed. New York: McGraw-Hill.

Mehrabian, A. (1976). *Public Places and Private Spaces.* New York: Basic Books.

Nelson, M., and Sieber, S. D. (February 1976). Innovations in Urban Secondary Schools. *School Review, 84*(2), 213–231.

Rogers, E. M. (1962). *Diffusion of Innovations.* New York: Free Press.

Sharpe, D. T. (1974). *The Psychology of Color and Design.* Chicago: Nelson Hall.

Sinofsky, E. R., and Knirk, F. G. (March 1981). Color: It Can Make a Difference. *Instructional Innovator.* Reprinted in *Education West* (September 1981). Choose the Right Color for Your Learning Style, 3(1), 1–2.

Spangenberg, R. W. and Smith, E. A. (December 1975). *Handbook for the Design and Implementation of Air Force Learning Center Programs.* AFHRL-TR-75-69. Air Force Human Resources Laboratory, Brooks Air Force Base, TX: Air Force Systems Command.

Springer, S. P., and Deutsch, G. (1981). *Left Brain, Right Brain.* San Francisco: W. H. Freeman.

Tart, C. T. (1975). *States of Consciousness.* New York: E. P. Dutton.

Van Horn, R. W. (June 1980). Environmental Psychology: Hints of a New Technology? *Phi Delta Kappan,* 696–697.

Weinstein, C. S. (Fall 1979). The Physical Environment of the School: A Review of the Research. *Review of Educational Research,* 577–610.

Appendices

A. Sources of Instructional Materials: Distributors, Evaluations, and Sources of Information by Instructional Medium

General Sources

The National Information Center for Educational Media (NICEM), University Park, University of Southern California, Los Angeles, CA 90007, is one of the best single sources of information on where to obtain instructional materials. The materials are organized by topic and by medium of instruction. This data set can also be searched by computer. Dialog Information Retrieval Service includes the NICEM database and the NICSEM database, which is oriented at materials for handicapped children.

Brown, L. G. *Core Media Collection for Elementary Schools*, 2nd ed. New York: R. R. Bowker, 1978.
————. *Core Media Collection for Secondary Schools*, 2nd ed. New York: R. R. Bowker, 1979.
Multimedia Approach to Children's Literature: A Selective List of Films, Filmstrips, and Recordings Based on Children's Books, 2nd ed. E. Greene and M. Schoenfeld, eds. Chicago: American Library Association, 1977.

A Reference List of Audiovisual Materials Produced by the United States Government.
Washington, DC: National Audio Visual Center, 1982.

Audiotapes

The major source of information on the location of audiotapes is the *National Tape Recording Catalog*, National Center for Audiotapes, University of Colorado, Stadium Building, Boulder, CO 80302.

American Library Association, 50 E. Huron St., Chicago, IL 60611.
Columbia Records, Educational Division, 51 W. 52nd St., New York, NY 10019.
Educator's Guide to Free Audio and Video Tapes. Randolph, WI: Educator's Progress Service (annual).

Computers

The following are, in some cases, primarily sources of computer hardware, but they also refer to sources of software/courseware.

ADCIS International Headquarters, 409 Miller Hall, Western Washington University, Bellingham, WA 98225. $30/year.
Apple Computer Inc., 10260 Bandley Dr., Cupertino, CA 95014.
Control Data Corp., 8100 34th Ave., South Minneapolis, MN 55420.
Digital Equipment Corp., 146 Main St., Maynard, MA 01754.
EFLA Film Evaluations, Educational Film Library Association, 17 W. 60th St., New York, NY 10023.
Hewlett-Packard, Inc., 11000 Wolfe Rd., Cupertino, CA 95014.
IBM, Thomas J. Watson Research Center, Box 218, Yorktown Heights, NY 10598.
Index to Computer Based Learning. A. C. Wang, ed. Milwaukee, WI: University of Wisconsin, 1981.
NEA Educational Computer Service, 4720 Montgomery Lane, Bethesda, MD 20814.
Radio Shack, 2617 W. Seventh St., Fort Worth, TX 76107.

The following are primarily listings of courseware or sources of evaluated courseware.

EPIE Micro-Courseware Pro/Files (EPIE & Consumers Union, Box 620, Stony Brook, NY 11790). This joint activity by the Educational Products Information Exchange and Consumers Union provides a source of information on courseware for K–12 schools.

The 1983 Educational Software Preview Guide is a good source of computer courseware evaluations. The guide was developed by the Educational Software Evaluation Consortium, which represents seventeen organizations involved in computer education in North America. The selection of titles is based on a critical evaluation conducted by participating organizations and participants at the California Software Evaluation Forum. Over two hundred materials are indexed by curriculum area, topic, grade level, and computer brand. Additional source and price information is included. Copies are available from the California TEC Center Software Library and Clearinghouse, SMERC Library, San Mateo County Office of Education, 333 Main Street, Redwood City, CA 94063.

MicroSIFT (Northwest Regional Educational Laboratory, 300 Southwest Sixth Ave., Portland, OR 97204) serves as a clearinghouse for microcomputer course information. They have over fifty reviews currently available. The evaluation procedure uses criteria in the areas of content and instructional and technical quality.

Swift's Directory of Educational Software (Editions for the IBM-PC, and the Apple II), 7901 S. IH-35, Austin, TX 78744. Breaks software into subject areas. A listing of programs, no evaluation. Updated semiannually.

School Microware Reviews, Box 246, Dresden, MA 04342.

Digest of Software Reviews: Education, 1341 Bulldog Lane, Suite C, Fresno, CA 93710.

Electronic Learning, 902 Sylvan Ave., Englewood Cliffs, NJ 07632.

AEDS Monitor, Association for Educational Data System, 1201 Sixteenth St., NW, Washington, DC 20036.

Motion-Picture Films

Free films

Many public libraries as well as school districts have film libraries from which teachers may obtain free films.

Association of Instructional Materials, 2221 S. Olive St., Los Angeles, CA 90007. (Write for free catalog.)

Educator's Guide to Free Film. Educators' Progress Service. Randolph, WI.

Modern Talking Picture Service, 5000 Park St. North, St. Petersburg, FL 33709; or 6735 San Fernando Rd., Glendale, CA 91201.

Rental films

American Educational Films, 9304 Santa Monica Blvd., Beverly Hills, CA 90210.

Association Films, 600 Madison Ave., New York, NY 10022.

Bailey Film Associates, 11559 Santa Monica Blvd., Los Angeles, CA 90025.

Carousel Films, Coronet Building, 65 E. South Water St., Chicago, IL 60601.

Churchill Films, 662 N. Robertson Blvd., Los Angeles, CA 90009.

Contemporary Films/McGraw-Hill, 330 W. 42nd St., New York, NY 10036.

Coronet Instructional Media, 65 E. South Water St., Chicago, IL 60601.

The Educational Film Locator of the Consortium of University Film Centers and R. R. Bowker, 2nd ed. New York: R. R. Bowker, 1980.

Encyclopaedia Britannica Educational Corp., 425 N. Michigan Ave., Chicago, IL 60611.

Landers Film Reviews. Landers Associates, Box 69760, Los Angeles, CA 90069.

McGraw-Hill Book Co., Text-Film Division, 1221 Avenue of the Americas, New York, NY 10020.

Moody Institute of Science, Educational Film Division, 12000 E. Washington Blvd., Whittier, CA 90606.

National Education Media, 15250 Ventura Blvd., Sherman Oaks, CA 91403.

National Film Board of Canada, 1251 Avenue of the Americas, New York, NY 10021.

Pyramid Film Producers, Box 1048, Santa Monica, CA 90406.

Sterling Educational Films, 241 E. 34th St., New York, NY 10016.

Technicolor, Inc., AV Systems, 299 Kalmus Dr., Mesa, CA 92627.

Time-Life Multimedia, 1271 Avenue of the Americas, New York, NY 10020.

University of California, Extension Media Center, 2223 Fulton St., Berkeley, CA 94720.

Walt Disney Educational Media, 500 S. Buena Vista St., Burbank, CA 91521.

Walt Disney Films, 800 Sonora, Glendale, CA 91201.

Filmstrips

The major source for information on 35mm filmstrips is the *Index to 35mm Educational Filmstrips,* National Information Center for Educational Media, (NICEM), University Park, University of Southern California, Los Angeles, CA 90007.

Basic Skill Films, 1355 Inverness, Pasadena, CA 91103.

BFA Educational Media, 2211 Michigan Ave., Santa Monica, CA 90404.

Coronet Instructional Media, 65 E. South Water St., Chicago, IL 60601.

Dukane Corp., 2900 Dukane Dr., St. Charles, IL 60174.

Educator's Guide to Free Filmstrips. Educator's Progress Service, Randolph, WI 53956 (annual).

Filmstrip House, 6633 W. Howard St., Niles, IL 60648.

Guidance Associates, 757 Third Ave., New York, NY 10017.

Jam Handy Organization, 2843 E. Grand Blvd., Detroit, MI 48211.

McGraw-Hill Book Co., 1221 Avenue of the Americas, New York, NY 10020.

Moody Institute of Science, Educational Film Division, 12000 E. Washington Blvd., Whittier, CA 90606.

Time-Life Multimedia, 1271 Avenue of the Americas, New York, NY 10020.

Slides

Demco Educational Corp., Box 1488, Madison, WI 53701.

Museum of Modern Art, 11 W. 53rd St., New York, NY 10019.

Society for Visual Education, 1345 W. Diversey Parkway, Chicago, IL 60614.

Microfiche / Microfilm / Microform

A major source for information on microforms is the *Guide to Microforms in Print,* printed annually. Author-title entries. The volume is companion to *Subject Guide to Microforms in Print.*

Dennison Manufacturing Co., Framingham, MA 01701.
Eastman Kodak Co., 343 State St., Rochester, NY 14650.
National Cash Register Co., 3100 Valleywood Drive, Dayton, OH 45429.
Xerox University Microfilms, 300 N. Zeeb Rd., Ann Arbor, MI 48106.

Programmed Instruction

The best source of information on programmed instruction materials is *Programmed Learning: A Bibliography of Programs and Presentation Devices* by Carl Hendershot, 4114 Ridgewood Dr., Bay City, MI 48707.

Addison-Wesley Publishing Co., South St., Reading, MA 94025.
Behavioral Research Laboratories, Adera Professional Center, Box 577, Palo Alto, CA 94302.
Encyclopaedia Britannica Educational Corp., 425 N. Michigan Ave., Chicago, IL 60611.
Harcourt Brace Jovanovich, 1250 Sixth Avenue, San Diego, CA 92101.
Holt, Rinehart and Winston, 383 Madison Ave., New York, NY 10017.
McGraw-Hill Book Co., 330 W. 42nd St., New York, NY 10036.
Macmillan Co., 866 Third Ave., New York, NY 10022.
Sargent-Welch Scientific Co., 7300 N. Linder Ave., Skokie, IL 60076.
John Wiley and Sons, 605 Third Ave., New York, NY 10016.

Simulations and Simulation Games

Abt Associates, Games Control, 55 Wheeler St., Cambridge, MA 02138.
Academic Games Associates, 430 E. 33rd St., Baltimore, MD 21218.
Avalon Hill Co., 4517 Harford Rd., Baltimore, MD 21214.
Bobbs-Merrill Co., 4300 W. 62nd St., Indianapolis, IN 46268.
CONDUIT/Central, Box 388, Iowa City, IA 52240.
Cruickshank, Donald R., and Ross A. Telfer. *Simulations and Games: An ERIC Bibliography* (1979). (ERIC Clearinghouse on Teacher Education, Suite 616, One Dupont Circle, Washington, DC 20036; $3.50)
Horn, R. E., and A. Cleaves, eds. *Handbook of Simulation Gaming in Social Education,* 2nd ed. Beverly Hills, CA: Sage, 1980.
Horn, Robert E., ed. *The Guide to Simulations/Games,* 3rd ed. Cranford, NJ: Didactic Systems, 1978.
Instructional Simulations, 2147 University Ave., St. Paul, MN 55114.
Science Research Associates, 529 E. Erie St., Chicago, IL 60611.

Transparencies

Allyn and Bacon, Inc., A-V Department, 470 Atlantic Ave., Oston, MA 02210.
Creative Visuals Division, Games Industries, Box 236, Wilmette, IL 60091.
Encyclopaedia Britannica Educational Corp., 425 N. Michigan Ave., Chicago, IL 60611.
Keuffel and Esser, 20 Whippany Rd., Hoboken, NJ 07960.
Lansford Publishing Co., Box 8711, San Jose, CA 95155.
McGraw-Hill Book Co., Text-Film Division, 1221 Avenue of the Americas, New York, NY 10020.
Ozalid Division, General Aniline and Film Corp., 140 W. 51st St., New York, NY 10020.
Rand McNally and Co., Box 7600, Chicago, IL 60680.
United Transparencies, Inc., Box 688, Binghamton, NY 13902.
Visualcraft, Inc., 12842 S. Western Ave., Blue Island, IL 60406.

Videotapes

Agency for Instructional Television, Box A, Bloomington, IN 47401.
Children's Television Workshop, 1 Lincoln Plaza, New York, NY 10023.
Great Plains National Instructional Television Library, Box 80669, Lincoln, NB 68501.
Instructional Television Cooperative, Skyline Center, Suite 1207, 5205 Leesburg Pike, Falls Church, VA 22041.
National Association of Educational Broadcasters, 1346 Connecticut Ave., NW, Washington, DC 20036.
Public Broadcasting Corporation, 475 L'Enfant Plaza West, SW, Washington, DC 20024.
University of Mid-America, Box 82006, Lincoln, NB 68501.

Books

Bonanza Books, "Bargain Reprints," One Park Avenue, New York, NY 10016.
Educator's Progress Service, Inc., "Educator's Grade Guide to Free Teaching Aids," 214 Center Street, Randolph, WI 53956.
Publishers Central Bureau, "Catalog of Books, Prints, and Records," One Champion Avenue, Avenel, NJ 07131.
United Nations Publications, Room A-3315, New York, NY 10017.
U.S. Government Printing Office, Superintendent of Documents, Washington, DC 20402.

Commercial Instructional/Training Software Producers (no specific medium)

Allen Corporation of America, 401 Wythe Street, Alexandria, VA 22314.
BITS International Training Systems, 3500 S. Figueroa, Suite 211, Los Angeles, CA 90007.

Calspan, Box 235, Buffalo, NY 14221.

Courseware, Inc., 9820 Willow Creek Rd., San Diego, CA 92131.

Education and Training Consultants Co., Box 2085, Sedona, Arizona 86336.

Educational Computer Applications, 13941 Garber St., Arleta CA 91331.

Encyclopaedia Britannica, Educational Corporation, 425 N. Michigan Ave., Chicago IL 60611.

Frozen Leopard Inc., 3500 S. Figueroa, Suite 205, Los Angeles, CA 90007.

McDonald and Associates, Inc., 988 Woodstock Rd., Suite 136, Orlando, FL 32803.

Mathetics, Inc., Box 26655, San Diego, CA 92126.

National Training Systems, 330 Washington St., Los Angeles, CA 90401.

Professional Development Inc., Terminal Tower, Cleveland, OH 44113.

Spectrum of America, Inc., 1040 Woodcock Rd., Suite 214, Orlando, FL 32803.

TRATEC Co. (Division of McGraw-Hill), 2999 Overland Ave., Los Angeles, CA 90064.

Video Systems, Inc., 12530 Beatrice Street, Los Angeles, CA 90066.

XYZYX, 21116 Van Owen Street, Canoga Park, CA 91303.

B. Sources of Instructional Media

The most current source of information on projectors is found in the National Audio-Visual Association's *Audio-Visual Equipment Directory,* which is revised annually. Available from NAVA, 3150 Spring St., Fairfax, VA 22030. The following are a few selected sources of projectors and other A-V equipment.

American Optical Co., Eggert Road, Buffalo, NY 10036.
Ampex Corp., Audio-Video Systems Division, 401 Broadway, Redwood City, CA 94063.
Audiotronics Corp., 7428 Bellaire Ave., N. Hollywood, CA 91605.
Bell and Howell Co., 7100 McCormick Rd., Chicago, IL 60645.
Califone International, 5922 Dukane Dr., St. Charles, IL 60174.
Dukane Corp., 2900 Dukane Dr., St. Charles, IL 60174.
Eastman Kodak Co., 343 State St., Rochester, NY 14650.
Kalart Victor Corp., Henius Street, Plainville, CT 06062.
Newcomb Audio Products Co., 12881 Bradley Ave., Sylmar, CA 91342.
RCA Victor Division, RCA, Audiovisual Marketing Div., Front and Cooper Streets, Camden, NJ 08102.

3M Co., Mincom Division, 3M Center, Building 223-5E, St. Paul, MN 55101.
Viewlex AV, Inc., Broadway Ave., Holbrook, NY 11471.

Projection-Screen Sources

A-Lite Screen Co., Inc., Box 629, Warsaw, IN 46580.
Eastman Kodak Co., 343 State St., Rochester, NY 14650.
Knox Manufacturing Co., 111 Spruce St., Wood Dale, IL 60191.
TransLux News Sign Corp., 625 Madison Ave., New York, NY 10022.

C. Professional Organizations

The following organizations are relevant to instructional technologists as they provide current information in a wide variety of associated fields. Most of these organizations offer substantial student discounts. All have annual meetings to promote an exchange of ideas.

American Educational Research Association (AERA), 1230 Seventeenth St., NW, Washington, DC 20036. Publishes the *Review of Educational Research* and a number of other journals to provide current research activities, reports, and trends.

American Psychological Association (APA), 1400 N. Uhle St., Arlington, VA 22201. Publishes *The American Psychologist* and other journals that provide current psychology-related information and theory.

American Society for Training and Development (ASTD), Box 8250, Washington, DC 20024. Local chapters are very active in bringing instructional development personnel from schools and industry together to share new developments.

Association for the Development of Computer-Based Instructional Systems (ADCIS), 409 Miller Hall, Western Washington University, Bellingham, WA 98225. Publishes the *ADCIS News* six times a year to provide CAI- and CMI-related information, and the monthly *Journal of Computer-Based Instruction* with theory and research articles. Individual membership, $30 annually.

Association for Educational Communications and Technology (AECT), 1126 Sixteenth Street, NW, Washington, DC 20036. Publishes *The Instructional Innovator, The Journal of Instructional Development*, and other journals that provide information for A-V producers, instructional designers, and instructional managers.

Association for Educational Data Systems (AEDS), 1201 Sixteenth Street, NW, Washington, DC 20036. Publishes the monthly *AEDS Monitor*.

Human Factors Society, Box 1369, Santa Monica, CA 90406. Publishes *Human Factors* to provide for interchange of ideas among engineers, physiologists, psychologists, and other scientists involved with human factors.

National Society for Performance and Instruction (NSPI), 1126 Sixteenth St., NW, Suite 315, Washington DC 20036. Provides information to the instructional developer working in industry or the military.

Society for Applied Learning Technology (SALT), 50 Culpepper St., Warrenton, VA 22186. A military training-oriented group that sponsors many conferences related to instructional systems development.

D. Reference Documents and Publications

Books

Annual Review of Information Science and Technology. ". . . to describe and appraise the publication and trends in the field of information science and technology."

Audiovisual Market Place, R. R. Bowker (annual). Directory of A-V industry listing producers and distributors, equipment, services, organizations, conventions, film festivals, and publications on media (films, filmstrips, slides, etc).

Educational Media Yearbook, R. R. Bowker (annual). The purpose is to "review and capsulize significant aspects of the current status of educational media-related activities, developments, and projected plans in interrelated fields of instructional-educational technology, librarianship, information science, and telecommunications."

Information Science Abstracts (quarterly). Provides abstracts of books, journals, conference proceedings, reports, and patents in the field of information science.

Media Review Digest (annual). Indexes media reviews published in a wide range of periodicals.

Minor, E., and Frye, H. R. *Techniques for Producing Visual Instructional Media,* 2nd ed. New York: McGraw-Hill Book Co.

NAVA AudioVisual Equipment Directory, National AudioVisual Association (annual). Illustration and description of the major types of A-V equipment available in the United States.

Oates, S. C. *Audiovisual Equipment Self-Instruction Manual*, 4th ed. Dubuque, IA: Wm. C. Brown Co., 1979.

Simonson, M. R., and Volker, R. P. *Media Planning and Production*. Columbus, OH: Charles E. Merrill, 1984.

Thomas' Register of American Manufacturers (annual). Products and services are listed alphabetically by company names and brand names.

Periodicals

AEDS Journal, Association for Educational Data Systems
AEDS Monitor, Association for Educational Data Systems
Audio-Visual Communications
Computers and Education
Creative Computing
Digest of Software Reviews: Education
Educational and Industrial Television
Educational Communication and Technology Journal
Educational Technology, Educational Technology Publications
EFLA Bulletin, Educational Film Library Association
Electronic Education (good CBI references)
Electronic Learning, Scholastic Inc.
EPIEgram: Equipment, Educational Products Information Exchange Institute
EPIEgram: Materials.
EPIE Review, Educational Products Information Exchange. Reports field-tested courseware; and *EPIE Micro-Courseware Pro/Files*
Futurist: A Journal of Forecasts, Trends and Ideas about the Future
Info World
Instructional Innovator, Association for Educational Communications and Technology (monthly)
Interface Age
International Journal of Instructional Media
Journal of Computer-Based Instruction
Journal of Educational Technology Systems
Library Journal
Media and Methods
Media in Education and Development
Media Review
Microcomputers in Education
MicroSIFT
On Computing
Personal Computing
Popular Computing
Review of Educational Research, American Educational Research Association (quarterly)

School Library Media Quarterly, American Association of School Librarians
School Microware Reviews
Simulation and Games
T.H.E. Journal: Technological Horizons in Education
Training: The Magazine of Human Resources Development
Training and Development Journal, American Society for Training and Development

E. Materials and Program Management

One type of media facility instructional technologists may supervise is an Instructional Materials Center (IMC). Upon accepting the responsibility for an IMC, the new "director" should (re)examine the functions of the center. The following questions should clarify his or her responsibilities:

1. Is the center intended for use by students or teachers?
2. Is the center designed to assist student learning?
3. Is the center to assist teachers in preparing instructional materials (not required in all IMCs)?
4. Is the material to be programmed for individualized instruction?
5. Is the center to be used for instruction of groups or classes?
6. Is the center responsible for producing testing materials or teaching materials, or keeping student records?
7. Is the center to operate an "A-V distribution" operation to assist teachers in obtaining the necessary films or other materials and projectors?

273

Once the functions of the center have been confirmed, the director will want to examine the activities to be performed. The general competencies required of an administrator are:

1. Establish goals of the program.
2. Develop and maintain a long-range plan.
3. Prepare and administer a fiscal plan based on operational needs.
4. Seek information regarding supplemental funding.
5. Organize services to meet the goals.
6. Plan media facilities. Allocate and monitor space according to program requirements.
7. Assess the degree to which the operations meet the program goals.

To accomplish these competencies, the systems specialist in IT must be trained in personnel management, materials production, educational psychology, library science, media services, and evaluation techniques.

An IMC director should be able to help instructors in the following ways:

1. Previewing and selecting instructional materials.
2. Developing an awareness of new materials.
3. Providing facilities where materials can be previewed and shown to students.
4. Developing an awareness of journals or other materials.
5. Assisting in the evaluation of (a) student progress and (b) instructional materials.

It may be desirable for the IMC director, or other instructional technologist, to write proposals for outside funding to provide for some services. Parent organizations may also be utilized as a support group.

Quantitative standards for materials collections can assist an IMC director in obtaining support by using the standards as a basis for recommendations to supervisors. "Joint Standards In School Media," adopted by the American Association of School Librarians (AASL) and the Association for Educational Communications and Technology (AECT), suggests that an IMC should have between 6000 and 10,000 titles or twenty volumes per student, whichever is greater. There should be 500 to 1000 titles or three prints per student for filmstrips.

The three most important environmental considerations that affect the longevity of instructional materials are temperature, humidity, and dust. To increase the life expectancy of film- or magnetic tape-based materials it is important to keep them as dust-free as possible; keep the temperature as near 65 degrees F. (18 degrees C.), and the humidity at or a little below 50 percent. These same conditions are also recommended for equipment.

Color films and books have a greater life expectancy with the temperature approaching 32 degrees F. (0 degrees C.). As the temperature increases, cellulose film becomes brittle, acids in books destroy the paper, colors rapidly change, and polyester tapes begin to shrink. High humidity encourages fungal growth on films, and tapes become abrasive and promote excessive head wear. As the humidity decreases below 50 percent film becomes brittle and curls, and electrostatic charges on magnetic tapes increase the noise.

The use of projectors and amplifiers increases the need for ventilation and cooling. It decreases the need for heating. A 500-watt lamp in a projector will give off as much heat as five people, so additional ventilation must be designed into areas where media will be used.

Humidifiers or dehumidifiers can be employed to maintain the desired humidity level, and air conditioning can cool the storage area. Windows in audio-visual storage areas are undesirable due to heat, light control, and security. Ultraviolet rays will affect the color of materials and deteriorate furnishings. Infrared rays will cause the heat-related problems discussed above.

Dust-proof containers are recommended for storage of most materials. Books, films, records, and tapes should be stored vertically. Magnetic tapes should be stored away from any possible magnetic fields such as fluorescent lights, motors, or transformers. All materials should be stored away from heating units.

Index